Responding to Abuse in Christian Homes

The House of Prisca and Aquila

OUR MISSION AT THE HOUSE OF PRISCA AND AQUILA IS TO PRODUCE QUALITY books that expound accurately the word of God to empower women and men to minister together in a multicultural church. Our writers have a positive view of the Bible as God's revelation that affects both thoughts and words, so it is plenary, historically accurate, and consistent in itself; fully reliable; and authoritative as God's revelation. Because God is true, God's revelation is true, inclusive to men and women and speaking to a multicultural church, wherein all the diversity of the church is represented within the parameters of egalitarianism and inerrancy.

The word of God is what we are expounding, thereby empowering women and men to minister together in all levels of the church and home. The reason we say women and men together is because that is the model of Prisca and Aquila, ministering together to another member of the church—Apollos: "Having heard Apollos, Priscilla and Aquila took him aside and more accurately expounded to him the Way of God" (Acts 18:26). True exposition, like true religion, is by no means boring—it is fascinating. Books that reveal and expound God's true nature "burn within us" as they elucidate the Scripture and apply it to our lives.

This was the experience of the disciples who heard Jesus on the road to Emmaus: "Were not our hearts burning while Jesus was talking to us on the road, while he was opening the scriptures to us?" (Luke 24:32). We are hoping to create the classics of tomorrow: significant and accessible trade and academic books that "burn within us."

Our "house" is like the home to which Prisca and Aquila no doubt brought Apollos as they took him aside. It is like the home in Emmaus where Jesus stopped to break bread and reveal his presence. It is like the house built on the rock of obedience to Jesus (Matt 7:24). Our "house," as a euphemism for our publishing team, is a home where truth is shared and Jesus' Spirit breaks bread with us, nourishing all of us with his bounty of truth.

We are delighted to work together with Wipf and Stock in this series and welcome submissions on a wide variety of topics from an egalitarian inerrantist global perspective. The House of Prisca and Aquila is also a ministry center affiliated with the International Council of Community Churches.

For more information, contact housepriscaaquila@comcast.net.

Responding to Abuse in Christian Homes

A Challenge to Churches and their Leaders

EDITED BY NANCY NASON-CLARK,
CATHERINE CLARK KROEGER,
AND BARBARA FISHER-TOWNSEND

WIPF & STOCK · Eugene, Oregon

RESPONDING TO ABUSE IN CHRISTIAN HOMES
A Challenge to Churches and their Leaders

Wipf & Stock
An Imprint of Wipf and Stock Publishers
199 W. 8th Ave., Suite 3
Eugene, OR 97401
www.wipfandstock.com

ISBN 13: 978-1-61097-178-2

Manufactured in the U.S.A.

Contents

Contributors

EDITORIAL TEAM

Nancy Nason-Clark, PhD, is a Professor and Chair of the Sociology Department at the University of New Brunswick, Fredericton, Canada, where she has taught for the past 25 years. She received her PhD from the London School of Economics and Political Science, London, England. Her books include: *The Battered Wife: How Christians Confront Family Violence*, *No Place for Abuse: Biblical and Practical Resources to Counteract Domestic Violence* and *Refuge from Abuse: Hope and Healing for Abused Religious Women* (both with Catherine Clark Kroeger), and several co-edited books including *Woman Abuse: Partnering for Change* and *Feminist Narratives and the Sociology of Religion*. She served as editor of the international journal, *Sociology of Religion: A Quarterly Review* from 2000-2006. She directs the RAVE Project, funded by the Lilly Endowment.

Catherine Clark Kroeger, PhD, is an Adjunct Associate Professor of classical and ministry studies at Gordon-Conwell Theological Seminary. She has edited several books: *Woman Abuse and the Bible*, and *Healing the Hurting* (with James Beck), and the *IVP Women's Bible Commentary* (with Mary Evans). With Nancy Nason-Clark, she has written *No Place for Abuse: Biblical and Practical Resources to Counteract Domestic Violence* and *Refuge from Abuse: Healing and Hope for Abused Religious Women)*. Together with husband, Richard Kroeger, she wrote *I Suffer Not A Woman*. She is the co-founder of Christians for Biblical Equality and President and founder of Peace and Safety in the Christian Home.

Barbara Fisher-Townsend, PhD, is employed as an Assistant Professor in the Department of Sociology at the University of New Brunswick, Fredericton, Canada, after having completed a post-doctoral fellowship with the RAVE project. For six years she served as an editorial assistant on the international journal, *Sociology of Religion: A Quarterly Review*. She teaches courses at the University of New Brunswick and is completing a book (with Nancy Nason-Clark) on religious men who act abusively.

CHAPTER CONTRIBUTORS

Terry Atkinson is the Senior Pastor at Brunswick Street Baptist Church in Fredericton, New Brunswick. He holds both a MSW degree and a D. Min.

Laurie Cooper is research assistant to Dr. René Drumm in the School of Social Work at Southern Adventist University. She is a member of the university's multi-disciplinary research teams on domestic violence and adolescent residential treatment. Her contributions to the research process have included data collection and management, literature review, professional presentations, and publication editing and co-authorship.

René Drumm is Dean of Social Work, Southern Adventist University, in Collegedale, Tennessee. In 2009 she co-edited with Marciana Popescu a special issue of the journal *Social Work and Christianity* focussed on religion and intimate partner violence.

Jacqueline Dyer received her PhD from Boston College Graduate School of Social Work. She has over 19 years in the field post-MSW, and is currently Assistant Professor at Eastern Nazarene College. Jacqueline is also a licensed social worker in Massachusetts where she continues to provide clinical supervision in the community, in addition to volunteering with a Christian domestic violence community support group.

Victoria Fahlberg has a PhD in Clinical Psychology and a Master of Public Health in Population and International Health from Harvard University. From 1989 to 1997 she lived in Brazil where she founded ACODE, a social service/mental health clinic in a large *favela* (City of God) in Rio de Janeiro, initiated the first graduate program in Brazil in family violence at *Pontificia Universidade Catolica*, and directed a national research project on child abuse in Brazil. She returned to the US in 1997 and has been working with immigrants and refugees since 2001. She has worked as a consultant for UNICEF, was a member of the Governor's Commission for Domestic and Sexual Violence from 2003-2007, and was the Executive Director of ONE Lowell, a community based organization in Lowell, Massachusetts from 2002 -2010.

Anjuli Ferreira-Fahlberg earned a Bachelor's in International Relations and Peace & Justice Studies from Tufts University in 2007. She was raised in Rio de Janeiro, Brazil, and is fluent in Portuguese, Spanish, and French. From 2007 to 2010 she worked as a domestic violence advocate, focusing primarily on advocating for immigrant victims of abuse. Since July, 2010, Anjuli has been a regional director at Horizons for Homeless Children, overseeing a network of 24 shelters and 230 volunteers.

Catherine Holtmann, MDiv, MA, is a Catholic feminist interested in education and social justice. Her professional experience involves pastoral ministry, music ministry, workshop facilitation, social movement organization and university teaching. She is a doctoral student in the Sociology Department of the University of New Brunswick and works with The RAVE Project team as a graduate research assistant.

Steve McMullin, MATS, is completing his PhD in Sociology at the University of New Brunswick, where he has been researching churches in decline and working with the RAVE Project. A pastor for 27 years, Steve has recently joined the faculty at Acadia Divinity College at Acadia University, in Wolfville, Nova Scotia.

Julie Owens, BA, is a survivor of DV who has worked in the field of violence against women for almost 20 years. The daughter of a prominent pastor, her personal story of survival is featured in the documentaries, "Broken Vows" and "When Love Hurts." She trains faith leaders for the FaithTrust Institute and Peace and Safety in the Christian Home (PASCH) and was a Site Coordinator for the RAVE Project.

Robert Owens is a retired Presbyterian (PC-USA) pastor and pastor emeritus of First Presbyterian Church of Honolulu, Hawaii. He knows from personal experience the pain and devastation that occurs in the aftermath of domestic violence. Bob has been involved in domestic violence education since 1988 when he and his daughter Julie were attacked by her estranged husband. His powerful preaching has taken him and his wife Norma around the world where they have served in numerous capacities.

Marciana Popescu, PhD, is an Associate Professor, Fordham University Graduate School of Social Service in New York City. In 2009 she co-edited with René Drumm a special issue of the journal *Social Work and Christianity* focussed on religion and intimate partner violence.

The Very Rev. Robert Pynn served as Archdeacon and later as Dean of the Anglican Diocese of Calgary as well as Prolocutor of the General Synod. He was a founding Advisory Board Member of the Chair of Christian Thought at the University of Calgary. Throughout his career Bob has inspired, and helped found, many social programs, including HomeFront and FaithLink. His first collection of poetry, *LifeLines,* was published in 2007.

Michael Rothery, PhD, has recently retired from teaching at the Faculty of Social Work, University of Calgary. For many years he has researched and published in the area of domestic violence and was a founding member of FaithLink, a Calgary-based organization.

Dan Schaefer, PhD, is a licensed psychologist who is director of Person to Person Resources Inc., a private group of mental health professionals located in Northwest Ohio. He has been running 2-3 domestic violence groups for men every week for about 7 years and presents regularly at national conferences on the topic. He teaches counselling courses at Spring Arbor University.

Ty Schroyer and Barbara Jones-Schroyer, MSW, are a husband and wife team on the staff of the Domestic Abuse Intervention Project in Duluth Minnesota. In 2003 they began a faith based men's non-violence program called Changing Men, Changing Lives (CMCL) in collaboration with the Duluth program. Besides operating two Christian intervention groups, they offer certified training courses in batterer intervention.

Irene Sevcik, PhD, is the Director of FaithLink, a Calgary-based organization focused on raising awareness of family violence and increasing capacity of spiritual/religious communities to respond to disclosures of abuse, as well as building collaborative working relationships between spiritual/religious communities and secularly-based service providers. She is currently completing a book on domestic violence and religion.

Steve Tracy, PhD, is author of *Mending the Soul: Understanding and Healing Abuse*, and director of Mending the Soul Ministries. His research centers on the effect of patriarchy on domestic violence. Steve and his wife, Celeste, conduct a flourishing ministry in healing, training and addressing issues of domestic abuse with a widespread community outreach in Phoenix. They travel worldwide in offering their seminars.

Introduction

Catherine Clark Kroeger and Nancy Nason-Clark

DOMESTIC ABUSE IS A horror. It lurks beneath the surface of our collective existence, sometimes raising its ugly head where least expected—in the church, or within families of faith.

Are we—individually or collectively—ready to respond? What can, or should, congregations and their pastoral leaders do? And, as we survey the Christian landscape across the United States and Canada, are we as the community of faith stepping up to the challenge presented by violence in the family?

There is no easy answer to the problems that surface when abuse impacts the Christian family. But each of the authors contributing to this volume believes fervently that it is imperative that followers of Jesus and their spiritual shepherds respond to the cries for help. To respond well necessitates both knowledge and a willingness to act.

Take any given month, like last month, in the work-lives of Cathy, Nancy and Barb.

- One of us received a call from a huge megachurch asking for guidelines to provide safety when an offender stalks a victim within a church;

- One of us was asked to prepare training for church leaders to assist them in responding to violence in the Christian family;

- One of us was approached by students wanting more information on issues of safety as it relates to victims of battery;

- One of us listened as a young man disclosed that the police were now involved in his escalating violence;

- All of us were called upon to bring information, healing and hope to those families who had been impacted.

The need is great—and sometimes it can seem like the laborers are few. Perhaps you feel that way as you pick up this collection of essays. You may find yourself needing help and not being able to find it. You may find yourself being called upon to help others and yet lacking vital information about the issue or resources to respond to those impacted by it. You may want to speak out about abuse but feel that you do not know how. We have good news.

This book is here to help. It represents a collective effort to bring all of us a step further in our journey of walking with Christ over a sea of troubled waters. None of us know as much as we should, but all of us can learn from one another. In the pages to follow, we provide an opportunity to examine a diversity of perspectives, with the hope that each will in some way advance our understanding of the complexity of domestic violence issues in our midst—within our churches and the communities where our churches minister.

> I will listen to what God the Lord will say;
> He promises peace to his people, his saints—
> But let them not return to folly.(Psa 85:11)

Bringing a collection of essays—and poetry—to print involves a great many people. First, it involves assembling the written work of many individual contributors. Thanks to each one who accepted our invitation to be part of this venture. The behind-the-scenes work often proceeds unacknowledged but without it good ideas for a book would remain just that—good ideas.

Thanks to all those who walked alongside us. In particular, we would like to thank Aida and Bill Spencer and all their colleagues at Prisca and Aquila for their enthusiasm for our project. We appreciated Barton Freeman's meticulous editorial eye, prompt turn-around and supportive spirit. The staff at Wipf and Stock, especially Diane and Christian, are accommodating and helpful. All in all, we are grateful for such a group of colleagues as these—represented in the chapters themselves and in ensuring that our collective efforts reach you, the reader. We trust that those who pick up this book will find its contents provide a challenge and then a roadmap. May God help us all on that journey.

PART ONE

The Call to Peace and Safety

GRATITUDE

Remember your gratitude
even when the beasts are at the door.

Do not hold it hostage to your happiness.

It is embedded in your heart.
Let it out,
Even while you're weeping.

ROBERT PYNN

1

Let us Grow up unto Him in all Things

Catherine Clark Kroeger

THE WALLS AND RAFTERS of Wolsey Hall reverberated with the impassioned hymn singing and fervent worship responses at the fiftieth reunion of the Yale class of 1949. This was the generation who had won World War II, and now they were gathered in a memorial service. Though many had been lost, those who remained found joy in this heartfelt expression of their indomitable faith.

They were a small part of the men who returned from military service at the end of the World War II, while most of the women had stayed at home praying for them. Those men had found God in fox-holes and battle fields, on the high seas, above those seas and under them, in prison camps and hospitals, in foreign lands and dreary office jobs at home. As they re-entered civilian life, they brought a new Christian commitment that invigorated existing churches and spun off tens of thousands of vibrant new ones, along with thousands of parachurch organizations to further the Gospel. Theirs was a determination to live out Christian conviction in every aspect of life.

Funded by the GI bill, a host of new developments sprang up with housing for veterans, together with places of worship filled with their burgeoning families.

The new evangelicalism reached into the political realm as well, beginning with President Jimmy Carter, who announced unabashedly that he had been born again. All of us were swept along in the zeal and the new affirmation of faith, rejoicing in the reawakening that we had prayed for so very long. All of us were determined that Christ should be lived out in our family relationships.

In such a situation, it is possible for the pendulum to swing too far in a misunderstanding of the biblical mandates. Admittedly there were some misguided efforts, and some that were attuned to special needs. In St. Paul, Minnesota during the seventies the first shelter in the nation opened "for battered women," a phrase that I had never heard before. This was not all that was happening in the city.

A HARSHER REALITY SETS IN

The Civic Auditorium in St. Paul was filled to capacity as a supposed expert held forth for a whole week on how to build constructive relationships within the family. At the time, he was enormously popular with the Christian public. The event had been widely promoted by churches and parachurch organizations, and I too had been encouraged to attend. I sat there, along with many thousands of others, watching as the "expert" drew a diagram of a man and woman standing side by side in a dating relationship. Then, while sketching the downward swoop of an arrow, he explained that after marriage, the woman dropped below her husband to a servant status.

There followed another cartoon of the husband as a hammer pounding down on the wife, who was depicted as a chisel hacking away at the children. There were as well other symbols that were harsh and violent, such as the military image of a chain of command. I could not bring myself to attend the last two nights, but friends told me that they were present when women were instructed to praise God for their husbands *even when they were beating them.*

Within the following week, I was speaking with the Christian education director of a church located near a psychiatric hospital. There a single psychiatrist was treating three patients who required hospitalization as a result of their attendance at those meetings. Another therapist told me that he too had been busy treating both male and female clients in the aftermath of that particular program. Time moved on, and the "expert" lost a good deal of his popularity, but some of the impressions that he created lingered. Was it not the Apostle Paul who warned us "*not to go beyond what is written*" (1 Cor 4:6).

I attended another event sponsored by the Greater Minneapolis Association, this time at First Baptist Church in Minneapolis. Here another family life expert explained how he had repeatedly knocked his teen-aged son to the ground in order to gain his compliance. This was followed by an example of having forced his daughter into the car when she was unwilling to attend a week night prayer meeting. One could not miss the implication that sometimes force and violence were useful tools in promoting orderly family life. Veterans understood very well how to command, control, and coerce; and we came to consider this a biblical pattern.

Obviously such instances of warped instruction are now an embarrassment to many of us who participated in the events, or acted on the advice of those gurus. But the influence is still with us.

Other Christian leaders adopted some of the concepts in a more modified form, concepts nevertheless that could lend themselves quite readily to abuse. Usually the argument is made that these concepts are biblically based, but here is where we must examine what is being propounded. There is much that we need to rethink. As a good Christian mother, I spanked my children, but now I regret having used corporal punishment. As we deal with delicate issues of domestic abuse, it is important to deal carefully and faithfully with the Word of God.

MOVING ON IN CHRISTIAN THOUGHT

Commencing in the seventies, there began to be a growing awareness of the widespread existence of domestic abuse. Originally many of us maintained that no such evil was to be found among those who had been born again; but the evidence proved us wrong. It was evident that the Gospel called us to minister to both victims and perpetrators inside and outside of the fold of faith. All too often there has been a vast gulf between those grappling with a profound social problem and the voice of the church.

Clearly Christians needed to rethink what the scriptures and the Fathers of the church were telling us about family relationships. Misconceptions have led to tragic forms of abuse and misery that call for correction. None are more susceptible to misinterpretation than the biblical statement that man is the head of woman. How often it has led to abuse! This was recognized very early in the life of the church. One such voice was that of the greatest early biblical exegete, St. John Chrysostom. He perceived that women are often wonderfully attuned to the concerns, needs, and emotions of those around them, and have a gift of responding sensitively and sympathetically. Their gifts enable them to create an environment of care and loving support for the entire family. But abuse and brutalization deprive a wife of the ability to give freely of herself to those around her. Chrysostom wrote:

> For when she has been subjected to her husband through force, fear, and violence, it will be more unbearable and unpleasant than if she commands him with total authority. Why do you suppose this is? Because this force drives out all love and pleasure. If neither love nor desire are present, but instead fear and duress, how valuable can the marriage be henceforth?[1]
>
> For someone can subdue a slave through fear, but even he will soon try to escape. But your life partner, the mother of your children, the source of every joy, must not be bound through fear and threats, but by love and a kind disposition.[2]

Christianity is not a faith about who should be the boss but about each one of us assuming the role of a servant (Phil 2:3–8). How often we fail to notice that the practice of Christianity requires mutuality. We are told to be subject one to another (Eph 5:21). Indeed, the word *allelos* ("one another") occurs no less than one hundred times in the New Testament! Our trademark is to be meekness, humility, and a concern for others. We might think of Jesus' declaration:

> You know that those who are regarded as rulers of the Gentiles lord it over them, and their high officials exercise authority over them. Not so with you. Instead whoever wants to become great among you must be your servant, and whoever wants to be first must be slave of all (Mark 10:42–43. cf. Matt 20:25–28; Luke 22:24–27).

Jesus said that we would know a tree by its fruits and that we must beware a message based upon a mistaken ideology (Matt 7:15–20; 12:33; Luke 6:44). He called for a differentiation to be made between those commandments that are truly given in the scripture and those that develop from human misconception (Matt 15:6–9). If we have embraced a theology that requires further development, now is the time get on with the work of reconsideration.

1. De Virginitate 54.1 (SC 125:302).
2. In Eph. Hom. 20.2 (PG 62:137).

BEWARE THE TWISTING OF SCRIPTURE INTO A LAUNCHING PAD FOR SELFISH GAIN

After a spate of eight domestic murders in Massachusetts during a span of thirty-one days, a front page article in the Boston *Globe* declared:

> These were cases with much in common, for this kind of killing is among the least random of crimes: Assailant and victim, by definition, know each other intimately. Power, and the unnatural need for it, is the recurrent motive.[3]

The article states that authorities were seeking a pattern and could find none. Yet the journalist herself sees a "recurrent motive" in "power and *the unnatural need for it.*" We have heard a thousand times over that issues of power and control lie at the heart of domestic abuse, but the concept of an unnatural need for power could move our thought in new directions. Have we been guilty of promoting a doctrine of male privilege that permits domination, possession, and even the power of life and death? Surely Vienna's famed psychiatrists demonstrated the lust for power that dwells within our sinful human breasts, but have we in the church of Jesus Christ exacerbated that lust? Have things been said in church contexts that have led to unnatural extremes? Have we been swept along when we should have been considering the biblical warnings?

Sometimes we have been guilty of claiming over others an authority that is not biblically sanctioned. In particular there has often been an emphasis on the exercise of power by the male over the female. All too often that has led to methods of control that destroy family life. The Scriptures caution us against the dangers of distorting the words of St. Paul. St. Peter wrote:

> Some of his [Paul's] comments are hard to understand, and those who are ignorant and unstable have twisted his letters around to mean something quite different from what he meant, just as they do other parts of Scripture and the result is disaster for them. I am warning you ahead of time, dear friends, so that you can watch out and not be carried away by the errors of these misguided people. I don't want you to lose your own secure footing (2 Pet 3:15–170). Peter warns as well not to use honest biblical values as a cover-up for evil (1 Pet 2:16) nor as a selfish occasion to serve one's own flesh (Gal 5:13).

3. Schweitzer, "The Dangers were Plain, but the Killings went on."

> O members of the household of God, you have been called to lib-
> erty, but *not as a starting point for gaining your own selfish objects.*
> Rather serve one another out of love. Indeed. The entire law is
> fulfilled in this: "You shall love your neighbor as yourself." For
> if you bite and gnaw at one another, watch out that you are not
> totally destroyed by one another (Gal. 5:13–15).

How very often we see this scenario played out among those who
claim Jesus Christ as Lord and Saviour! In the above text, I have translated the Greek word *aphorme* as "starting point" though it is often
translated as "pretext" in this verse. Two of its essential meanings are "a
military base of operations" or "a means of war."[4] The terminology led
me to contemplate instances of other military and violent images that
were used by evangelicals in the last half century. Do we not need to deal
with a doctrine that in many instances has inappropriately become a
springboard for injustice and abuse?

ISN'T THE HUSBAND SUPPOSED TO BE THE BOSS?

Although some will insist that the Bible teaches male dominance, this is
stated only in the book of Esther.

> The king sent dispatches to all parts of the kingdom, to each
> province in its own script and to each people in its own language,
> proclaiming in each people's tongue that every man should be
> ruler over his own household (Est 1:22).

The decree is issued after an enormous drinking party by a king angered
because his queen had refused to appear in a compromising situation
before the royal court. The rest of the story of Esther deals with how the
valiant heroine subverts both this decree and the order for the extermi-
nation of all Jews in the empire. King Ahasueres (aka Xerxes), known
in other circumstances for his lack of good judgment, ultimately recognizes the wisdom of Esther and vests her with authority. Other than this
statement, the Bible does not say that the man should be the boss. The
question we must ask is whether that position does not lead to conclu-
sions that may provide justification for the demeaning, degradation, and
brutalization of women.

But does not the scripture speak of the husband as head of the wife?
It does indeed use this metaphor, and it is important for us to understand

---

4. Liddell et al., *Classical Greek Lexicon.*

that in this instance the apostle Paul is using a figure of speech. When we approach his writings, we are dealing with an ancient language and ancient thought patterns. Of course the head is the uppermost member of the physical body. Clearly Paul was not using "head" literally but as a figure of speech, as a metaphor for some other value or relationship.

Frequently there are difficulties in understanding a language different from our own. Even if a person understands basic English grammar and vocabulary, she or he might not be familiar with our idioms and our metaphors.

Metaphors can hold different values in different cultures. For instance in our English context to "harden one's heart" means to determine not to show compassion, while in the African Fulani language it implies being courageous.[5] We use many idioms in our own language that must be understood in order to grasp the intention of the author or speaker. As an example, we could say that someone had "tied one on" or was "three sheets to the wind" and it might be impossible for a person from another culture to understand the sense even if they knew the words.

In the same way "head" is a metaphor that in the English language can be used to imply "boss, chief" or "one in charge." This was seldom true in Greek, the original language in which the New Testament was written. Other languages, such as French, do not necessarily use the word in this way. In Greek too "head" seldom meant the ruler or leader, although it does indeed have that sense in Hebrew. Indeed the Septuagint, the ancient translation of the Old Testament from Hebrew into Greek, carefully uses other Greek words when the Hebrew text employs "head" as meaning chieftain or ruler.

When used as a metaphor by ancient Greek writers, "head" often had the sense of "beginning, source" or "point of beginning." Today, even in English, we speak of the "head" of a river. That first great exegete of Christian scripture, Chrysostom, whose native language was Greek, discussed what relationship the apostle Paul intended to designate when he used the term "head." Chrysostom asked, how then should we understand "head"? And he answered, understand it in the sense of "perfect unity and primal cause and source."[6]

In classical literature we find many statements attesting to the Greek belief that the head was the source from which the rest of the

5. De Waard and Nida, *From One language to Another*, 34.
6. Chrysostom, *Commentary on the First Epistle to the Corinthians*, 216.

body grew.[7] Even the art of the ancients demonstrates their concept that new life sprang from the head. Ancient scraps of poetry speak of Zeus as head and source of all things, while a well-known myth tells of the wisdom goddess Athena as springing full grown from his head. Sometimes a bearded head of either man or bull was set up at a fountain or source of a river because, as Eusthatius explained, the river's head is that which generates the whole river.[8]

In statuary buried for two thousand years by the eruption of Mount Vesuvius, fountains burst from the heads of mythological figures. Both the actual fountains and the frescoes depicting them still remain.[9] In the ancient tombs of Magna Graecia are to be found both statements of the belief in the transmigration of souls and figurines depicting the re-incarnation of the soul as it issues forth from the head of Persephone, queen of the underworld. Around the emerging souls cluster tiny leaves, demonstrating the belief in head as the source of life and growth.

The statements of St. Paul himself demonstrate the same concept of life springing from the head as it promotes growth.

> From the head the entire body *grows* with the *growth* of God as it is supplied by the head and held together by every ligament and sinew. (Col 2:19)

Here and in Eph 4:15–16 are the only two instances where he gives us his understanding of the function of the head and how he applies it metaphorically. The head causes the body to grow, and thus he invites his readers to grow up in Christ.

> Let us grow up in all things unto Him who is Christ, the Head. He *causes the body to build itself up in love* as the head provides empowerment according to the proportion appropriate for each member as they are bound and supported by every sinew (Eph 4:15–16. See also Col 2:19).

In the following chapter, St. Paul holds Christ to be the Head of the Church as the man is head of the wife. Here the husband is encouraged

---

7. For a developed listing, see Clark Kroeger, Appendix III "Then Classical Concept of *Head* as 'Source'" in Hull, 267–83. Clark Kroeger, "Toward an Understanding of Ancient Conceptions of 'Head.'"

8. Homer, *Odyssey* IX, 140, XIII, 102, 346; Onians, *The Origins of European Thought*, 232.

9. Jashemski, *The Gardens of Pompeii*.

to take Christ as model in causing his bride to grow, to realize her full potential, to become all that she can be, nourishing and cherishing her (Eph 5, 25–27). It is the power to build up rather than to tear down (See 2 Cor 10:8; 13:10).

The Bible tells us many things about growth, and surely all of us need to mature in the things of Christ. In some areas, the need can be particularly urgent. Sometimes historic and social events have ways of changing us. In the early days of the church, there were many church councils and much heat was generated as believers struggled to understand theological truths. There needed to be numerous corrections made along the way. Distorted ways of thinking were addressed as God's people were challenged to think more carefully and to respond articulately. Out of it all, new convictions grew, and faithful believers moved on. The Holy Spirit is still at work in our midst. Let us, as Paul admonishes, grow up unto Christ in all things.

REFERENCES

Chrysostom, John. *Commentary on the First Epistle to the Corinthians*, Homily 26. Migne, PG 61.214, 216.

De Waard, Jan and Eugene Nida. *From One language to Another: Functional Equivalence in Bible Translating*. Nashville, TN: Thomas Nelson Publishers, 1986.

Homer. *Odyssey IX*, 140, XIII, 102, 346. London: Duckworth Publishers (BCP Greek Texts), 1980.

Jashemski, Wilhelmina. *The Gardens of Pompeii, Herculaneum and the Villas Destroyed by Vesuvius*, Vol. 1 and 2. Aristide d Caratzas Publ *passim*.

Kroeger, Catherine Clark. "Toward an Understanding of Ancient Conceptions of 'Head.'" *Priscilla Papers* (2006) 4–8.

———. Appendix III. "Then Classical Concept of *Head* as 'Source.'" In *Equal To Serve: Women And Men Working Together Revealing The Gospel*, edited by Gretchen G. Hull, 267–83. Grand Rapids, MI: Baker, 1998.

Liddell, Henry, et al. *Classical Greek Lexicon*. Perseus Digital Library. http://www.perseus.tufts.edu/hopper/collections.

Onians, R.B., *The Origins of European Thought about the Body, the Mind, the Soul, the World, Time, and Fate*. Cambridge: Cambridge University Press, 1951.

Schweitzer, Sarah. "The Dangers were Plain, but the Killings went on." *Boston Globe*. Sunday, May 16, 2010, 1.

2

The Shepherd's Conduct

—Putting Scripture into Practice

Robert Owens

Tend the flock of God that is your charge, not by constraint
but willingly, not for shameful gain but . . .

(1 PET 5:2–3, RSV)

WHENEVER WE DISCUSS THE crisis of domestic violence as members of the Body of Christ, we also need to address a crisis of pastoral leadership in the ministry of caregiving in North American Christianity. It is not enough to acknowledge the sin most churches deny, the sin of silence and denial with regard to the existence of family violence in our churches. We must also recognize a crisis of pastoral care in the practice of ministry as shepherding—a crisis in the conduct of ministers as pastor-shepherds, actually putting scripture into practice by faithfully feeding, tending, guiding, guarding, and healing the sheep in God's flock entrusted to their care by the *"Chief Shepherd"* (1 Pet 5:4, RSV). This crisis is especially important for the sheep that have been attacked, and are suffering from wounds inflicted by their attackers. Instead of tending their wounds, as Christ has commanded us (John 21:16), we must sadly confess that abused women have often been further victimized by too many pastors in their misuse of power and authority, as well as their abuse of scripture. Their interpretations of "headship" and "submission" have been more hurtful than helpful, more harmful than healing. Furthermore, those pastors who have treated spouse abuse as a marriage problem, suggesting marriage counseling, have unfortunately failed to address the real problem—which is the husband's abuse of his wife. Such pastors, who usually adhere to a concept of marriage that includes the military image of a "chain of command," have often even encouraged wounded women to remain in abusive relationships, in the hope of eventually seeing their husbands changed, even converted. At a Family Life Conference in Dallas, Texas, a prominent pastor had been encouraging women in the congregation to be submissive to their husbands, *"as to the Lord"* (Eph 5:22, RSV), when one wife stood up during the discussion period and asked, "Well, what if your husband, who is a leader in the church, is a batterer? What should you do?" Without any hesitation or embarrassment, the pastor gave the abused woman this advice: "Just go back and take another beating!"

Most of us would like to believe that such abuse of pastoral power and leadership is rare, but the patriarchal perspective continues to nourish this kind of masculine mentality in too many parts of the Body of Christ, among both clergy and laity; encouraging women of faith to accept subservience under the guise of submission (passive obedience) to their husbands, which many pastors always insist is God's design for marriage. These pastors base their views on the words of the Apostle Paul, who says: *Wives, submit to your own husbands* (Eph 5:22, NKJV). That verse is often lifted out of its context, and the preceding verse, which calls for mutual submission, is usually ignored: *Be subject* (the same word) *to one another out of reverence for Christ* (vs. 21). Furthermore, the Greek word that is translated both *"submit"* and *"subject"* does not imply domination and subjugation. In his *Letter to the Ephesians*, Paul is plainly calling for mutual regard and respect in the covenant of Christian marriage, for a love that is not selfish, a love that is not dominating, a love that is other-person centered, a love that cherishes and nourishes, a love that is self-giving, like the love of Christ, who *". . . loved the Church (His Bride), and gave Himself up for her"* (vs.25–30, RSV). Paul is making his appeal for that kind of spiritual leadership.

We are living in a time when this scriptural understanding of leadership, including the proper exercise of power and authority, needs to be recovered and restored in both Christian marriage and pastoral ministry. In biblical history authority was bestowed by God for the common good, and then confirmed and conferred by the faith community for a ministry of caring and sharing, for doing justly, showing mercy, for proclaiming good news to the poor, for binding up the wounds of the afflicted, for comforting the brokenhearted, and for freeing the oppressed (Isa 61). Power was entrusted to leaders for empowering the powerless. Those who were chosen by God and placed in positions of leadership in the faith community were responsible and accountable for the ministry of caregiving, providing for the needs of God's people, serving for the welfare of all. Privilege always involved responsibility, as well as account-ability for one's actions. Those in positions of leadership, including the shepherds, were to set an example in serving others, rather than seek-ing to be served. Any attempt to control or dominate others in order to satisfy one's own needs was the very opposite of what was called for in terms of a caring and serving style of leadership in both ministry and marriage, as well as in the vocations of our common life. However, this kind of servant leadership is rare in today's world, even in the faith community, for it has been largely replaced by the "over and under" style of leadership so prominent in our secular society. It is the style of leader-ship that accompanies a world-view that is hierarchical—that presumes inequality—and values personal control at the expense of healthy inter-personal relationships. It is self-serving at the expense of others. It is in fact a serious distortion of biblical teachings, where authority actually becomes abusive, where submission actually becomes subservience, and where the interests of those in power actually become more important than the needs of the powerless.

This is the style of leadership that is seen in the attitude and ac-tions of abusive husbands who "lord it over" their wives, who are *"the weaker sex"* (1 Pet 3:7)—that is weaker physically, the most defenseless, the most powerless, and the most vulnerable. It is seen in pastors who support such abusers rather than their victims. It is seen in husbands who pray on their knees on Sunday, but prey on their wives the rest of the time. It is seen in pastors, who actually blame abused women for their husband's violence, asking: "What did you do to provoke him?" It is seen in the twisted thinking of husbands who believe that a good way to demonstrate spiritual leadership is to assert yourself as boss, and even to bully your wife into submission if necessary, in order to gain and main-tain control over your spouse. It is seen in pastors who try to find some excuse for such abuse, when there is absolutely no excuse for abuse! It is seen in the conduct of pastors who maintain that when a wife refuses to be *"subject"* to her husband, she is also undermining his God-given role as the spiritual leader in the family. Therefore, such pastors even lay an additional burden of guilt and shame on victims of abuse, blaming them for their husband's failure to provide the spiritual leadership that God expects of them. This kind of counsel is not only a flagrant abuse of pastoral power and authority, but also further abuse of those women who have already been subjugated, dominated, and humiliated by their controlling husbands.

Pastors are called to be channels of God's love, instruments of God's peace, providing care and comfort to all who are suffering, especially those who are some of the most powerless and helpless among us in the Body of Christ. Perhaps a recovery of the biblical concept of shepherding is our best hope, if pastors are going to model the ministry of caregiving to which they have been called, serving as *"examples to the flock"* — *". . .not as domineering over those in "their charge,"* but humbly tending the flock (1 Pet 5:2–3, RSV), as models of servant leadership, caring leadership, in a community of equals. Reclaiming this biblical metaphor for pastoral care, and restoring this radical vision of a community of faith where there is no place for subjugation or domination, will require a dismantling of the scaffolding that Old Testament patriarchal ideologies have constructed over such New Testament concepts as mutual submission and gender equality. Then, and only then, will we see a restoration of the Church as that unique fellowship described in Paul's *Letter to the Galatians,* where *". . . there is neither Jew nor Greek, neither slave nor free, neither male nor female; for all are one in Christ"* (3:28, RSV); and where old structures of domination are to be no more, just as Jesus said: *You know that the rulers (leaders) of the Gentiles (unbelievers) lord it over them, and those who are great exercise authority over them. Yet it shall not be so among you . . . even as the Son of Man came not to be served, but to serve* (Matt 20:25–28, NKJV).

This shepherding metaphor has real potential for the recovery of that New Testament vision of the Church as a fellowship in which pastoral power and authority are exercised without regard for race, culture, class, sex, or status, but exercised with equal concern for all of the sheep in *"the flock of God"* (1 Pet 5:2), without discrimination or favoritism. The question is not whether pastors, and their fellow elders, should exercise power and authority in the ministry of caregiving, but what kind of power and authority should they wield? Jesus answered that question once and for all, not only by what he said, but what he did, by how he used his power as our Servant Lord, by how he modeled servanthood.

His final lesson as our Servant Lord was stooping to wash the dirty feet of his disciples, telling them: *"I have given you an example"* (John 13:15, RSV). It was an acted-out parable of servanthood that they would never forget. However, the greatest demonstration of his humiliation and humanity was seen in his offering of himself as a sacrifice for the sins of the world, when as Paul says: . . . *being found in human form, he humbled himself and became obedient unto death, even death on a cross* (Phil 2:8, RSV). He had called himself *"the Good Shepherd,"* who would *". . . lay down his life for the sheep"* (John 10:11, 15 RSV).

Jesus used this shepherding image so many times in his teaching ministry, not only to describe himself and his relationship with his followers, as well as the purpose for which he had come into the world, but also to illustrate the kind of ministry to which he was calling all of his followers. It is significant that the Risen Christ gave this final command to the Apostle Peter, who was destined to become the pastor-shepherd of the "Mother Church" in Jerusalem: *"Feed my lambs,"* and *"Tend my sheep"* (John 21:15–16, RSV). This was obviously one of the major concerns of our Lord before his final departure from his disciples and his ascension into heaven. He wanted to be sure his sheep would be cared for faithfully and lovingly. In fact, the resurrected Lord told Peter this was the way he would be able to prove his love for him, by shepherding the sheep of his flock. He even said it three times for emphasis (vs. 15–17). Of course, this is by no means the only image Jesus used to illustrate the ministry to which he was calling his disciples. However, the shepherding metaphor is the most important one he used to convey the purpose and priorities of pastoral care. It is also the most common one, and undoubtedly the best one, to illustrate the kind of leadership pastor-shepherds are called to model in Christ's Church. It is certainly the most helpful one for our purposes in discussing putting scripture into practice in the ministry of caregiving. This is true for several reasons. First, it offers an important corrective in the way it joins authority and caring, power and service. The shepherd is the authority figure, in charge of the sheep. He is responsible for seeing that all members of his flock are cared for equally. However, he must not neglect those that are wounded, but always provide special care for the sheep that have been attacked. Therefore, this particular metaphor helps correct those patterns of behavior in ministry which ignore or exclude any of the sheep of God's pasture, especially those that are suffering from wounds inflicted by ravaging wolves, or other beasts of prey. Second, it also conveys the trustworthy exercise of power as protective action for the safekeeping of all the sheep in a particular sheepfold, to keep them from any further danger. In other words, this metaphor helps pastors to understand what is most important and essential for the ministry of authentic pastoral care, including responsibility for the weakest, the most powerless, the most helpless, and therefore the most vulnerable sheep entrusted to their care. Third, it calls for accountability to the One who owns the sheep, and who has put pastors in charge of the flock for which he or she is responsible (Pss 79:13, 100:3; Jer 23:1; Ezek 34:31). Finally, this metaphor contradicts the contemporary practice of pastoral ministry as essentially that of chief executive officer, church administrator, and supervisor in the life and work of Christ's Church, rather than the one primarily responsible for the ministry of caregiving, under the direction and supervision of the Chief Shepherd, who is Jesus Christ our Lord (I Pet 5:4).

It is not difficult to see why this metaphor is also used so frequently in the Old Testament when we remember that Israel was a semi nomadic people. The patriarchs had many flocks, with shepherds to care for their sheep. God called Moses from keeping the flock of Jethro, after his escape from the land of the pharaohs, where he had become a fugitive for killing an Egyptian. David, the greatest of Israel's kings, became known as the "Shepherd King." God had called him when he was a lad tending his father's sheep. All the kings of Israel were expected to be shepherds, and their Messianic King would be the greatest of all the shepherd-kings, of whom David was a type. In the writings of the prophets we are told God was both grieved and angered, because his chosen people were "*. . . like sheep with none to gather them*" (Isa 13:14, RSV). They had become like "*. . . lost sheep*" because their shepherds had "*. . . led them astray*" (Jer 50:6, RSV). Ezekiel had issued these stern warnings to the shepherds who had not tended, guarded, and protected the sheep of God's pasture:

> *The word of the Lord came to me: Son of man, prophesy against the shepherds of Israel, and say to them . . . the weak you have not strengthened, the sick you have not healed, the crippled you have not bound up, the strayed you have not brought back, the lost you have not sought, and with force and harshness you have ruled them. So they were scattered, because there was no shepherd, and they became food for all the wild beasts. . . . As I live, says the*

*Lord God, because my sheep have become a prey, since there was no
shepherd . . . behold, I am against the shepherds; and I will require
my sheep at their hand, and put a stop to their feeding my sheep . . .*
(Ezek 34:2–4, 5,10, RSV).

The shortage of faithful and responsible pastors was not only a problem in Israel before the coming of Christ, it continued to be a problem
during the intertestamental period. We are also told in the gospels that
there was still a shortage of good shepherds during the time of Christ's
ministry. He told his disciples: *The harvest truly is plentiful, but the laborers are few. Therefore, pray the Lord of the harvest to send out laborers into
his harvest* (Matt 9:36–8, NKJV). What kind of laborers? The context
gives us the obvious answer: shepherd-laborers! Why? Because he had
seen so many who were scattered and helpless *". . . like sheep without
a shepherd."* Jesus knew the lack of enough caring and compassionate
shepherds to care for the sheep in God's flock would continue to be a
serious deficiency in the Church he was going to build (Matt 16:16).
Furthermore, he knew there was only one way to solve the problem, and
that was through prayers of faith. Believers would need to pray for God
to supply more pastor-shepherds, whose conduct and care would be motivated by a deep love for all God's people, and a desire to not only feed
and lead the sheep of His pasture, but to tend and defend them, to guide
and guard them, to protect them and provide for their safety. Therefore,
knowing this would always be a crucial need in his Church through the
ages, Jesus instructed his disciples to pray, and to pray as he had taught
them to pray, faithfully, confidently, earnestly, fervently, hopefully, and
persistently. For there was going to be a great harvest of souls!

We *can* safely assume that his followers did exactly what the Master
had told them to do. They prayed, and prayed, and kept on praying for
more shepherds! How else can we explain what happened following the
crucifixion, the resurrection, the ascension, and Pentecost? More than
three thousand people were added to Christ's Church in one day (Acts
2:41), and the number of converts continued to increase dramatically.
Furthermore, the number of shepherds also increased as the number of
Christians grew at such a phenomenal rate, for all those converts needed
to be cared for. They had to be nurtured in the faith, for they were babes
in Christ. They were helpless lambs that needed to be protected from
those wolves in sheep's clothing who would seek to lead them astray.
Many of them would be attacked, and they would need special care.

Some of those suffering believers would continue to be in danger and would need to find someplace where they could be safe. The apostles were continuing the ministry of Jesus in the power of the Spirit, and everywhere the believers went preaching the Gospel, people were being converted and baptized into the Body of Christ (Acts 8:1). People were being saved daily, and new churches were being planted in Israel, Judea, Samaria, and throughout the Greek-speaking world. In Luke's history of the Early Church, we are told how pastors and elders were appointed to serve those young churches as pastor-teachers and shepherds, and how elders and deacons were also chosen and ordained to share the ministry of caregiving (Acts 6:3–6, 14:23).

In every place where a new church was planted, the leaders in those churches were admonished: *Take heed to yourselves and to all the flock, in which the Holy Spirit has made you overseers, to care for the church of God which he obtained with the blood of His own Son* (Acts 20:28, RSV).

> In his letters to some of those young churches, Paul not only reminded the leaders in those newly established fellowships of their personal shepherding responsibilities, but also emphasized their calling to *". . . equip the saints" (i.e. all believers) for their own "work of ministry"* (Eph 4:12, RSV), which was not only a ministry of preaching and teaching, but also a ministry of caregiving. In his Corinthian correspondence, Paul used the analogy of the human body to teach how the Body of Christ is supposed to function, when it is functioning properly: *For just as the body is one and has many members, and all the members of the body, though many are one body, so it is with Christ . . . For the body does not consist of one member, but of many . . . . and the parts of the body which seem to be weaker are indispensable . . . God has so composed the body, giving the greater honor to the weaker parts, that there may be no discord in the body, but that the members may have the same care for one another* (1 Cor 12:12, 14, 22, 24–25, RSV).

In other words, there was to be no place for feelings of superiority or inferiority in Christ's Church, and no partiality was to be shown in the ministry of shepherding. However, there was always to be a special concern for the wounded and weaker members of the Body of Christ. In biblical times those were usually the *"widows and orphans"* (Pss 146:9; 1 Tim 5:5; James 1:27). Therefore, these were often named to represent those needing special care (Acts 6:1–3), lest some among them be neglected. Today it could be the women who are victims of spouse abuse who are the most powerless and most vulnerable members of the Body of Christ, the scared and scattered ones, like those of whom Jesus was speaking when we are told he saw them like sheep in need of a shepherd. The Apostle Paul saw believers in those young churches the same way, through the eyes of a pastor-shepherd. For example, he wanted those in the Corinthian church to care equally, and deeply, for one another: *If one member hurts, all members hurt* (1 Cor 12:26, RSV). And in his *Letter to the Romans*, he gave these instructions:

> *By the grace given me I bid every one among you not to think of himself more highly than he ought to think . . . . For as in one body we have many members, and all the members do not have the same function, so we, though many, are one body in Christ, and individually members one of another. Having gifts that differ according to the grace given to us, let us use them. Let love be genuine; hate what is evil, hold fast to what is good; love one another with brotherly affection; outdo one another in showing honor. Never flag in zeal, be aglow with the Spirit, serve the Lord. Rejoice in your hope, be patient in tribulation, be constant in prayer. Contribute to the needs of the saints. . . . (12: 12:3, 4–6, 9–13).*

The Greek New Testament word that is translated *"needs"* does not only refer to material and financial needs, but to all kinds of needs: mental, emotional, psychological, physical, and spiritual—the need for care, the need for comfort, the need for counsel, the need for guidance, the need for protection, the need for healing, the need for safety. The word translated *"contribute"* means simply *"to provide for"*—in other words, providing for all the needs of all the sheep in any part of God's flock. There are times when praying for one another is not enough! Isn't this where we so often fail in the Body of Christ, when we do not go beyond praying, when we fail to follow through on our prayers? We do not actively seek to become a part of the answer to the prayers of intercession we have offered. We simply expect God to do everything, rather than guiding us and using us to become a part of His answer to our prayers, especially for those saints with so many special needs. Jesus certainly wanted his disciples to do more than pray. They knew they would need to be *"doers of the word"* (James 1:22). Jesus had warned them: *Not everyone who says to me (who prays to me), 'Lord, Lord,' shall enter the kingdom of heaven, but he who does the will of my Father who is in heaven* (Matt 7:21, RSV) — *I have given you an example . . . a servant is not greater than his master; nor is he who is sent greater than he who sent him. If you know these things, blessed are you if you do them* (John 13:16–17) — *Truly, truly, I say to you, he who believes in me will also do the works that I do* (John 14:12).

Jesus was talking about the work of ministry: serving (rather than seeking to be served); loving (loving one another as he has loved us); listening (listening is loving); caring (bearing one another's burdens); healing (binding up the wounds of the afflicted); sharing (but when you give, *". . . sound no trumpet before you, as the hypocrites do in the synagogues, that they may be praised by men. . . . Let your giving be done in secret; and your Father who sees in secret will reward you"* (Matt 6:4, RSV). It is this kind of ministry that is known as "doing the Gospel," which is to be modeled by pastors and their fellow-elders as leaders in Christ's Church. Those in authority are expected to be *"examples to the flock"* (1 Pet 5:4). Jesus said this is the way to prove that we are his disciples, not by the love we are also *expected to have for those outside the Church, but by the quality of love we are commanded to show for those inside the Church: By this,* Jesus said, *"all men will know that you* are *my disciples, if you have love for one another"—as brethren* (John 13:35, RSV) — *By this my father is glorified, that you bear much fruit, and so prove to be my disciples. As the Father has loved me, so have I loved you; abide in my love. If you keep my commandments, you will abide in my love . . . . This is my commandment, that you love one another as I have loved you* (John 15:8–9, RSV). It was the deep love those early Christians had for one another that amazed non-believers—Jews and Gentiles alike, slaves and free, male and female (Gal 3:28), caring so deeply for one another, in spite of their racial, sexual, cultural, and economic differences. They were so kind to one another, so tenderhearted, loving one another *". . . with brotherly affection," outdoing one another in showing honor," rejoicing with those who rejoiced, and weeping with those who wept"* (Rom 12:10–13; Eph 4:32, RSV) — loving one another equally and unconditionally, as *"God's chosen ones,"* just as Jesus had loved them, with *". . . compassion, kindness, lowliness, meekness, and patience"* (Col 3:12–13, RSV). Their ministry to one another was a ministry of humble service, like the ministry Jesus, who told his disciples: *You call me Teacher and Lord; and you are right, for so I am. If I then, your Lord and Teacher, have washed your feet, you also ought to wash one another's feet. For I have given you an example* (John 13:13–15, RSV).

When writing to the saints in Corinth, in Galatia, in Ephesus, in Philippi, in Thessalonica, in Rome, Paul was not only writing to counsel them, or to chastise them. He was also writing to comfort them, and to encourage them. He knew about their hardships. He had received reports of their suffering. He was aware of their struggles, and was very sad because of the abuse they had endured. In his love letters, Paul relates to them as a fellow struggler, as well as a pastor-shepherd. He speaks out of his own experience, saying: *We do not want you to be unaware, brothers and sisters, of the affliction we have experienced. . . for we were so utterly, unbearably crushed that we despaired of life itself* (2 Cor 1:8); *We are afflicted in every way, but not crushed; perplexed, but not driven to despair; persecuted, but not forsaken; struck down, but not destroyed; always carrying in the body the death of Jesus, so that the life of Jesus may also be made manifest in our bodies* (4:8–10). No one had suffered more for Christ than Paul; he had been beaten, stoned, imprisoned, shipwrecked, and smuggled out of one city after another. Everywhere Paul went, he caused either a revival or a riot! He had endured so many forms of abuse for the sake of the Gospel, and had been exposed to constant threats and dangers, even death. He knew what it was like to be a victim, to wonder if there was any place where he would be safe. He knew how much he needed the support and assistance of other believers who were concerned for his safety, and even willing to put themselves at risk in order to protect him.

He also knew how much his brethren needed him, and how much they needed each other. They had such a deep love for Paul, the same kind of love he had for them. All of them were also motivated by the love of Christ to care for one another. Paul is the best example we find in the New Testament of a loving pastor-shepherd. He wrote to his Philippian friends that he had them in his heart, telling them *". . . it is right for me to feel this way about all of you"* (Phil 1:7, RSV). One of the most tender scenes is found in the *Acts of the Apostles* when Paul was meeting with the Elders of the church in Ephesus, and Luke tells us how *". . . they all wept as they embraced him and kissed him"* (Acts 20:37, RSV). Those elders were not ashamed or afraid to unwrap their emotions, as some pastors and elders are today. We usually think of Paul as a preacher, as a missionary, as a church planter, and seldom think of him as a pastor. However, if we study his letters, especially his prayers for his brothers and sisters in the churches he had planted, then we can see clearly that he had the heart of a pastor. Although usually he was on the move, Paul was continually hurting because he knew his brethren were hurting. He carried a heavy burden as a pastor-shepherd, for he constantly felt the pressure of concern for all those believers in the young churches –buildings with steeples. There were no structures that had been erected, or buildings that had been converted, where the followers of Jesus could gather safely for worship, for prayer, for study, for fellowship, for support, to be mutually encouraged by each other's faith and testimony: *Let us hold fast to the confession of our hope without wavering, for he who has promised is faithful. And let us consider how to provoke one another to love and good deeds . . . meeting together . . . encouraging one another* (Heb 10:23–5).

We do indeed need spiritual support and encouragement if we are going to remain steadfast and unwavering in our faith (1 Cor 15:58). We do need spiritual guidance and counsel that is scriptural (2 Tim 3:14-17), for we are weak and need to be strengthened; our faith wavers from time to time and needs renewing. We can find ourselves growing weary, and the Bible promises: *The Lord . . . gives strength to the weary, and increases the power of the weak. . . . Those who wait on the Lord will find their strength renewed* (Isa 40:31, RSV). As believers, we claim such promises by faith, and we can find ourselves clinging to those scriptures in the crisis times of life, and also using them to encourage other believers to do the same when they find their faith being tested. There are times when all of us as believers are very much aware of our need for other Christians who will agree with us in prayer, knowing that the place of agreement is the place of power when God's people pray together. Jesus said: *"I tell you, if two of you agree on earth about anything you ask, it will be done for you by my Father in heaven"* (Matt 18:19). Of course, this promise is not a *"blank check,"* for our Lord always emphasized that we must pray according to the will of God, following his own example (Matt 6:10; Luke 22:42). Victims of domestic violence who are believers are usually desperate for other believers who will pray with them and for them.

Studies have shown that when a Christian woman is being abused by her husband, who is, in many instances, also a professing Christian and a member of the same church, she will ordinarily first seek prayer support from her own pastor. She may also seek the prayer support of others in the church who are brothers and sisters in Christ she believes she can trust. She knows she needs the prayer support of believers who will be willing to become prayer partners with her. She also knows she needs spiritual counsel and comfort from other Christians who know the scriptures, and who have themselves been comforted by the promises of God (2 Cor 1:3–7).

God's prophet, Ezekiel, not only uses the shepherding metaphor, but also the metaphor of the *"watchman"* to dramatize the pastor's responsibility for watching over the sheep, and to also underscore the importance of being alert at all times to any possible threat. Pastoral ministry is too complex for any one metaphor to suffice, so combining these two biblical images reinforces the fact that pastors must be vigilant day and night, conscious of the fact that danger may be lurking in the darkness. The "shepherd" and "watchman" must always be ready to warn the people of God of any approaching danger, any possible violence: *If the watchman sees the sword coming and does not blow the trumpet to warn the people, and the sword comes and takes the life of any of them . . . . I will hold the watchman accountable . . . their blood I will require at the watchman's hand* (Ezek 33:6, RSV).

- *Pastor-shepherds should never treat spouse abuse as a marriage problem, or suggest marriage counseling until there is proof that the violence has definitely stopped, and for an extended period of time.* Ordinarily, this will only happen after an abuser has participated willingly and faithfully in a batterer's intervention program. Then, and only then, can a victim and her abuser work together on other problems in their marriage, with any real hope of recovery, reconciliation, and restoration of the relationship.

- *Pastor-shepherds must always hold perpetrators responsible and accountable for their actions, so they will stop blaming their victims for their own power and control problem.* Promises to change are not sufficient. Such promises must be accompanied by actions that show a continuing commitment to counsel and treatment for as long as necessary.

- *Pastor-shepherds can provide counseling and offer spiritual help, but they should not attempt to minister beyond the boundaries of their own expertise.* They should be prepared to refer both the victim and perpetrator to professionals who are better qualified to deal with some of the specific problems surrounding the abuse, more capable of providing proper treatment, and able to make any additional referrals.

- *Pastor-shepherds should focus on the scriptural and theological issues that secular professionals are not qualified to deal with.* People living with the crisis of domestic violence, who are people of faith, are in need of spiritual support and direction, which pastor-shepherds can and should provide, seeking to identify the specific religious questions or spiritual aspects of a particular victim's struggle. This is probably the most important contribution pastors can make, but it is still not enough.

- *Pastor-shepherds should communicate and cooperate with secular agencies and advocates,* so that all the needs and concerns of both the abused and their abusers can be addressed and all available resources "from the steeple to the shelter" utilized most effectively. Both spiritual and secular counselors have important roles to play, and it is this kind of collaboration that provides the balanced approach that is most successful in counseling both victims and offenders.

- *Pastor-shepherds should never accept an abuser's explanations, excuses, or rationalizations for his acts of violence.* This includes attempts by some abusive husbands, who pose as godly men, to search for some kind of biblical justification for their abuse of their wives, such as "keeping them in line" as submissive wives. Abusers who are believers often say, "We have these verses in the New Testament mandating a wife's submission to her husband, so what is wrong with husbands demanding obedience?"

- *Pastor-shepherds should never allow abusers to further victimize victims in this manner, for selfish and destructive purposes.* Those who enjoy taking such Bible verses out of context, and adding them to their arsenal of abusive weapons, should always be reminded of those biblical passages that speak directly to Christian husbands, such as the command to love their wives "*. . . as Christ loved his Church, when he gave himself up for her*" (Eph 5: 25, RSV); and to "*. . . live considerately*" with their wives . . . *treating them with respect,*" so their prayers will not "*be hindered*" (1 Pet 3:7, RSV). When abusers, who are professing Christians, begin wondering why their own prayers are not being answered, they should be encouraged to take a long hard look at how they have been treating their wives!

- *Pastor-shepherds, whenever providing marriage counseling for both victims and their abusers, should focus on biblical passages that teach gender equality and command mutual submission in the covenant of marriage.* When husbands and wives are submitting to one another "out of reverence for Christ," as God's Word commands (Eph 5:21, RSV), with the desire to know ". . . *what the will of the Lord is,*" and a common commitment to actually do ". . . *what pleases the Lord*" (vs. 10-12,17)— always praying to ". . . *be filled with the Spirit*" (literally, ". . . *being filled,*" for this is a continuous process, which means being controlled by the Spirit), then the Holy Spirit will be producing in them those qualities that Paul calls the "fruit of the Spirit" in his *Letter to the Galatians:* ". . . *love, joy, peace, patience, kindness, goodness, faithfulness, gentleness, and self-control*" (5:22-23, RSV). This leaves no room for abuse of any kind!

In his Letter to the Colossians, Paul gives these specific commands to both husbands and wives: *Wives, submit to your husbands, as is fitting in the Lord. Husbands, love your wives and do not be harsh with them* (3:18-19, RSV). Then, in his correspondence to the believers in Galatia, Paul gives us his strongest statement on gender equality, reminding us that we are all children of God through faith in Jesus Christ, with equal rights, privileges, and responsibilities: *There is neither male nor female, for you are all one in Christ* (Gal 3:26–28, RSV). This emphasis on gender equality should never be overlooked, either in pre-marital or marriage counseling, but especially when pastors are counseling men who are not treating their wives with the respect and honor God's commands, as equal partners in the covenant of Christian marriage.

- *Pastor-shepherds must be willing to strongly refute and reject any behavior that indicates a denial of gender equality, which so often contributes to the harsh and abusive treatment of women by men who believe God has put them in authority over them, and who insist that their wives should always submit willingly and obediently to their spiritual leadership in the family.*

Whenever pastor-shepherds do not respond strongly to men who not only seek to dominate and subjugate their wives or intimate partners, but also objectify the opposite sex, then the abuse of women will not only continue, but usually escalate. Furthermore, when such abusers in Christ's Church are not confronted and challenged by pastors, their victims are often forced to make a very difficult and painful decision: not only to leave their abusers, but to leave their faith communities as well. That is a decision no victim of abuse in the Body of Christ should ever be forced to make!

3

Calling the Evangelical Church to Truth
—Domestic Violence and the Gospel

Steven R. Tracy

If you look for truth, you may find comfort in the end;
If you look for comfort you will not get either comfort or truth
Only soft soap and wishful thinking to begin, and in the end, despair.

C. S. Lewis

I GREATLY APPRECIATE THE title the editors chose for this chapter—
"Calling the Evangelical Church to Truth." It bristles with irony, provo-
cation, and hope. At first blush it might seem strange to "call evangelicals
to the truth" regarding the sin of domestic violence (DV). After all, truth
and sin, particularly physical abuse, are fundamental to evangelical faith.
Evangelicals, by definition, believe in propositional truth and furthermore
believe it is found in the trustworthy, authoritative Word of God. We
evangelicals should be well-versed in this subject, since the Scriptures we
follow have so much to say about abuse—in the world and in the community of faith. Furthermore, we evangelicals, by definition, are characterized
by a personal commitment to the *"euangelion"*—the "good news" of the
gospel. The gospel affirms that we live in a fallen, alienated world in which
humans are innately, inexorably inclined to sin. Thus, throughout human
history, suffering, evil and violence have reigned. The breath-taking irony
and hope of the gospel is that God sent his Son to suffer grotesque physical
abuse to redeem us from sin and death. All humans need forgiveness. And
all humans, including abusers and their victims, can find redemption in

Christ. Therefore, as evangelicals we are well-postured to understand and embrace the ugly reality of physical abuse.

CHALLENGES TO FACING THE TRUTH ABOUT ABUSE

The very nature of evangelical faith should naturally lead us to confront the truth of domestic violence. However, what is straightforward in theory is often messy and vexing in practice. In reality, facing domestic violence in our homes and churches is a daunting challenge for several reasons.

It Forces Us to Confront Dark, Anguishing Realities

Domestic violence is painful for everyone. It is an ugly subject we naturally prefer to avoid. Sappy cheerfulness quickly evaporates when we let the prevalence of domestic violence and resultant human misery sink in. Humanly speaking, I would rather not hear, let alone reflect on, the fact that over one-third of the adult women in my home city of Phoenix report being physically abused by an intimate partner, that one out of five adolescent girls in America report being physically or sexually assaulted by a dating partner, and that adult men and women suffer over two-and-a-half million physical injuries annually from intimate partner violence (IPV).[1] The harder one looks at the reality of violence in the home, the more painful it becomes. Those of us who devote our lives to ministering to the abused are haunted by the stories, the faces, and the pain of those we aid. So the pull to avert our eyes is powerful.

Several months ago I was shipping some boxes to Uganda. We have been ministering to physical and sexual abuse survivors in East Africa for several years. This particular day I was sending supplies to our daughter in Uganda. She lives in the slums of Kampala and ministers to street children. A high percentage of these children are on the streets because they had experienced extreme physical violence in their homes. The clerk who assisted me was quite curious about my boxes. When I explained it was supplies for African children, he immediately began asking me a series of brief questions, primarily wanting to know whether you "see sad things in Africa." I explained that you do witness suffering but you also observe and experience beauty and joy as you share with the needy. He immediately

1. "Domestic Violence Survey," provided by Phoenix Councilwoman Peggy Bilsten; Silverman et al., "Dating Violence against Adolescent Girls," 572–79; "Adverse Health Conditions," 113–17.

declared that he would never go to Africa because he "just couldn't handle seeing and knowing about people's suffering." While most people aren't as forthright, we can all relate to the temptation to simply close our eyes to others' anguish, to make our distress over their pain disappear by pretending that their distress has disappeared.

There is another dynamic at work—opening our eyes to physical abuse forces us to confront ugly realities in our own lives. Seeing abuse around us has an unnerving way of triggering our own painful personal and family histories. King David is a classic example of this impediment. In Second Samuel thirteen David refuses to acknowledge lucid warnings signs of impending family abuse. He is mute and paralyzed after it strikes. While other family members recognized ominous emotional changes in David's son Amnon, who had developed such perverse incestuous lust for his own sister that he became ill, David was so oblivious to the problem that he unwittingly approved a wicked plan which allowed Amnon to rape his sister Tamar. Afterwards, when David heard about the rape "he was furious" yet did absolutely nothing (v. 21). This in turn allowed one of David's other sons, Absalom, to concoct a plan to murder Amnon in revenge for abusing his sister. Tragically, David was again oblivious to his son's homicidal intentions. Yet again, he conceded to a plan that allowed Absalom to commit fatal family violence. Years later David again refused to recognize abusive warning signs, which culminated in Absalom staging a conspiracy, sexually abusing David's concubines, and attempting to murder David himself. David's bizarre, chronic denial of physical and sexual abuse in his own household is best explained by his own physical and sexual abuse surrounding his abusive relationship with Bathsheba (2 Sam 11). Though God had forgiven him, his sons' abuse must have triggered such shame that he simply couldn't open his eyes to the fact that they were following squarely in his wayward steps. Ironically, the foundational truth that initially allowed David to quit hiding his own sin and experience God's forgiveness and healing is this: *the painful truth and God's lovingkindness are inextricably connected*. In Psalm fifty-one, in the context of his confession after being confronted by Nathan the prophet, David's states: "Have mercy on me, O God, according to your unfailing love; according to your great compassion blot out my transgressions. Surely you desire truth in the inner parts" (v. 1, 6).[2] Closing our eyes to family violence is a tempting way to

---

2. Unless otherwise stated, all Scripture citations are from the New International Version. David repeatedly connects God's loving kindness with his truth: Ps 25:5–6; 26:3; 40:10; 69:5, 13; 138:2. Other Scripture writers also make this connection.

mute painful truth, but it comes at a very high price—our experience of the redemptive power of God's love.[3]

It Upsets our Desired Vision for the Church and Family

As evangelicals we believe the home and church are two foundational institutions ordained by God. We lament the attacks on the family all around us and are powerfully tempted to identify the "outside secular world" as the enemy of the family, refusing to take a hard look at violence in our homes and churches. Or, when we are forced to deal with family violence in our congregations, we often resort to simplistic, ineffective strategies for "saving" violent marriages. Research repeatedly shows that one of the greatest evangelical impediments to recognizing and responding effectively to domestic violence is an "idealized" view of marriage which fails to account for the destructive realities of DV.[4] For instance, according to Knickmeyer et al. (2004), one abused woman recounted that when she went to her church leaders for help, they didn't prioritize her physical and emotional well-being but offered spiritual platitudes:

> "'pray, pray more. God can change anyone. God can change him.'
> It wasn't 'get out of there now.' It was 'God is able to change him.
> And you just have to pray more and God can work this out for
> you . . . God's will is that we hang together as a family. So just keep
> praying. God is going to change him.'"[5]

Surveys of abused Christians reveal that this type of "spiritualization of abuse," often flowing from a simplistic attempt to preserve the family, is one of the greatest obstacles to dealing with abuse in the church.[6] It is also counter-productive to the well-being of families and abused women, for it minimizes the prevalence and gravity of abuse and the characteristics of unrepentant abusers.

3. For a theological development of the importance of facing the truth of abuse, see Tracy, *Mending the Soul*, 131–40.

4. Nason-Clark, "Christianity and the Experience of Domestic Violence," 386–87; Levitt and Ware, "Religious Leaders' Perspectives," 212–22. For specific examples from evangelical marriage literature, see Tracy, "What Does 'Submit in Everything' Really Mean?" 285–312.

5. Knickmeyer et al., "Responding to Mixed Messages," 38.

6. Giesbrecht and Sevcik, "The Process of Recovery," 235; Nason-Clark, "Conservative Protestants and Violence against Women," 121.

Similarly, in one of the largest surveys of Christian leaders' views on domestic violence over five thousand North American Protestant ministers were queried. In spite of the fact that over eighty percent indicated they had some pastoral ministry experience with family violence, twenty-seven percent said that if a wife would begin to submit to her abusive husband God would honor her obedience and the abuse would stop or God would give her the grace to endure the beatings. Furthermore, almost one-fifth of the church leaders surveyed said no amount of violence from an abusive husband would justify a wife leaving.[7] Seemingly, marriage is more sacred than life itself. It is important to understand that the vast majority of abused Christian women believe in the sanctity of marriage. In fact, that is why they often endure years of abuse, don't seek help, agonize over leaving a husband they love, and feel great shame that they must have somehow failed and deserve some of the abuse they suffer.[8] They want the violence to end, not the marriage.

In summary, when we put on a happy "game face," unjustifiably pretending that all is well in our homes, or offer glib spiritual platitudes in response to the grave, devastating sin of domestic violence, this only drives the ugly truth deeper into the darkness, perpetuates the problem, dishonors the gospel, and keeps us from experiencing the beauty and transforming power of Christ. We do well to remember Jeremiah's warning to the religious leaders of his day who were minimizing abuse and oppression, offering superficial responses: "They dress the wound of my people as though it were not serious. 'Peace, peace,' they say, when there is no peace. Are they ashamed of their loathsome conduct? No, they have no shame at all" (Jer 8:11–12).

It Confronts Us with our Limited Knowledge and Power

Research among pastors reveals that the vast majority care about domestic violence and have dealt with it in their congregations, but most feel quite insecure about having the requisite knowledge and skills to help abusive families. One recent study of southern pastors revealed that

---

7. Alsdurf and Alsdurf, *Battered into Submission,* 153–58. More recent surveys of pastors are a bit more encouraging, but continue to reveal a prioritization of marriage over the well-being and physical safety of women and children. See for example Levitt and Ware, "Religious Leaders' Perspectives," 212–22.

8. Ringel and Park, "Intimate Partner Violence," 349; see also Giesbrecht and Sevcik, "The Process of Recovery," 229–48.

only a fraction of them (8%) felt "very equipped" to counsel domestic violence victims, and less than one-third felt they possessed adequate knowledge to refer victims to community resources.[9] Domestic violence creates complex, seemingly intractable dynamics in families. When Christian leaders do try to help abused women or their abusive husbands, it often doesn't go well. This creates a terrible "double bind" for pastors—they want to shepherd their flock but often feel impotent to do so. As evangelical leaders who believe in the veracity and power of God's Word, this is a particularly vexing dilemma, tempting us to overlook abuse in our families. It is hard to face a problem when you feel you lack the knowledge and power to deal with it. But this is precisely where we must apply "gospel theology." In a context of ministry effectiveness, Paul confesses, "[n]ot that we are adequate in ourselves to consider anything as coming from ourselves, but our adequacy is from God" (2 Cor 3:5, NASV). Furthermore, it is essential that we as Christian leaders recognize the foolishness of thinking that we have innate wisdom and power to change lives. At the end of the day, God does not work through our strength, rather, his life changing power is "made perfect in [our human] weakness" (2 Cor 12:9).

A recent study of abusive religious men highlights the importance of Pauline "weakness theology." These men had been recruited from court-mandated anger-management groups. Each admitted physically abusing a female intimate partner and almost all said that having a relationship with God was "important in their lives." One of the key findings of this unique study was that these men were trapped in a terrible double bind. On one hand, in the course of the interview they came to recognize that fear, particularly of being perceived as weak or unmanly, triggered their violence, yet at the same time they overwhelmingly believed that to admit fear, inability, or weakness would only invite humiliation and rejection. They were convinced that their female partners would prefer their rage to a confession of vulnerability.[10] It is not surprising that these men are isolated and mistrust others, particularly religious leaders who

9. Brennan et al., "Family Violence in Congregations," 18–46. In Nason-Clark's clergy research clergy also revealed that only eight percent felt well equipped to deal with DV, "When Terror Strikes the Christian Home." In *Beyond Abuse in the Christian Home*, 174.

10. Levitt et al., "Male Perpetrators' Perspectives," 443–45. The role "power oriented" masculinity and gender role insecurity play in the etiology of male perpetuated DV is well established. See Schwartz et al. "Gender-Role Conflict," 109–113.

seem to have all the answers. Thus, it is important and powerful for male Christian leaders to acknowledge their own weaknesses and fears, thus modeling reliance not on their abilities but on the sufficiency of Christ.

Now that we have identified some of the specific challenges to facing the truth, we will identify cardinal truths to accept.

SPECIFIC TRUTHS THE EVANGELICAL CHURCH MUST EMBRACE

Human Depravity is Universal and Results in Violence in the Home, Including Christian Homes

Scripture gives a shockingly brutal record of human conflict, bloodshed, abuse, and oppression. This is the product of universal human depravity, which results in those with more physical or social power taking advantage of those with less, particularly females, the poor, widows, orphans, and aliens.[11] Most often women have considerably less physical and often less social power than their husbands. The following research data demonstrates that DV is still prevalent and has a particularly virulent impact on women.

- Twenty-two to thirty-three percent of North American women will be assaulted by an intimate partner in their lifetime.[12]

- Between 2001 and 2005 nonfatal IPV represented 22 percent of nonfatal violent victimizations against females twelve years of age or older, whereas intimate partner victimization represented only 4 percent of nonfatal victimizations against males twelve years of age or older.[13]

- A 2005 Justice Department report revealed that 84 percent of spouses and 86 percent of boyfriends/girlfriends who experience

11. Eccl 4:1–4; Jer 7:6; Ezek 22:6–7, 29; Amos 5:11–12; Zech 7:9–10; Mal 3:5; Jas 5:1–6.

12. One of the largest and most cited U.S. surveys of DV is the Violence against Women Survey. It found a female lifetime intimate partner assault rate of 22 percent, Tjaden and Thoennes, *Prevalence, Incidence, and Consequences of Violence against Women*. Using a screening tool recommended by the American Medical Association, other researchers found a 31 percent lifetime prevalence for DV among adult American women, Siegel et al. "Screening for Domestic Violence," 874–77.

13. Catalano, *Intimate Partner Violence in the United States*.

IPV are females, and eight in ten murderers who killed a family member are male.[14]

- Intimate partner homicides account for 40 to 50 percent of all murders of women in the United States, and in 70 to 80 percent of intimate partner homicides, no matter which partner was murdered, the man abused the woman prior to the murder.[15]

- Seventy-five percent of the victims of violent family crimes are female.[16]

Male perpetuated gender oppression, including domestic violence, is anticipated in Gen 3:16 when God predicted that as a result of the fall the man would "rule" over the woman.[17] The first biblical account of domestic violence is found in the very next chapter of Genesis after Adam and Eve's sin in the Garden of Eden, when Cain killed his brother Abel (Gen 4:8–11). The first instance of DV towards a spouse is most likely also in Genesis four, when Lamech emphatically told his two wives, "listen to me . . . hear my words. I have killed a man for wounding me. . . . If Cain is avenged seven times, then Lamech seventy-seven times" (v. 23–24). Domestic violence is widely understood to involve not just the actual use of physical violence against a family member, but also the threat of force.[18] This appears to be the point of Lamech's haughty, chilling boast to his wives. Physical abuse soon became so widespread that God told Noah "I am going to put an end to all people, for the earth is filled with violence because of them" (Gen 6:13). The threat and/or experience of physical abuse occasioned the writing of many of the Psalms.[19] Physical violence and oppression is a dominant theme in most of the Major and Minor Prophets.[20] In addition to idolatry, the perpetration of

14. Durose et al., "Family Violence Statistics," 1.

15. Campbell et al., "Assessing Risk Factors for Intimate Partner Homicide," 118.

16. "Special Report: Violence among Family Members and Intimate Partners," 344.

17. Most commentators recognize that "He shall rule over you" is no divine proscription but a tragic predication of sin's effects on the human race. The Hebrew verb for "rule" found in Gen 3:16 (*mashal*) is the same term found in Gen 4:7 of Cain's need to harshly dominate that which would harm him, i.e., sin.

18. Verbal threats of violence are characteristic of physical abusers. See for instance 1 Kgs 19:1–2; 22:27; 2 Kgs 18:27–35; Ps 73:6–8; Acts 4:21, 29; 9:1.

19. For example, Ps 5, 10, 35, 37; 52, 59, 64; 140.

20. For example, see: Isa 59:1–5; Jer 7:6–11; Ezek 11:5–12; Hos 4:1–2; Joel 3:19; Amos 5:11–12, 24; Obad 10; Jonah 3:8–9; Mic 3:10; 6:8; 7:2–3; Nah 3:1–3; Hab 1:2–3, 9;

oppression and physical abuse precipitated the Babylonian Captivity (Jer 7:5–15). Paul apparently believed that the sins of physical and verbal abuse are so predictable and common in our fallen world that he used them to support his assertion of universal human depravity: "[t]heir mouths are full of cursing and bitterness. Their feet are swift to shed blood" (Rom 3:14–15). The "fruit of the flesh" anticipates physical abuse, for left to our own sinful instincts humans exhibit "hatred, discord, jealousy, fits of rage" (Gal 5:20). Furthermore, Scripture anticipates that physical abuse will actually increase in the last days when people will be characterized as "lovers of self," "arrogant," "abusive," "heartless," and "brutal" (2 Tim 3:2–4, ESV).

Believers are certainly not exempt from committing physical violence. There are numerous biblical examples of physical abusers, including domestic abusers, among God's covenant people. Notable examples include Cain, King Saul, David, Absalom, King Ahab, Queen Jezebel, Manasseh, the priests and rulers of Israel, Jewish parents of small children, Herod, the Pharisees, Herodias, and Saul, the religious zealot and fatal abuser who eventually became the greatest evangelist and theologian of the early church.[21] The Apostle Paul was so realistic about the potential for believers, including church leaders, to physically abuse that he listed this as a disqualifier for church eldership in 1 Timothy 3:3—"not violent."

The human heart hasn't changed since Scripture was written millennia ago. Humans continue to be born sinful, and this is often reflected in physical violence perpetuated by believers and unbelievers alike. When my wife Celestia and I first began ministering in East Africa, we were shocked to learn that two of the African countries which have experienced some of the worst indigenous physical and sexual violence, Rwanda and the Democratic Republic of the Congo, are two of the most "Christianized" countries in Africa.[22] Research on American families reveals that violence in Christian homes is roughly at parity with violence rates in secular families. Based on several studies which independently corroborated each others' finding, we can be more specific: conservative

---

Zeph 3:1–4; Zech 7:9–10; Mal 2:16.

21. Gen 4:8; 1 Sam 18:10–11; 20:33; 2 Sam 11, 13; 1 Kgs 21; 2 Kgs 21:16; Mic 3:9–12; 2 Kgs 17:17; Matt 2:16; 23:29–35; Matt 14:8; Acts 26:10–11.

22. At the time of the 1994 genocide, Rwanda was the most Christianized country in Africa. For a discussion of the role of the Rwandan churches in the genocide, see Rittner, et al. eds., *Genocide in Rwanda: Complicity of the Churches.*

Protestant men who attend church regularly are the least likely to engage in domestic violence, while conservative Protestant men who are irregular church attendees are the most likely to batter their wives.[23]

Given the clear biblical teaching on the prevalence of physical abuse among believers as well as unbelievers it is surprising that evangelicals so frequently assume that family violence rarely if ever happens in their congregations. Denial of abuse in the church is widespread even when abuse is prevalent in the surrounding community. For instance, a survey of forty-four pastors in Texas revealed the vast majority (83%) believe that less than ten percent of the families in their congregation have experienced domestic violence, in spite of the fact that they live in a state where seventy-four percent of the adult population acknowledges having either experienced violence or having a friend or family member who have experienced some form of domestic violence.[24] Likewise, two different studies of church leaders in Memphis found that almost all of them believe domestic violence to be exceedingly rare in their congregations, apparently so rare that they need not preach on it or otherwise address it. This is an incredible assumption in a city which has very high domestic violence and domestic homicide rates, and which, at the time of the surveys, was ranked "the second most violent metropolitan area" in the United States.[25]

Believers can and do continue to sin. We need the transforming power of the gospel until we are glorified. Christians, including church leaders, are not "above" the sin of abuse. There is a sin continuum here and we are all on it. We need to recognize the fact that there are "seeds" of abuse in all of us—harsh words, harmful angry outbursts, inappropriate use of power, etc. Biblical teaching on physical abuse as well as current research on families make it patently clear that the evangelical church, particularly pastors, *must* teach on abuse. Battered Christian women re-

23. Ellison and Anderson, "Religious Involvement and Domestic Violence among U.S. Couples," 269–86; Ellison, et al., "Are There Religious Variations in Domestic Violence?" 87–113; Wilcox, *Soft Patriarchs, New Men: How Christianity Shapes Fathers and Husbands*, 181–83.

24. Homiak and Singletary, "Family Violence in Congregations," 21.

25. Horne and Levitt, "Shelter from the Raging Wind: Religious Needs of Victims of Intimate Partner Violence and Faith Leaders' Responses," 83–97. Nason-Clark's research with Canadian evangelical clergy is identical—they estimate DV in Christian homes as much lower than the general population, "Conservative Protestants and Violence against Women," 119.

port that the single most important thing their religious leaders can do to help abused women in their congregations is to teach on abuse from the pulpit, and acknowledge that it occurs in Christian families.[26]

Justice and Mercy, Particularly for the Oppressed and Physically Abused, Is a Cardinal Moral Priority[27]

From Genesis to Revelation justice and mercy for the oppressed and abused is an overwhelmingly dominant ethical theme. It is not simply one of many biblical imperatives; it is fundamental to biblical morality. More specifically, ministry to the physically abused/oppressed in the form of care, protection, and confrontation of abusers, is a cardinal biblical moral priority for the following reasons:

1. *It reflects God's moral priorities;* he abhors physical abuse and abusers and gives justice/mercy to those they abuse and oppress.

    > bloodthirsty and deceitful men the Lord abhors. Ps 5:6 (See also Prov 6:16–18). The LORD examines the righteous, but the wicked and those who love violence his soul hates. On the wicked he will rain fiery coals and burning sulfur; a scorching wind will be their lot. For the Lord is righteous, he loves justice; upright men will see his face. Ps 11:5–7 (See also Isa 5:6–8; 59:1–15).

2. *It summarizes what God desires of his people and what it means to know God.*

    > Do what is just and right. Rescue from the hand of his oppressor the one who has been robbed. Do no wrong or violence to the alien, the fatherless or the widow, and do not shed innocent blood in this place. He [King Josiah] defended the cause of the poor and needy, and so all went well. *Is that not what it means to know me?* declares the Lord. But your eyes and your heart are set only on dishonest gain, on shedding innocent blood and on oppression and extortion. Jer 22:3, 16–17 (See also Job 29:12–17).

He has showed you, O man, what is good. And what does the Lord require of you? To act justly and to love mercy and to walk humbly with

---

26. Knickmeyer, et al., "Responding to Mixed Messages," 51.

27. For a development of the biblical primacy of justice and mercy for the vulnerable, oppressed, and abused, see: Haugen, *Good News about Injustice: A Witness of Courage in a Hurting World*; Stassen and Gushee, *Kingdom Ethics: Following Jesus in Contemporary Context*; Wolterstorff, *Until Justice and Peace Embrace.*

your God . . . The godly have been swept from the land; not one upright man remains. All men lie in wait to shed blood; each hunts his brother with a net. Mic 6:8, 7:2 (The context of justice and mercy is clearly physical abuse/oppression. Similarly, see Amos 5:11, 21–24).

3. *It forms the basis for particularly rich divine blessing.*

> Is not this the kind of fasting I have chosen: to loose the chains of injustice and untie the cords of the yoke, to set the oppressed free and break every yoke? . . . Then your light will break forth like the dawn, and your healing will quickly appear; then your righteousness will go before you, and the glory of the Lord will be your rear guard. Then you will call, and the Lord will answer; you will cry for help, and he will say: 'Here am I.' If you do away with the yoke of oppression. Isa 58:6–9 (The context clearly includes physical abuse—59:3. See also the rich blessings promised in Isa 33:14–17).

4. *It forms the basis for particularly harsh divine judgment.*

> Her officials within her are like wolves tearing their prey; they shed blood and kill people to make unjust gain . . . The people of the land practice extortion and commit robbery; they oppress the poor and needy and mistreat the alien, denying them justice...So I will pour out my wrath on them and consume them with my fiery anger, bringing down on their own heads all they have done, declares the Sovereign Lord. Ezek 22:27–31 (See also Isa 59:1–4).

5. *It is foundational to godly leadership. Spiritual and civic leaders have a particular responsibility to care for and protect the abused/ oppressed.*

> Endow the king with your justice, O God, the royal son with your righteousness. He will defend the afflicted among the people and save the children of the needy; he will crush the oppressor. He will take pity on the weak and the needy and save the needy from death. He will rescue them from oppression and violence, for precious is their blood in his sight. Ps 72:1, 4, 13–14 (See also Ps 82:2–4; Isa 1:15–17; Jer 22:2–3).

A final piece of evidence that justice and mercy for the oppressed and physically abused is a cardinal biblical priority is seen in one of the most dramatic acts of judgments in all of Scripture—God's punishment on Sodom and Gomorrah. The sin that precipitated God's wrath is one that evangelicals most frequently cite yet least understand. There are solid exegetical reasons for asserting that the inhabitants of Sodom and Gomorrah were judged for homosexual acts. But this was not the only sin that brought judgment. In fact, Ezek 16:49 only highlights one sin—their neglectful apathy toward the needy. And these people were needy because they were being oppressed/abused. Moses says "the outcry against Sodom and Gomorrah" is what stimulated divine judgment (Gen 18:20, ESV). The Hebrew word used for "outcry" (*za'áqat*) is "a technical word for the cry of pain or the cry for help from those who are being oppressed or violated."[28] Jer 23:10–14 also links the sin of Sodom and Gomorrah with abuse and oppression.[29]

As Evangelicals, We Have Not Responded Well to Domestic Violence

Historically, we evangelicals have been slow to address domestic violence. Evangelical pastors rarely preach on abuse. Few evangelical seminaries offer courses on abuse in general or domestic violence in particular. Evangelical churches rarely have specific protocols or resources for ministry to violent families. When churches do respond to abuse, they often do so in unsound and harmful ways. Their self-assessments are often inaccurate—they exaggerate the care they provide survivors of family violence, and minimize actions and teaching which may harm violent families.[30] It saddens me to issue such a strong negative assessment, but the evidence is overwhelming. We must be willing to face the truth about our collective failures and take corrective action.

28. Wright, *The Mission of God: Unlocking the Bible's Grand Narrative*, 359. *za'áqat* is used to refer to the cry of the poor (Prov 21:13), outcry due to famine and destruction (Jer 18:22), and the cries of the oppressed and afflicted (Job 16:18; Isa 15:5; 65:19), including the oppressed Israelites (Neh 5:6; 9:9; Esth 9:31).

29. Condemnation of Judah's oppression/abuse, particularly physical abuse, is a dominant theme throughout Jeremiah's ministry, cf. Jer 2:34–35; 5:25–31; 7:4–6; 19:4–5; 22:1–4, 13–17; 23:2–5, 13–17; 32:32–35.

30. For instance, in one study of almost two hundred parishioners, including fifty-seven battered women, there was a dramatic difference between the perceptions of battered versus nonabused parishioners regarding whether the church offered financial support to battered women, church teachings contributed to a climate that fostered DV, and whether DV was addressed in sermons, Manetta et al., "The Church-Does it Provide Support for Abused Women? Differences in the Perceptions of Battered Women and Parishioners," 5–21. Similarly, while 31% of clergy surveyed report having preaching a sermon on abuse, 95% of Christian women surveyed report never having heard a sermon on abuse, Nason-Clark, "When Terror Strikes," 174.

Reverend Al Miles surveyed 158 pastors regarding various aspects of domestic violence. Many of those surveyed, particularly the male pastors, asserted that there were no abused women in their congregations. Thirty pastors refused to participate, reasoning that there was no evidence of domestic violence in their church. Not surprisingly, most of the fifty-three abuse survivors he surveyed were disappointed and hurt by the way their pastors responded to them when they reported experiencing DV. Miles' study findings left him both worried and hopeful.

> [The pastors surveyed] were unanimous in condemning domestic abuse and all other forms of violence against women and children. They call domestic abuse criminal, deplorable, and sinful. Some of the ministers are confronting perpetrators with their accountability for the damage they have caused. But sadly, the vast majority of spiritual leaders could not describe any plans for programs in which they are involved to address this pervasive problem.[31]

I highlight the church's historic unhealthy response to abuse as an evangelical ethicist who loves the church. I have been a pastor for fifteen years and a lay leader for many more. For several years after graduating from seminary and entering the pastorate, I also failed to understand, prioritize, or respond properly to domestic violence. I shudder at recalling some of the abuse situations in my first two pastorates which I ignored or minimized. I have apologized to several of these individuals. By God's grace, I purposed to educate myself on abuse and make justice mercy for survivors and perpetrators a life priority. Our widespread failure to prioritize what God prioritizes and to hate what God hates is no trivial matter; it is grave. Thankfully, it is correctable. Many of us need to repent for our failure to address domestic violence and take corrective action. The good news is that when we do, we will often discover astounding ministry opportunities.

As We Face the Truth of Domestic Violence in our Homes and Churches, the Gospel Will Transform Lives and Give Hope

While family violence is ugly, painful, and complex, it is not insurmountable! Most abuse survivors as well as perpetrators carry deep psychological and spiritual wounds. Satan confuses and misdirects them with

---

31. Miles, *Domestic Violence: What Every Pastor Need to Know*, 50, 93, 153.

entrenched lies and shame. Change comes slowly. Sometimes it doesn't seem to come at all. Drawing on our own resources, we will not have the insight or power to minister effectively to violent families. It is essential that we draw on God's resources, embrace his promises, and develop a true "gospel mindset."

The gospel does miraculously change lives, but this is not a "quick fix" for family violence. The gospel truth sets us free by exposing our sin and by bringing us to the end of ourselves. Thus, the mandate of the church is to proclaim the all sufficiency of Christ in our weakness and brokenness, not in our beauty and perfection (cp. 2 Cor 4:7–18). Christ came for the sick not for the healthy (Matt 9:9–13). The church is for broken sinners who have the same problems and needs as the rest of the fallen world. We are all in constant need of the grace of God (1 Cor 15:10). Ministry to survivors and perpetrators of DV is living out the truth of the gospel in a pure and beautiful manner. God promises to honor and empower those who engage in ministry to the oppressed and broken. It is a sacred, beautiful, and uplifting privilege to have an abuse survivor entrust us with the most personal and painful parts of their lives, and to walk along side them and witness their amazing courage and sacrifice to grow and heal. Thus, while facing the truth of family violence is painful and difficult, it is among the most strategic, God honoring, and rewarding types of ministry.

CONCLUSION

We evangelicals showcase the beauty and power of the gospel when we actively face the reality of abuse in all its ugliness. Many of us have, at times, ignored the truth and failed to respond to family violence in a godly and redemptive manner. Thankfully, by God's grace, this can change. And for many evangelical leaders and churches it is changing. I would like to conclude with a testimony from one of my former seminary students.[32] Kim's story highlights the tremendous healing power churches can have in the lives of those shattered by family violence, even when the abuser doesn't appear to repent or allow the church to minister to him or her.

Kim and Bill were missionaries. They returned from the field so Kim could go to seminary, a plan Bill fully supported. Unfortunately,

32. I have changed their names to protect their identity.

these events intensified areas of insecurity and unhealthiness in Bill, and he became increasingly abusive. The following is a condensed description of events that occurred over five years in which Kim, with the help of seminary and church leaders (in two different congregations) sought to heal their abusive marriage.

> The abuse continued to intensify and I began to fear for my safety after Bill started using Rev 2:20–23 ["the spirit of evil Jezebel"] against me, saying that I would not go unpunished from my continued rebellion. Shortly after this I packed a suitcase and left our apartment under the guise of going to a retreat, since he was watching my every move. This would be the first time I would separate from Bill. Unfortunately, some of our friends and ministry supporters turned their back on us and withdrew their assistance after they learned of our marital problems. The support I received from what I would call my "first healing community" included material support along with unconditional love and grace as I tried to find my way through the confusion and devastation. My church mentor allowed me to stay in their home temporarily while I looked for employment so that I could support myself. Feelings of shame and failure seemed insurmountable at times, so my support community's aid was an especially important extension of God's grace that gave me hope for the future.

I loved my husband and greatly desired to have my marriage restored, so with the help of my mentor I prepared a plan of reconciliation which gave the steps Bill needed to take for us to reconcile. My spiritual advisors recommended Bill get more extensive professional counseling, to which he agreed. He said he was sorry for all of his abuse and appeared truly committed to personal and marital health. So I moved back into our home. Many times through the next five years Bill would "repent" after being confronted but the abuse would inevitably reappear, often in different forms.

Bill became increasingly unsafe at home and at church. So I went and explained everything to the senior church staff. They extended love and grace to both of us. Unfortunately, Bill would not accept their repeated offers of help. He utterly rejected their spiritual care, insisting they were ungodly and he was being persecuted. His abusive behavior at home intensified. When I was forced to separate from Bill for the second time, the church helped me to move into a new place and provided extra financial assistance. They offered to pay for counseling for both of us. Sadly, Bill's abuse and increasingly bizarre behavior continued. Eventually I was left with no other choice but to file for divorce.

It would have been easier for my church leaders to say I needed to go on to greener pastures but they stood by me, advocated for me, and showed their support in a myriad of ways. Most importantly, they believed me and did not ostracize me or make me feel inferior because I was being abused and having to make difficult decisions for my own safety and health. The leadership was open to learning more about domestic violence. The church and God's people became a place where I could be reassured of God's love, grace and truth.

God used my situation powerfully to say to our church: we are all broken; we are all in need of healing; you can find safety, unconditional love, and encouragement to become a whole and healthy disciple of Jesus Christ here in this church. I continue to be amazed and grateful to God who led me to this community of believers. God is now bringing many abused people to our church because we are ready to receive and minister to them. They are safe with us. This is the ultimate demonstration of God's love and redeeming grace.

Kim's story powerfully illustrates many of the principles discussed in this essay—the challenges as well as the redemptive power of God. Her church and seminary leaders agonized over how to best help her and her husband. They found the situation confusing and vexing. So they wisely and humbly reached out for help. They listened to Kim. They sought the assistance of others with expertise in ministry to violent families. They kept on reaching out to Bill, even though he repeatedly rebuffed their efforts. We can only imagine how difficult it was for Kim and Bill's two churches to face the reality of abuse in their marriage. After all, they were missionaries. She was a seminary student. We can only imagine how frustrating and disheartening it must have been after all the efforts by their church leaders (and Kim) over five years to learn that the abuse still had not stopped, that Bill still wasn't safe, that Kim felt she had no other choice but to file for divorce. But as difficult as this must have been, it reflects post-Eden biblical realities. Scripture simply does not promise that this side of eternity, in a fallen world containing sin, violence, and unrepentant abusers, we will all live "happily ever after." Yet just because real life does not produce care-free fairy tale endings, it need not produce Shakespearean tragedies. In fact, Scripture assures us that God does some of his most beautiful, powerful work in and through pain, brokenness, and abuse. Our very salvation is the supreme example of this startling truth.

The fact that Kim, in spite of her husband's failure to repent, is healing and thriving spiritually, and that her church has become an oasis for the abused, speaks of the miraculous power of God to redeem. It also speaks of the incredible ministry opportunities in local churches that are willing to reach out to those shattered by abuse. Kim's closing words should encourage and motivate us: offering love and safety to the broken in the name of Jesus is "the ultimate demonstration of God's love and redeeming grace." May God give us the courage and grace to face the truth that we might offer his grace to the broken.

REFERENCES

"Adverse Health Conditions and Health Risk Behaviors Associated with Intimate Partner Violence—United States, 2005." *Morbidity and Mortality Weekly Report* 57 (February 8, 2008) 113–17.

Alsdurf, James and Phyllis Alsdurf. *Battered into Submission: The Tragedy of Wife Abuse in the Christian Home*. Downers Grove, IL: InterVarsity, 1989.

Catalano, Shannan. *Intimate Partner Violence in the United States*. Washington, D.C.: U.S. Department of Justice, Office of Justice Programs, Bureau of Justice Statistics, rev. 2007.

"Domestic Violence Survey." Wirthlin Worldwide, 2000. Provided by Phoenix Councilwoman Peggy Bilsten.

Durose, Matthew R., et al. "Family Violence Statistics: Including Statistics on Strangers and Acquaintances." Washington, D.C.: U.S. Department of Justice, Office of Justice Programs, Bureau of Justice Statistics, 2005.

Ellison, Christopher G, et al. "Are There Religious Variations in Domestic Violence?" *Journal of Family Issues* 20 (1999) 87–113.

Ellison, Christopher G. and Kristin L. Anderson. "Religious Involvement and Domestic Violence among U.S. Couples." *Journal for the Scientific Study of Religion* 40 (2001) 269–86.

Giesbrecht, Norman, and Irene Sevcik. "The Process of Recovery and Rebuilding among Abused Women in the Conservative Evangelical Subculture." *Journal of Family Violence* 15 (2000) 229–48.

Haugen, Gary A. *Good News about Injustice: A Witness of Courage in a Hurting World*. Downers Grove, IL: InterVarsity, 1999.

Homiak, Katie Brennan, and Jon E. Singletary. "Family Violence in Congregations: An Exploratory Study of Clergy's Needs." *Social Work & Christianity* 34 (2007) 18–46.

Horne, Sharon G., and Heidi M. Levitt. "Shelter from the Raging Wind: Religious Needs of Victims of Intimate Partner Violence and Faith Leaders' Responses." *Journal of Religion & Abuse* 5 (2003) 83–97.

Knickmeyer, N., et al. "Responding to Mixed Messages and Double Binds: Religious Oriented Coping Strategies of Christian Battered Women." *Journal of Religion and Abuse* 5 (2004) 29–53.

Levitt, Heidi, et al. "Male Perpetrators' Perspectives on Intimate Partner Violence, Religion, and Masculinity." *Sex Roles* 58 (2008) 435–48.

Levitt, Heidi M., and Kimberly N. Ware. "Religious Leaders' Perspectives on Marriage, Divorce, and Intimate Partner Violence." *Psychology of Women Quarterly* 30 (2006) 212–22.

Manetta, Ameda A., et al. "The Church-Does it Provide Support for Abused Women? Differences in the Perceptions of Battered Women and Parishioners." *Journal of Religion & Abuse* 5 (2003) 5–21.

Miles, Al. *Domestic Violence: What Every Pastor Need to Know.* Minneapolis: Fortress, 2000.

Nason-Clark, Nancy. "Christianity and the Experience of Domestic Violence: What Does Faith Have to Do with It?" *Social Work & Christianity* 36 (2009) 379–93.

———. "Conservative Protestants and Violence against Women: Exploring the Rhetoric and the Response." *Religion and Social Order* 5 (1995) 109–30.

———. "When Terror Strikes the Christian Home." In *Beyond Abuse in the Christian Home: Raising Voices for Change,* edited by Catherine Clark Kroeger et al., 167–83. Eugene, OR: Wipf & Stock, 2008.

Ringel, Shoshana, and Juyoung Park. "Intimate Partner Violence in the Evangelical Community: Faith-Based Interventions and Implications for Practice." *Journal of Religion & Spirituality in Social Work: Social Thought* 27 (2008) 341–60.

Rittner, Carol, et al., eds. *Genocide in Rwanda: Complicity of the Churches.* Minneapolis: Paragon House, 2004.

Schwartz, Jonathan P., et al. "Gender-Role Conflict and Self-Esteem: Factors Associated with Partner Abuse in Court-Referred Men." *Psychology of Men & Masculinity* 6 (2005) 109–113.

Siegel, R. M., et al. "Screening for Domestic Violence in a Community Pediatric Setting." *Pediatrics* 104 (1999) 874–77.

Silverman, Jay G., et al. "Dating Violence against Adolescent Girls and Associated Substance Abuse, Unhealthy Weight Control, Sexual Risk Behavior, Pregnancy, and Suicidality." *Journal of the American Medical Association* 286 (2001) 572–79.

"Special Report: Violence among Family Members and Intimate Partners." Washington, D.C.: Federal Bureau of Investigation, revised January 2005.

Stassen, Glen H., and David Gushee. *Kingdom Ethics: Following Jesus in Contemporary Context.* Dowers Grove, IL: InterVarsity, 2003.

Tjaden, P., and N. Thoennes. *Prevalence, Incidence, and Consequences of Violence against Women: Findings from the National Violence against Women Survey.* Washington D.C., U.S. Department of Justice and Centers for Disease Control, 1998.

Tracy, Steven R. *Mending the Soul: Understanding and Healing Abuse.* Grand Rapids: Zondervan, 2005.

———. "What Does 'Submit in Everything' Really Mean? The Nature and Scope of Marital Submission." *Trinity Journal* 29 (2008) 285–312.

Wolterstorff, Nicholas. *Until Justice and Peace Embrace.* Grand Rapids: Eerdmans, 1983.

Wilcox, W. Bradford. *Soft Patriarchs, New Men: How Christianity Shapes Fathers and Husbands.* Chicago: University of Chicago Press, 2004.

Wright, Christopher J. H. *The Mission of God: Unlocking the Bible's Grand Narrative.* Downers Grove, IL: InterVarsity, 2006.

4

"Changing Men, Changing Lives"

—Calling Men to Peace

Barbara Jones-Schroyer and Ty Schroyer[1]

Is not this the kind of fasting I have chosen:
to loose the chains of injustice and untie the cords of the yoke,
to set the oppressed free and break every yoke?

(Isa 58:6)

IN THIS CHAPTER WE offer both a description of the Changing Men, Changing Lives program and some of what we believe are integral points related to calling men to peace. This program, developed by us in collaboration with the Domestic Abuse Intervention Program, expands the Duluth curriculum with the addition of faith related materials and approaches.

The Domestic Abuse Intervention Program (DAIP) is the most recognized model, both nationally and internationally, for responding to domestic assault and offers a variety of trainings and resources for the prevention and intervention of domestic violence. This system-wide

1. Ty Schroyer, B.A. and Barbara Jones-Schroyer, M.S.W., are a husband and wife team that have been involved both individually and as a partnership in domestic violence work since the late 80s. In 2003 they began a faith based men's nonviolence program called Changing Men, Changing Lives (CMCL) in collaboration with the Domestic Abuse Intervention Programs (DAIP) in Duluth, MN, USA. CMCL provides 27 weeks of court approved classes for men who have been arrested for domestic violence or have an Order for Protection filed against them by a domestic partner. CMCL receives referrals from the DAIP, directly from the court system, from churches and also self referrals from volunteers.

intervention strategy is being taught and applied throughout the world as part of a coordinated community response (CCR) to violence. A coordinated community response is composed of a network of agencies communicating together and made up of women's shelters, batterer intervention programs, the criminal justice system, human service agencies, and most recently, churches. This type of response involves written policies, practices and strategies regarding domestic violence and advocates swift consequences for violations of court orders and failures to comply with program rules.

We believe it is critical for a batterer intervention program or class to be part of a CCR, thus *Changing Men, Changing Lives* does not stand alone in the community. As a partner in the CCR we share the primary goal of protecting women from harm, preventing abusive behavior and intervening when necessary, and providing opportunities for men to change.

FROM DESTRUCTION TO REDEMPTION: TY'S STORY

My father was a football player in high school who prided himself on being tough, strong, and in control. Those characteristics carried on throughout his life. As a married man, it was clear that he was the "head" of our family and the ultimate decision maker. At that time, his position was culturally supported and socially sanctioned (and legally sanctioned in times gone by). No matter what part of society I was being molded by during my childhood (music, art, media, politics, school), the notion of a hierarchical relationship between men and women was being reinforced. I learned that I needed to be superior, or indeed that I was superior, to girls. I needed to win in every activity—the chess game, the race, or even the argument—or risk ridicule from the boys and the girls. I believed I needed to embrace a rigid masculinity and avoid and even reject anything feminine. Interestingly, my dad was the kind of man that would have defended a woman in public from male disrespect and yet behind closed doors was violent to my mother, my brothers, and me. My mother became the peacemaker and protector of her sons.

At age ten, my brother and I vowed never to be like our dad. Yet at age 21, I was arrested and jailed for domestic assault. The police responded to our home three different times before my actual arrest although on each occasion I had assaulted my partner. Unfortunately for her and for me, the mandatory arrest policy wasn't fully implemented in

1981. I didn't need an anger management class to teach me to breathe, to count to ten, or to take a time out in order to stop raging when the police arrived at our door. Even intoxicated, I knew how to act in this new hierarchal police-alleged perpetrator relationship where I no longer had the authority to get my own way or to punish my girl friend for some real or imagined transgression. I was fairly calm, cool, and collected while I helped her appear the crazy, angry one.

On this third occasion, the police told me that I would need to stay somewhere else for the night, and I reluctantly obliged but then went around the block and attempted to get back into our home. The police followed me and approached with irritation as I banged on the door. They stated that they were angry with me for not following their directives, and I momentarily forgot that in this hierarchal relationship they had socially sanctioned authority that I didn't have. I swore and mouthed off to them, producing negative consequences for me much like the consequences I had levied on my partner thirty minutes earlier. They threw me to the ground, handcuffed me, and brought me to jail with charges of domestic assault. The difference of course is that I was acting out of beliefs of male privilege and a sense of entitlement and the police really did have legal authority.

I heard Ellen Pence (founder of DAIP) say something at a training session that made so much sense—she said "the social relationship in which you find yourself will determine the limits you place on your behavior." You probably will only have to reflect momentarily to find examples of this in your own life. I certainly set different limits on my behavioral choices with the police than the person I had just assaulted.

I am so grateful that I was arrested and subsequently ordered into the DAIP program. It changed my life and perhaps saved a life. I discovered that what I was doing was not only morally wrong but that it was also a crime—not a relationship issue. Today I know that my partner would not have had to change anything for me to be nonviolent—nothing at all! I learned that I was 100% responsible for the choices I had made to cause harm. My actions were intentional, not out of control, as I attempted to get her to do something, get her to stop doing something, or to punish her.

Our relationship ended while I was in the DAIP program due to the destruction that I had caused. Perhaps it was also because, with the activation of the coordinated community response, she was made to feel safe enough and had the necessary support to leave the relationship.

HISTORY OF CMCL

Many years after this arrest and jail term, Ty became the Men's Program Coordinator for the DAIP, the very program he had been ordered into as a young man. Gradually during his sixteen year tenure in the position, the program recognized the value of having a culturally specific class for one of Duluth's non-white populations—Native American men. To meet the needs of this population, a culturally specific class for Native American men was developed. Native men then had the freedom to practice their spirituality not only through a mainstream group process, but also through culturally traditional activities such as smudging, sweat lodge, offering tobacco, and prayer. The men felt understood in a group created for them and led by native facilitators.

Christian men also have a comprehensive spiritual belief system, unique language, customs, prayer, and rituals which are pertinent to their culture. Just as the native men's class was created to be sensitive to the Native American community with the hope of optimizing the learning environment, Christian men needed a class that would be culturally sensitive to them, with God included in the change process. We were seeing that men with conservative Christian beliefs often did not respect the facilitators who held different spiritual beliefs from their own. Frequently this would result in either vigorous debate between participants and facilitators or the participant would not engage in the class, remaining silent. Neither outcome was helpful in creating change for Christian men, as debating or silence reinforced their religious justifications for abuse and violence.

In 2003, after fifteen years of facilitating secular classes, we realized our desire to become a teaching/facilitator team and we were ready to engage this specific population of Christian men. After much discussion and prayer, Ty presented our proposal to the management team at the DAIP and they agreed that this was an idea whose time had come and the staff gave their skeptical "thumbs up." We had wanted their buy-in because we believed the work should be a collaborative partnership with the DAIP. However, we also believed there needed to be freedom to develop and conduct the classes under the direction of the Holy Spirit.

CMCL helps men to:

- Define and identify controlling behavior;

- Examine thoughts, attitudes and beliefs and their connection to emotions and actions;

- Explore the effects of controlling/abusive behavior;

- Recognize and understand minimizing, denying, and blaming as obstacles to positive change and personal growth;

- Deal with the past to be able to live effectively in the present;

- Identify and learn to express feelings appropriately;

- Enhance healthy relationship skills;

- Explore scriptural basis for biblical equality.

We encourage men with this scripture: "Let us not become weary in doing good, for at the proper time we will reap a harvest if we do not give up." (Gal 6:9, NIV).

Initially, the CMCL classes met at DAIP's Center for Nonviolence facility and we began our first faith based class with only four men. We did not have a Christian curriculum at that time, but we had the DAIP curriculum and our beliefs about what the Bible really has to say about marriage, submission, and headship. We had so much enthusiasm and energy our first day that we couldn't fall asleep that night after class. There we were with all of our experience, knowledge, and skills, finally facilitating a class to "our" people and we were very excited about it! After CMCL met for a few months at the DAIP, we moved the class into a church facility. Interestingly, while the church was teaching the importance of taking the gospel out of the four walls of the church and bringing the message into the marketplace, as social activists we felt the need to take the class back into the church building.

DOUG AND BONNIE

Shortly after we began, a Christian man named Doug voluntarily joined the class. Doug had never used physical violence with his wife, but he had many control issues which caused his wife Bonnie to despair about whether their marriage could continue. She heard about the class from Barbara and "drew a line in the sand" with Doug, insisting that he needed to attend. Out of desperation he enrolled and told Bonnie that he would do whatever it took to repair their marriage. True to his word, in humility he worked earnestly on his issues. There were many months when he did not get through a class without crying in brokenness as the Holy Spirit revealed to him the truth about how he had treated his wife. As this happened and we set an atmosphere of trust, accountability, and encouragement, little by little Doug changed. He took home the new behaviors he was learning and practiced them, along with learning to change his thinking. As he did this, it had a profound effect on his marriage and restoration began to happen. Doug and Bonnie's life became attractive to others and they freely shared with friends and family what was going on in their relationship.

Doug became an "evangelist" for CMCL, which resulted in a number of Christian men volunteering into CMCL. Doug completed the twenty-seven weeks and continued to come to class for the next three years, acting as a mentor and leader to other men. Eventually our class grew quite large. To meet this growth opportunity, Doug and Bonnie attended the DAIP's intensive three day training that we taught, so they could become class facilitators. Following a close mentoring program, we started our second CMCL class with them as the facilitators. (To see more about Doug's story go to the video at: www.changingmenchanginglives.org.)

WOMEN'S VOICES

While conducting our men's groups we also worked with the DAIP to develop a faith based support group for Christian women because we believed it was imperative that this group be led by a skilled woman of faith who could help battered women become safe, honor their faith, and guide them through a process of healing and personal empowerment. Pat, a Christian woman and a women's advocate for the DAIP, has been faithfully facilitating this group. The group meets every other week in a local church which provides free space. The support group is open and free to any woman, not just those whose partners are in CMCL.

As a result of our ongoing work with both men and women, the DAIP became interested in the success of the faith based classes and in 2006 they wrote a grant for a Christian curriculum to be written and the development of a documentary DVD of CMCL.

Before we wrote the curriculum, we held two focus groups comprised of Christian women who were either currently in an abusive intimate relationship, or had been in their recent past. Most of the partners of these women participated in our classes. The purpose of the focus groups was to hear directly from abused Christian women what their experiences, thoughts, and feelings were, especially in relationship to their spirituality. Before we began we received their permission to tape record the sessions, for later transcription. We assured the focus group participants that their identities would remain anonymous and with that in mind, they agreed.

What the women shared in the focus groups was heart wrenching. They frequently talked about the church valuing their marriages more than their lives. In other words, it was a greater sin to separate or divorce than to remain in the marriage (often with children), continue to be abused, and possibly lose their lives. A woman whose church withdrew its support when she filed for divorce asked, "Where is the church discipline for the violence?" The women also spoke of the fear that disclosing the abuse would bring shame to the church, particularly if a woman's husband was a pastor or was active in ministry. The following are comments offered during those groups:

> There was no voice; I wasn't allowed to say what was really going on. [The church counselor] didn't want to really hear it, that whole thing about "Don't tell the secret, don't tell anybody what's really going on in your life, nobody wants to hear it…that whole thing about the church telling women to keep silent."
>
> When you're a Christian woman and your spiritual leadership does not understand abuse or they're not educated in it, and they're reinforcing the abuse and using Scripture . . . it makes you have this subtle resentment and anger toward God. And whether you realize it or not, it's happening, and it's putting a barrier between you and God.
>
> The church has been both wonderful and abominable at different times.[2]

When the church turns away or minimizes the abuse that a woman experiences, her reality is denied and her safety is compromised. This increases the abuser's power and lessens his opportunities for meaningful change. At the same time, the women related examples of when and how their pastor or others in their spiritual community had been understanding and supportive:

- Believing her when she came forward;

- Validating her decision to leave the relationship;

---

2. Jones-Schroyer et al., "Changing Men," 25.

- Providing a safe place to stay;

- Providing financial support;

- Providing books and other readings for contemplation;

- Grounding support in Scripture that validated women's worth and equality.

"I felt like the chains were taken off my brain" was how one woman described the experience of finding a pastor who believed her. At the core of this support was someone who acknowledged that a woman's life counted—she did not have to lose her safety, her self, or her life in order to count before God.[3]

THE CHANGE PROCESS

CMCL is predicated on the principles of safety for women, accountability for men, and real opportunities for change. We value the covenant of marriage, but not over a woman's life. We believe in biblical equality and mutuality in marriage.

There is no longer Jew or Greek, there is no longer slave or free, there is no longer male and female, for all of you are one in Christ Jesus.

(GAL 3:28, NRSV)

In the Lord, however, woman is not independent, nor is man independent of woman. For as woman came from man, so also man is born of woman. But everything comes from God. (1 Cor 11:11–12, NIV)

We create a respectful but challenging classroom environment where Christian men who batter can look at their beliefs about abusive behavior, face the harmful effects this has on women, children and themselves, and move toward relationships of equality with women. This involves creating an encouraging atmosphere of trust, compassion, and accountability.

Participants are required to make a commitment to be nonviolent in order to attend. Classes are co-facilitated by men and women, assuring both a woman's and a man's perspective in the group process and modeling partnership. The classes use the curriculum of the DAIP and

3. Ibid.

the supplement "Changing Men, Changing Lives: Building Nonviolence with Christian Men," which adds the Christian faith perspective.

Men attend a general orientation at the DAIP and may choose the 27 week CMCL class to fulfill the court's requirements. We have noticed though, that to avoid being held accountable by other Christians, some Christian men will choose the secular/mainstream classes over CMCL in order to "hide." Christianity is defined by each participant—they do not need to attend church or be members of a particular denomination to participate in CMCL.

DIALOGUE AND CRITICAL THINKING

Men who batter use a variety of tactics to gain power and control over their partners. The justifications that Christian men give for their abuse may differ from men in the culture at large, even though their tactics are similar. Christian men often misuse scriptures to reinforce male "headship," to rationalize what they see as their God given authority, and to justify female submission.

In the CMCL classes we discuss male privilege, hierarchy, and oppressive social systems. Dialogue and critical thinking skills are used to analyze where these beliefs come from, what benefits and costs they bring to our relationships, and whether they are biblically accurate. We believe that the skills of critical thinking and reflection are essential to shifting core beliefs and changing abusive behavior. When programs avoid discussions regarding scripture, their effectiveness with abusive Christian men is reduced.

For men in class the change process is a journey through what we call the "5 R's." We learned these "Rs" from Rev. Dr. Marie Fortune at the Faith Trust Institute, Seattle, WA.[4] These characteristics are extremely useful as a measure and gauge of accountability during a man's process of change:

1. *Remorse*: he feels guilt and sorrow for his actions. This does not mean change, though! As Barbara often says "This is only tears and words; change remains to be seen;"

2. *Repentance*: he is willing to do whatever it takes to turn away from his actions. He acknowledges wrong doing and begins to change his thinking and subsequent behavior;

4. Adams and Fortune, *Against Women and Children*.

3. *Restitution*: he makes amends, joins program(s), pays his child support, and tells the truth to family and community about what happened;

4. *Restoration*: he begins to find healing within himself, in his relationship with God, and others (but not necessarily the marriage);

5. **Possible Reconciliation*: this is when the marriage relationship is able to be restored. This is not always possible and as Marie Fortune says, if the marriage cannot be reconciled, then it is our job to come alongside both people to help them mourn their losses.

The DAIP curriculum is divided into the following themes: nonviolence; nonthreatening behavior; respect and love; support and trust; honesty and accountability; sexual respect; partnership; and negotiation and fairness.

Six key roles for facilitators in batterer intervention programs using the Duluth curriculum are essential, and we strongly support them in Changing Men, Changing Lives:

1. Participate in interagency efforts to hold participants accountable for further violence and failure to complete the program;[5]

2. Keep the class focused on issues of violence, abuse, control and change;

3. Facilitate reflective and critical thinking in the class;[6]

4. Maintain an atmosphere that is compassionate, accountable and not colluding. (We add "to work toward social justice");

5. Provide new information and teach non-controlling relationship skills;[7]

6. Facilitate a positive and affirming class experience.

Many class participants have told us that they have been in a variety of Christian groups that were either religious and condemning or too loose ("greasy grace" as one man called it) with no accountability. In CMCL we try to maintain accountability in an atmosphere of genuine caring. It is a difficult atmosphere to create and maintain, but the only one in which we believe true change can happen.

5. DAIP. *Creating a Process of Change.*
6. *Ibid.*
7. *Ibid.*

"FLAGSHIP" VERSES

The following two verses are woven throughout the fabric of our classes:

> Do not conform any longer to the pattern of this world, but be transformed by the renewing of your mind then you will be able to test and approve what God's will is, his good, pleasing and perfect will. (Rom 12:2, NRSV)

> We demolish arguments and every pretension that sets itself up against the knowledge of God, and we take captive every thought to make it obedient to Christ. (2 Cor 10:5, NIV)

These verses are foundational because we believe the change process comes through changed thinking, changed beliefs, changed feelings, and changed actions.

THOUGHTS FOR PASTORS

Reverend Al Miles elaborates on the following steps that pastors must take in order to "avoid the many pitfalls an abuser will place before us, such as blaming his victim, manipulation, slick talk, and an early proclamation of being changed by God."[8]

- Put the woman's safety first;
- Seek training;
- Know your limits and work in collaboration with others in the community.

As a pastor you don't need to be an "expert" on domestic violence. Just as a paramedic responding to an accident doesn't attempt to perform surgery on a person but instead assesses the situation, administers life saving first aid, then takes the person to the specialist—you too can do the same thing—take her to the domestic violence specialists in your community and continue to be her pastor.

CLOSING THOUGHTS

We exhort the Church to become acquainted with the agencies and resources in their communities that are already working with domestic violence survivors and batterers. Take time to visit your nearest women's

8. Miles, Rev. Al., *Domestic Violence.*

shelter and batterer's program and partner with them. Find out where the women's support groups are and how your church can come alongside these programs. Join the CCR, speak up, teach and preach on domestic violence from the pulpit, take offerings for victims of domestic violence, and hold abusive men accountable. Get trained and start a faith based men's nonviolence class. Let the abused women in your congregation know that you will stand with them. Love the oppressed and help to set them free.

For more information regarding CMCL or to see their documentary video go to: www.changingmenchanginglives.org.

For information about the DAIP go to: www.theduluthmodel.org

REFERENCES

Adams, Carol, and Marie Fortune, eds. *Violence against Women and Children: A Christian Theological Sourcebook*, New York: Continuum Publishing, 1995.

Jones-Schroyer Barbara, et al., "Changing Men, Changing Lives: Building Nonviolence with Christian Men," unpublished curriculum, 2007.

Miles, Rev. Al., *Domestic Violence, What Every Pastor Needs To Know*, Minneapolis, MN: Fortress Press, 2000.

Pence, Ellen, and Michael Paymar, *Creating a Process of Change for Men Who Batter, The Duluth Curriculum*, Duluth, MN: DAIP, 2003.

5

Calling Women to Safety

Cathy Holtmann

A T THE DAWN OF the new millennium, world leaders recognized that it was time for big changes. Of the approximately 6 billion people alive on the planet at that time (it's now 6.6 billion and growing), the majority lived in poverty. Four billion people, most of whom were women and children, were living below the relative poverty line and of the 1.3 billion people living below the absolute poverty level, 70 percent were women.[1] An action plan for change was formulated called the Millennium Development Goals (MDGs) which focused on concrete improvements in eight areas: 1) poverty and hunger; 2) universal education; 3) gender equality; 4) child health; 5) maternal health; 6) HIV/AIDS; 7) environmental sustainability; and 8) global partnership. The MDGs had specific targets to reach by the year 2015, including halving the number of people living on less than a dollar a day, ensuring that all girls and boys have access to primary education, providing gender equality in access to secondary education, reducing child mortality rates by two-thirds, lowering the maternal mortality ratio by three-quarters, and halting the spread of HIV/AIDS.[2]

While some progress has been made it is clear that these targets will not be met, particularly poverty reduction in light of the recent global economic crisis.[3] According to the World Health Organization, while poverty is a barrier to positive health outcomes for both men and

---

1. WMW, "Advocacy Guide to Women's World Demands."
2. UN, "End Poverty: Millennium Development Goals 2015."
3. UN, "The Millennium Development Goals Report 2010."

women, poverty places a greater burden on women and girls' health.[4] Life expectancy is higher for women than men in most countries, but a number of health and social factors combine to create a lower quality of life for women. Unequal access to information, care, and basic health practices further increases health risks for women

Natural disasters and the effects of climate change are exacerbating this situation. In the wake of the January 2010 earthquake in Haiti, where unofficial estimates put the death toll as high as half a million, international aid agencies had difficulty getting emergency supplies and food to those most desperately in need. Non-governmental organizations (NGOs) began a policy of distributing relief supplies to women only, in order to ensure that they reached vulnerable people rather than the black market.[5] Increasingly those who work in the developing world are adopting a gendered approach to development because they recognize that ensuring the health and well-being of women and their dependents is the key to building a solid societal foundation. The Canadian Catholic Organization for Development and Peace, a faith-based NGO with a 42 year history of international development with partners around the world, stated the following:

> *Women at the heart of the matter:* If we have a preferential option for the poor, it means that we are therefore necessarily engaged in the struggles of women, for they constitute the majority of the poorest people on the planet. They are often the first victims of a conflict and sometimes even the target of pressure tactics against a community. Whether one is talking about agriculture or any other type of family economic activity, women are on the front lines but without the same recognition or rights as their brothers. In addition, all of our partners confirm that women are the keys to sustainable development, in their families and in their communities, and they are the main actors during any crisis. They are called upon to manage use of the Earth's resources—water, land and everything it produces.[6]

Another particularly troublesome aspect of this global picture is the high rate of violence against women. In 2008, the United Nations Secretary-General Ban Ki-moon launched the campaign *UNite to End*

---

4. WHO, "Women's Health."

5. CBC, "Women-Only Food Sites Open in Haiti."

6. CCODP, "2011-2016 Strategic Plan," 7.

Violence Against Women. This was designed as a multi-year effort aimed at preventing and eliminating violence against women and girls in all parts of the world. According to the UNite website:

- One in five women in the world will become a victim of rape or attempted rape in her lifetime;

- Violence against women during or after armed conflicts has been reported in every international or non-international war-zone;

- The most common form of violence experienced by women globally is physical violence inflicted by an intimate partner;

- One in three women have experienced beating, sexual assault or some other form of abuse by a spouse, boyfriend or common law partner.[7]

In today's globalized world not only is a chasm continuing to widen between a small minority of rich people and an overwhelming majority of poor, most of whom are women, but in addition to the vulnerability of poverty, women's physical and emotional safety is hugely at risk. The very people that women and children should be able to rely on for support in order to face difficult daily challenge—their fathers, husbands or boyfriends—are those that most frequently harm them. Love and compassion are what is needed by women dealing with widespread hunger, disease, and struggle, yet that is not what they can expect.

The extent of contemporary social issues such as poverty, disease, and violence, and their affects on women can be demoralizing particularly for those who, from the point of view of faith, believe that as Christians we are called to work to transform unjust social structures. The problems are huge and complex and the work to solve them is equally daunting. As a Catholic activist I have been committed over the years to taking part in collective struggles on a variety of issues including workers' rights in the face of free trade, participatory democracy, peace in times of war, ensuring the human right to water, calling Canadian mining companies to account for their human rights and environmental violations, working for food security, and trying to make poverty history. As an instructor of Religious Studies I have tried to teach undergraduate university students the ways in which religious traditions consider injustice and how religious people work for change on the basis of their faith.

7. UN, "UNite to End Violence."

The rich history of Catholic social teachings and the work of Canadian ecumenical justice coalitions have helped me in this regard.[8] I am also involved in the struggle for women's religious equality in the Catholic Church.[9] When I reflect on where my passion for social justice comes from, I know that it is rooted in faith and my personal experience.

I spent many years playing basketball in high school, at university, for the Canadian national team program, and overseas. By external measures, I was a successful elite athlete in that the teams on which I played won more games than they lost and I garnered many awards for my achievements. My university coach was also considered very successful, yet psychologically abusive to me and my teammates. At practice and during team meetings we were often yelled at and belittled. One line that still stays with me is, "You people are morons—completely incapable of thought!" Our mistakes were always occasions for punishment. We ran, we did pushups and sit ups, we did wall jumps, all in order to make up for our stupidity. Whenever we screwed up we were told so. I remember walking to practice with a teammate one afternoon after a tournament that we had not won. We were wondering what the punishment would be. She said to me, "I can take the drills and all that stuff, but it's the silent treatment that I find the hardest."

As elite athletes we were under the impression that such behavior from a coach was normal. This was supposed to toughen us up for competition and we heard stories from other athletes about their coaches that were worse than ours. But something inside told me that his tirades were wrong and I started to challenge them. Looking back now, so many years later, I do not remember exactly what I said or did, but I paid a price. For me, the abuse also included weekly "attitude adjustment" sessions. All I remember now about those meetings was that I would cry a lot and that I was self-conscious about how my face looked when I left his office. One of the secretaries in the athletic department said to me, years after I had graduated, "We all felt so bad for you whenever we saw you come out of that office."

All the time the abuse was going on however, I was an outstanding student. I loved university because it had opened up new ways of understanding the world. I felt like I had been freed—from the intellectual confines of my rural high school and from my family. My ability to ask

8. Lind and Mihevic, *Coalitions for Justice*; Sheridan, *Do Justice!*
9. Holtmann, "Resistance is Beautiful."

difficult questions was considered an asset rather than a liability. I received prestigious scholarships during my studies and got top awards at graduation. In addition to my music major, the courses I found most interesting were Religious Studies courses, particularly those that focused on the human search for meaning and justice. I was on my own search, obviously, looking for reasons to explain why I was working so hard yet feeling so badly about myself. One particular professor, a former basketball star and ordained minister in the United Church of Canada, inspired me with his stories of working with Latin Americans in resistance to American political, economic, and military domination. I developed a strong sense of solidarity with those who were struggling simply to build a life for themselves and their families yet were crushed by forces so much bigger and stronger than they. I realized that in life hard work and good intentions were not enough. Structurally, there were systems in place that fostered inequality and oppression. Christian theology from the point of view of the social gospel made so much sense to me. My experiences of pain and injustice could be used as a resource within myself in working for social change. I took comfort in the fact that my struggle was rather insignificant compared to that of others. How could I despair when so many were so much worse off? I learned to endure the tirades of my coach and my competitive spirit would not allow me to quit. After my basketball career, I studied theology and have devoted my life to working with others for social change.

It took me quite a while to figure out that what had gone on during those undergraduate years was not simply punishment, but psychological abuse. I spent the longest time wondering what was wrong with me. Years of being yelled at, criticized, and humiliated, both publically and privately, had fed feelings of low self-esteem, lack of self-confidence, and an eating disorder. On the surface I was a successful woman doing what I believed in—I had developed many strengths, but inside I was often miserable. In the words of sociologist Dorothy Smith, I was feeling the effects of a bifurcated consciousness.[10] I was split within myself, having worked hard to become a theologian, activist, and professional liturgical musician, yet when I used these gifts in the classroom, church, or activist community I was often in situations of conflict. I took these conflicts personally, seeing them as a product of my own inadequacies or inability to communicate clearly. It was through the help of a wise woman

10. Smith, *Institutional Ethnography.*

chaplain, companions in a women's spirituality group in the context of discovering feminist theology, and counseling, that I was able to name the abuse and its effects on my life.

It was particularly in the study of feminist theology and participation in feminist spirituality practices that I learned a language that began to describe my experience most accurately. While I had always found my Catholic faith to be a source of comfort and strength to me, until I discovered the feminist critique of patriarchy I had not realized that it too had contributed to my belief that there was something wrong with me, instead of being able to name the abuse (and its effects) for what it was. Patriarchy is a system of male dominance over women and children that is institutionalized. It is characterized by an ideology of hierarchical dualisms: men/women, white/black, spirit/matter, coach/athlete—with the former being somehow better or more powerful than the latter. Religious patriarchy affects both men and women, socially constructing patterns of relationship in which being male is understood as being the standard for human being and being female is not.[11] While recognizing that all theology is grounded in human experience, feminist theology takes as its starting point, women's experiences. Women's experiences within structures of religious patriarchy expose these structures as reflecting male experience rather than universal human experience. "Feminist theology makes the sociology of theological knowledge visible, no longer hidden behind mystifications of objectified divine and universal authority."[12] The effects of patriarchy are found in the social, economic, political, and religious inequality between men and women which is maintained through language, myth, symbol, and belief.[13]

In a patriarchal religion such as Catholicism, God is most often referred to as a loving Father and, in this male image, mirrored many of the stereotypical masculine qualities of men in our society. My own father was a dairy farmer who responsibly looked after his farm and family. He worked hard. As kids, my siblings and I were taught to respect our dad and not to question his authority. My mother supported my father through her work on the farm and served as an example of a good Catholic woman. Likewise, through participating in the liturgical life of the church I became Catholic, learning that male priests had special

11. Clifford, *Introducing Feminist Theology*, 28–32.

12. Radford Ruether, *Sexism and God-Talk*, 13.

13. Penner, *Healing Waters*, 6–12.

power. I was immersed in a religious culture where nuns and lay women served the church through work in education, fundraising, cooking and serving meals, and making music, while priests were held in the highest esteem. Most of the scripture stories proclaimed during mass were about men, exclusively masculine language was used in prayer, and even the fact that Jesus was a man was proof that being male was somehow better than being female. While the Catholic Church professed the equality of men and women through baptism, it did not practice this equality within its own structures or reflect this equality in its rituals. Religious imagery, language, and liturgy all reinforced masculine supremacy.

I grew to believe that God, imaged as powerful and judgmental, expected much from me, yet I could never live up to these expectations. As a teenager I regularly partook of the sacrament of reconciliation (confession) believing that only the priest could absolve my sins for a time. As Catholics, the moral bar was set very high, which left many of us feeling guilty about our inadequacy—no matter what we did. As well, sin was tightly bound up with sexuality, particularly female sexuality. In catechism I learned that women's sexuality was problematic. Eve was responsible for bringing sin into the world through giving in to temptation. Mary was an immaculate virgin who bore Jesus without having sex. The woman caught in adultery was saved by a man from her sin. Sex was acceptable only in marriage, which in itself was less holy than a life of celibacy. Birth control was taboo and even though most Catholics practiced it, they were nevertheless doing something wrong. Catholics were strongly urged to support the right to life movement and condemn abortion—considered the primary responsibility of women.

All of these elements of the Catholic faith can contribute to an inferior sense of self among women. For women it is a system of self-alienation and male domination.[14] In my case, I trusted male authority and believed that men had my best interests at heart. If a man in authority criticized me I automatically assumed that I had done something wrong. Growing up I had no positive role models of women in my life critiquing patriarchy, resisting men with power, or trying to deliberately change the system and do things differently. As a young adult, my Catholic identity and upbringing had fashioned me for personal abuse by my coach. The feminist critique helped me to understand the ways in which all women within patriarchal religious institutions and families are "set up" in the same way.

14. Schüssler Fiorenza, *Wisdom Ways*, 53–74.

Feminist theology and praxis helped me to take seriously my experiences, critically analyze my attitudes, reframe my past, find the liberating core of the Christian tradition, and strengthen my resolve to work with others so that women and oppressed people can become subjects of their own histories rather than objects of male domination and control.[15] Feminist biblical scholarship made me aware that the scriptures were originally written by men, for men. Yet beneath this patriarchal overlay there were also the seeds of its own dismantlement. Gradually I came to know the lesser known stories of biblical women—strong figures whose stories were not often told in Catholic circles.[16] Women such as Hagar, Rachel, Ruth and Naomi, Esther, Mary of Bethany, and Priscilla were brought out into the light along with their liberating actions and faith. Misogyny in the scriptures was highlighted and critiqued through the stories of Tamar, Queen Vashti, and Mary Magdalene. The image of Sophia, Wisdom of God, the divine feminine, and model for understanding the person of Jesus was reclaimed.[17] Women's roles in the history and development of the Christian church were uncovered.[18] Feminist work on ethics in the areas of sexuality and ecology raised the possibility that women's ways of making moral choices were both different and valid compared to men's.[19]

In coming to name some of my experiences as an athlete as psychological abuse, I cried a lot of tears—both of hurt and anger—but I know that I am a stronger person as a result of learning from them. In considering the effects of patriarchy, my experiences were not unique. My faith in the example of Jesus, someone who created a movement to challenge the abusive religious and political structures of his day, has deepened as a result. Jesus did not earn earthly accolades for speaking out against injustice but he did it because of his deep rootedness in the love of God, a love that seeks liberation and the fullness of life—a love that never tolerates abuse. I continue to learn about how patriarchal institutions and the cycles of control and domination in which we are all embedded affect me, other women, and all oppressed minorities.

In the years of reflection after the abuse, what has become very clear to me is that abuse, in whatever form it is manifest, is always wrong. I

15. Radford Ruether, *Women-Church.*
16. Winter, *Woman Wisdom, Woman Witness,* and *Woman Word.*
17. Rupp, *Prayers to Sophia;* Schüssler Fiorenza, *Wisdom Ways.*
18. Malone, *Women and Christianity;* Schüssler Fiorenza, *In Memory of Her.*
19. Gilligan, *In a Different Voice;* Eaton, *Introducing Ecofeminist Theologies.*

did not need the abuse from my coach in order to learn. Human beings can and will flourish in situations that are conducive to psychological and physical health and growth. Challenges and conflict are normal and will inevitably arise in relationships. but the need for inordinate power and absolute control over others is not. Relationships are about give and take. My task in this chapter, in terms of recounting my own abuse in the context of the pervasive structural inequality of women in society, is to call women to safety—particularly women of faith. Learning to recognize the signs of an abusive relationship is of critical importance. These signs include:

- a person's need to always be right, especially those in power;

- the opinions of those without power count for little or nothing;

- the critique of power or leadership is forbidden;

- accomplishments are belittled;

- mistakes are constantly pointed out;

- ridicule, disrespect, and name-calling;

- the needs of others are disregarded;

- there is a constant monitoring of behavior, either by those in power or by victims so as not to offend someone with power;

- conflict escalates and results in physical pain and/or injury;

- access to necessary resources such as financial, emotional, or material is limited or denied; and

- there is a cycle of continual blame rather than accepting responsibility for one's own actions.

Whenever any of these factors make themselves apparent in a relationship of any kind, women need to take them seriously. We need to teach our children to take them seriously. These are signs of potential abuse and action must be taken to either make the behaviors stop or to remove oneself from the relationship. In many cases, psychological abuse is the precursor to other forms of violence. Recognizing abuse and acting appropriately is difficult because we do not want to suspect that those we love or admire can be abusive or violent. But the reality is that the people who have the most potential to harm are those to whom we are in closest proximity—our fathers, husbands, lovers, brothers, teachers, doctors, ministers, or coaches. Being aware of the signs of abuse and violence does not mean that we cannot trust anyone, but it does mean that trust and respect are earned through the practice of healthy relationships. We need to hold those around us accountable and when our dignity as persons is being disrespected in any way we must speak up or walk away, acting on our own behalf.

A good strategy in situations of suspected abuse is to seek out the advice and counsel of a professional. Certainly a certified counselor, therapist or social worker is someone with whom you can talk about a relationship and about your feelings. He or she will help you decide how best to deal with abuse and violence. A professional will have your safety and wellbeing as her or his primary concern and will help you find ways to make it end. As awareness of the prevalence of violence and abuse grows among clergy, church leaders are becoming people that victims can also turn to in cases of abuse. Religious leaders can help you use your faith as a resource in bringing an end to abuse in your life. In all of these cases, if a professional suspects that your life is at risk, she will advise that you seek safety immediately.

In relationships with non-abusive adults, pointing out ways in which others make us feel uncomfortable or devalued will be received with empathy and a willingness to see things from another point of view. There will also be a willingness to work to change future interactions. In a relationship with an abusive person, such comments will heighten the controlling or violent responses. Those who are unaware of the ways in which they do damage to other people will continue to blame the victim and feel justified in what they have done. Sometimes words will not be enough to put a relationship back on the right track. In addition to identifying and naming the abuse or violence, finding physical and emotional safety should be a priority. Leaving an abusive or violent relationship is the right thing to do, even if the other person does not acknowledge the effects of his words and actions or blames the victim herself for the abuse. It is not a failure or a sign of weakness on the part of the person leaving the relationship. It is not a lack of commitment. It is a choice that means caring about oneself and others. Abuse cannot be allowed to continue for the sake of everyone involved. Leaving also does not mean the abusive person cannot or will not change. But it is *not* up to the victims to help abusers change. It is up to those on the receiving end of abusive or violent behaviors to identify the abuse and seek safety. You cannot love your neighbor as yourself without loving yourself enough to ensure your own safety. For those socialized to look after the needs of others before their own, this will be uncomfortable, but it is absolutely necessary. Drawing the line and bringing an end to an abusive relationship for the sake of your children is a loving act. It takes courage, but it is the courage that many millions of women, the world over, need to cultivate as we work to make the world a safer, more humane place. The gospels show that the courage to confront abusive and violent relationships with the truth and conviction is available to all who believe, not only from God but from the entire Christian community.

In recent years I have returned to graduate school to study sociology with a focus on the sociology of religion. During my first year of study, I was struck by the following passage from C. Wright Mills:

> Perhaps the most fruitful distinction with which the sociological imagination works is between "the personal troubles of milieu" and "the public issues of social structure." This distinction is an essential tool of the sociological imagination and a feature of all classic work in social sciences.[20]

From a sociological perspective the struggle to end intimate partner violence is done through consideration of both the personal and social. What occurs between two people in a seemingly private relationship is related to the abuse and violence that goes on in the wider societal context. The two are interconnected in that their causes and effects are embedded in social institutions. That rates of violence against women are so high in practically every country on the globe is an indication that this is not simply a product of "personal troubles" between couples or in certain families, but that domestic violence is a structural issue having to do with the very nature of relationships, the institutions of marriage and family, and the other institutions that bear upon them.[21] The solutions to this social problem therefore, are likewise both personal and social in nature.

In addition to my ongoing interest in religion, women, and social justice, I work with the RAVE Project team (Religion and Violence e-Learning) under the direction of Dr. Nancy Nason-Clark. One of the goals of the RAVE Project is to let people of faith know that while many people suffer from violence and struggle to overcome it, they are not alone. This is not simply a woman's problem—this is a societal problem

20. Wright Mills, *The Sociological Imagination*, 8.
21. Wright Mills, *The Sociological Imagination*.

with which all Christians should be concerned. Every individual woman's journey, while unique, is a collective journey as well. Feminists are adamant that as long as women and minorities anywhere are oppressed, we are all oppressed. We are deeply interconnected in the social fabric of society. Therefore, whenever we reach out to help victims of family violence, whenever we offer programs to educate people about the effects of violence, whenever we support agencies or shelters that help women and their children rebuild shattered lives, whenever we refer a woman to a lawyer for advice, whenever we preach a homily that denounces abuse, and whenever we teach young people the skills to maintain healthy relationships, we are part of a collective process of social change. The personal is the political and the political also involves people of faith.

The RAVE Project seeks to walk alongside victims and survivors on their journey to healing and wholeness. We do this primarily through a website located at www.theraveproject.org. In the privacy of their own homes, in a public library, or at an internet café, victims of abuse can access the website and find the resources they can use. Just as it took me time and conversation in order to understand and name my abuse, the website provides images, stories, and videos that provide ways for a victim to recognize the patterns of violence and abuse in her own life. Stained glass is prominent throughout the site and serves as a visual reminder of beauty but also brokenness. Jagged pieces of glass, rough to the touch and piercing to the skin can be reshaped, refigured, reset. The stained glass portrait is what a survivor of abuse experiences—moving from the chaos of brokenness to new beginnings. In essence, we retell the story of violence for women of faith through our *stained glass story of abuse* as it has been told to us, by countless numbers of women. Like the pieces of colored glass that make up a stained glass window, families bring together individuals with unique and varied hopes and dreams for the future. Violence and abuse shatters the dream of married life. Like a piece of glass that breaks, domestic violence brings chaos and brokenness to the lives of all family members. Over time and with tremendous patience and support, the broken shards of glass can be refigured into a new window, carefully reset within bonds of safety, honesty, trust, accountability, and faith. In fact, the new stained glass window, assembled from pieces of the old, is structurally stronger and more stable than the original glass. So too can the pieces of a family member's life be reclaimed through the process of naming and healing from abuse. The journey to wholeness will be unique for each person and the memory of violence will never be erased, just as the pieces of glass that are used to construct a new window are borne of the old. Inner strength and wisdom can be gifts gained during the journey to healing from abuse.

The stained glass is a visual depiction of every victim's story and invites visitors to the RAVE website to further explore information and stories about abuse and violence. It is rare that someone will openly say that she is battered or abused. There is a tremendous amount of shame involved in admitting this is going on. It is more likely that a woman will identify with certain elements of stories or with feelings expressed by another survivor. She might recognize the actions or words of her abuser for what they really are. That is why we share some of the stories that we have heard over the years. The "Resources for Women" section of the website has a talking circle wherein people can listen to stories of abuse and violence that women have shared with our research team. The Online Training tab features a "Mending Broken Hearts" section which retells stories of abusive relationships and how a variety of professionals might have responded. While these stories are designed for training religious leaders to bring an effective response to situations that may arise in their communities, they can also help victims recognize that they are not alone in their experiences and that there are people who are prepared to help them. In this section and throughout the website, we include a variety of perspectives on situations of abuse and violence. This is to show that no one approach to family violence is sufficient. Abuse may look differently when viewed through different lenses but it is nevertheless abuse.

The RAVE video section contains clips from a television series produced by Day of Discovery in which survivors of domestic violence tell their stories and the abusive behaviors of perpetrators are critiqued by scholars, clergy, and other professionals. Seeing the face of a survivor and hearing her voice provides a powerful role model to women thinking about seeking help. Also found here are videos which feature the stories of female victims of human trafficking—another troubling form of violence against women. In addition to helping victims to better understand their own narratives of abuse, taken together, the variety of stories on the RAVE website illustrates the pervasiveness and the many forms of abuse and violence in our society. For those who want to help address the problem of violence against women from a faith perspective, there is much work to be done both to raise awareness and prevention.

In the midst of these stories of abuse and the pain that victims have suffered, there is the presence of those who want to encourage victims to take the next step in ending the abuse or violence in their lives. When visiting the Stained Glass Advice page, a woman will see the faces of religious leaders. These people each have a unique and important message for victims, one that is intended to affirm them in their search for help in order to both name and bring an end to abuse. For example, Reverend Yvonne McJetters from the Center of Hope in Charlotte, North Carolina is there to remind visitors of the oppressed women who helped to transform biblical history into triumph. Both Steven McMullin and Terry Atkinson, Baptist pastors from New Brunswick, acknowledge that the church has not always been a safe place for women to seek help from situations of abuse but offer the hope that things are changing. They counsel victims to persevere in their quest for a better life with the help of their communities of faith.

Church women helping women suffering from violence is one of the most effective forms of church support we have encountered in our research.[22] The "resources for women" section highlights the efforts of some churches and can serve as an example to others of what can be done. In addition to direct support for services for battered women and their children, women of faith can become engaged in political work. Long-term government funding for shelters, transitions houses, and second stage housing is needed in order to ensure that these much-needed facilities remain available to those who need them. Unfortunately there is a shortage of refuge spaces and we must continually remind our elected officials of society's responsibility to support the victims of violence. Likewise we need additional supports such as legal aid, affordable housing, subsidized child care, and free counseling so that women can rebuild their lives. Imitating the persistent widow who demands justice from the unjust judge (Luke 18:1–8), we too must not remain silent in the face of government cutbacks to social services and organizations that support women. Letter writing and signing online petitions are two good responses. We know people in our local communities who are politicians or friends of politicians as well as those in business. As people of faith and conscience we need to talk to them and persuade them that responsible government means figuring out ways to better ensure that the needs of the victimized in society are being met. The measure of a good society is found in the ways that its most vulnerable members are treated.

22. Nason-Clark et al., "The RAVE Project."

Because the cycle of abuse and violence is so destructive and can turn deadly, one of the immediate concerns for everyone who works on the issue of family violence is the safety of victims. That is why the RAVE website has a bright red "Help Now" tab. That tab leads visitors to a series of maps for all of the provinces in Canada and states in the US. Three clicks of a mouse can help someone find the phone number of any shelter, whether she needs that information herself or she wants to pass it on to a friend. Scrolling down the initial "Help Now" web page reveals emergency phone numbers for a variety of crisis intervention services as well as links to U.S. and Canadian domestic violence coalition websites. The RAVE Project has the only website that offers this information all in one location, and it is updated regularly.

However, it must be kept in mind that the most dangerous time in the cycle of violence is when a victim begins making attempts to put an end to the abuse or leave the relationship. This is why many women remain in violent relationships—they are afraid and rightly so. Abuse is centered on issues of power and control and when the abuser feels that he is losing control, he will try to exert even more power over his partner. Most spousal homicides occur after a woman has left the relationship. Having a safety plan is essential. Such a plan needs to include reaching out to and receiving help from people in the community, including the church. The Resources Tab of the RAVE website has the outline of a safety plan that can be downloaded and printed. This can be helpful to an individual woman as she thinks through her "next steps" or to a mother who wants to help her daughter. The safety plan addresses such topics as what to do during a violent incident, how to prepare to leave a violent relationship, how to ensure safety when no longer living with the perpetrator, how to get a restraining order, how to work on your emotional health, and what to consider in regards to alcohol and drugs. The importance of knowing that there are people nearby that a woman can turn to when she needs to talk or seek refuge when things get dangerous cannot be overstated.

I am grateful to the people of faith, particularly the Catholic women who helped me to sort out my emotions and beliefs in the aftermath of my basketball career. They showed me how to utilize the theological and spiritual resources available in the Christian tradition for my own healing and for the work of social change. My journey continues to be one of transformation. I went from an unquestioning acceptance of my Catholic heritage to a critical appreciation for the wisdom of those whose struggles have led to a deepened understanding of what it means to follow Christ in the midst of an unjust and violent world. The "Women's Spirituality Circle" located under the Women's Resources section on the RAVE website offers some examples of spirituality gleaned through the emergence of Christian feminist theology. It is my hope that these varied voices can help a survivor fashion a unique spirituality that enables her to continue to live free from all forms of abuse, both personally and as a member of the larger society. Each of the voices in that circle join a global chorus of women, religious leaders, advocates, therapists, lawyers, judges, police officers, politicians, and sisters who are calling women to safety.

REFERENCES

Canadian Broadcasting Corporation. "Women-only food sites open in Haiti." *CBC News,* 31 January 2010. Online:http://www.cbc.ca/world/story/2010/01/31/haiti-women-food.html.

Clifford, A.M. *Introducing Feminist Theology.* New York, NY: Orbis Books, 2005.

Canadian Catholic Organization for Development & Peace. *2011–2016 Strategic Plan: Development and Peace Facing the Future.* Regional Meeting Discussion Document. Montreal, PQ, 2010.

Eaton, H. *Introducing Ecofeminist Theologies.* New York, NY: T & T Clark International, 2005.

Gilligan, C. *In a Different Voice: Psychological Theory and Women's Development.* Boston, MA: Harvard University Press, 1982.

Holtmann, C. "Resistance is Beautiful: The Growth of the Catholic Network for Women's Equality in New Brunswick." In *Feminist Theology with a Canadian Accent: Canadian Perspectives on Contextual Feminist Theology,* edited by M.A. Beavis et al., 200–219. Ottawa, ON: Novalis, 2008.

Lind, C., and J. Mihevic. *Coalitions for Justice: The Story of Canada's Interchurch Coalitions.* Ottawa, ON: Novalis, 1994.

Malone, M. *Women and Christianity,* 3 Volumes. Ottawa, ON: Novalis, 2000.

Nason-Clark, N., et al. "The RAVE Project: Developing Web-based Religious Resources for Social Action on Domestic Violence. *Critical Social Work* 10 (2009). No pages. Online: http://www.uwindsor.ca/criticalsocialwork/.

Penner, C. *Healing Waters: Churches Working to End Violence Against Women.* Toronto, ON: Women's Inter-Church Council of Canada, 2000.

Radford Ruether, R. *Sexism and God-Talk: Toward a Feminist Theology.* Boston, MA: Beacon Press, 1983.

———. *Women-Church: Theology and Practice.* San Francisco, CA: Harper and Row, 1986.

Rupp, J. *Prayers to Sophia: Deepening Our Relationship with Holy Wisdom.* Notre Dame, IN: Sorin Books, 2010.

Schüssler Fiorenza, E. *In Memory of Her: A Feminist Theological Reconstruction of Christian Origins.* New York, NY: Crossroad, 1989.

———. *Wisdom Ways: Introducing Feminist Biblical Interpretation*. New York, NY: Orbis Books, 2001.

Sheridan S. J., E. F. *Do Justice! The Social Teachings of the Canadian Catholic Bishops*. Toronto, ON: Jesuit Centre for Social Faith and Justice, 1987.

Smith, D. *Institutional Ethnography: A Sociology for People*. Walnut Creek, CA: Altamira Press, 2005.

United Nations. "UNite to End Violence Against Women: UN Secretary-General's Campaign." Online: http://www.un.org/en/women/endviolence/pdf/VAW.pdf

———. "The Millennium Development Goals Report 2010." Online: http://www.unfpa.org/public/site/global/lang/en/pid/6090.

———. "End poverty: Millennium Development Goals 2015." Online: http://www.un.org/millenniumgoals/.

World Heath Organization. "Women's Health." Online: http://www.who.int/topics/womens_health/en/.

Winter, M.T. *WomanWisdom: A Feminist Lectionary and Psalter, Women of the Hebrew Scriptures: Part One*. New York, NY: Crossroad, 1991.

———. *WomanWitness: A Feminist Lectionary and Psalter, Women of the Hebrew Scriptures: Part Two*. New York, NY: Crossroad, 1992.

———. *WomanWord: A Feminist Lectionary and Psalter, Women of the New Testament*. New York, NY: Crossroad, 1992.

World March of Women. "Advocacy Guide to Women's World Demands: Eliminating Poverty." Online: http://www.worldmarchofwomen.org/publications/cahier/c_03/en/base_view.

Wright Mills, C. *The Sociological Imagination*. New York, NY: Oxford University Press, 1959.

6

"Peace Upon This House"

—Issues of Submission and Substance

Catherine Clark Kroeger

O N HIS DEPARTURE FROM earth, Christ left no plans for a highly organized institutional administration. By contrast, he carefully planted a method of Gospel outreach, to be implemented by his superbly trained followers. When Jesus sent forth his disciples, he instructed them to find a suitable house in which to stay as they entered a town or village. They were not to move from house to house but to remain with the original hosts for their entire visit to a particular location. As they entered the abode that had been selected, the disciples were to say "Peace be upon this house." This was not simply the standard greeting of "shalom" (peace), for Jesus continued "If a child of peace is there, your peace will remain upon it. If not, it will return to you" (Luke 10:6 cf. Matt 5:9). The entry of the Gospel, then, was intended to bring peace and fulfillment.

Zechariah predicted that the Messiah was to proclaim peace to the nations (9:10). Those who brought good tidings are commanded to proclaim peace (Isa 52:7; Nah 1:15), and Zechariah foretold the mission of his son John the Baptist "to guide our feet into the way of peace" (Luke 1:79). Indeed, at Christ's birth the angels sang "peace on earth" (Luke 2:14). St. Peter declared "You know the message God sent to the people of Israel, telling the good news of peace through Jesus Christ who is Lord of all" (Acts 10:36), while the Apostle Paul instructed the faithful to have their feet "shod with the preparation of the Gospel of peace" (Eph 6:15). The proclamation of peace, then, was a major objective in the launch of earliest Christianity.

And with the Gospel messengers came their message. Those houses in which they stayed, graced by the ministry of the original disciples, served as prototypes of the homes that would later host tiny worshipping congregations throughout the Roman Empire and beyond. In contradistinction to the imposing pagan temples of the ancient world, Christian worship was rooted in the domestic sphere. House churches became the fundamental bases for the furtherance of the Gospel in their respective communities (Acts 10:22; 11:12; 16:15, 34; 18:7; 20:20; 21:8,16), with the hosts becoming "fellow laborers" (3 John 8). Believers gathered not in formal buildings but within the fold of individual families, sharing their lives, their challenges, and their faith. Essentially the nascent church moved in on top of the structure and space of an already existing family. The dynamics within the host family were especially open to examination, as well as emulation, since harmonious solidarity was urged upon all Christian households.

Strong committed families were an essential for the successful propagation of the gospel, and great care must be taken that nothing detrimental could be said about them. St Peter advised:

> Conduct yourselves honorably among the Gentiles, so that, though they malign you as evildoers, they may see your honorable deeds and glorify God when he comes to judge . . For it is God's will that by doing right you should silence the ignorance of the foolish. As servants of God, live as free people, yet do not use your freedom as a pretext for evil (1 Pet 2:12, 15–16).

Though viewed with suspicion, the Christian family presented a new paradigm in a world suffering from severe social disruption. Rome's conquests had driven many families from their farms into overcrowded cities. Large areas of land lay depopulated while the former residents sought to build their lives anew in a society that lacked meaningful cohesion. Those who had been trained for administrative posts were now displaced by oppressive foreign officials. Women who had managed much of family farm life had lost not only responsibilities but also meaningful occupation. Rome's ever-increasing wars produced slaves who could be purchased very cheaply to perform all household functions, and the existence of many a hard-working matron became idle and frivolous. While some families kept womenfolk severely secluded, in other households boredom drove women to ridiculous extremes. Christianity was to produce a markedly different pattern of life for women.

OLD TESTAMENT PRECEDENT

Among the ancient Hebrews family life had been the primary system for inculcating the faith. Children were to be instructed in the things of God as they walked along the way with their parents, as they sat with them at meals, and as they retired with them at night. The great Shema (hear O Israel, the Lord thy God is one) was affixed to the doorposts of the home, to be observed by all who entered therein. It was in the home that strangers were welcomed and taught the ways of God, that the needs of the poor were met and the helpless defended.

Central to the dynamic of the home was the bond between man and wife, based upon covenant and consummated love. From this union sprang new members of the family of the faith. The position of the woman is affirmed as a fruitful olive tree (Ps 128:3), the crown of her husband (Prov 12:4), a well of constant delight (Prov 5:15–19), a gift from God (Prov 18:22; 19:14), a faithful companion to her husband (Mal 2:14), and an instructor of the young (Prov 1:8; 6:20; 31:1, 26). It was the wise woman who built up her house while the foolish one tore it down (Prov 14:1).

Proverbs 31 describes an industrious woman who contributes not only to the life of her family but to that of the community as well. She is capable of making her own decisions, engages in creative and profitable enterprises. She is widely respected and enjoys the full confidence of her husband who is able to concentrate on the affairs of the city while he leaves household matters to her capable management. This is the most complete picture of family life in the Bible, and it focuses on the role of the woman.

THE WORLD OF THE NEW TESTAMENT

The New Testament family paradigm also required a strong bond between husband and wife, but this could not be so readily expected in the Greco-Roman world as it had been in Israel. Family ties were not nearly so strong, and even in Jewish homes divorce was not uncommon by the first century BC.

Husbands and wives often had very little contact or conversation with each other. Marriages, sometimes between people who had never before seen each other, were arranged for purposes of producing legitimate offspring to inherit family property. In many instances the bride, as well as her dowry and religious obligation, remained under the control of her birth family rather than that of her husband. Technically and legally her attachment was to her oldest male agnate, and on him she was dependent for any aid that she might require. Children and slaves belonged to the husband's family but not the wife who was married under the common *sine manu* legislation introduced by the Emperor Augustus.

In point of fact, it was possible for a woman's birth family to remove her from the home of her husband if they found it advantageous to do so. A social historian declared, "the only enduring relationship a married woman had was the one with her blood relatives."[1] Ancient social observers were aware of the fragmentation that the arrangement created not only within the family but within the mind of the woman herself. Writing about 7 B.C., Dionysius of Halicarnassus observed that divorce was rare in early Roman days because women looked only to their husbands and had no other recourse, while husbands knew that the wives belonged to them in a permanent relationship.[2] Thus *sine manu* marriage came to be recognized as a threat to the cohesion and permanence of marriage. Often the result was that women gave much less of themselves to their home life.

By the first century of the Common Era, moral looseness on the part of women was everywhere decried. The chaste Roman matron was replaced by her promiscuous granddaughter. Numerous extramarital affairs are celebrated in Latin poetry, and a major motif is the fun of outwitting the lady's husband. The beleaguered housewife often gave less than her best to her own household. Both Greek and Roman women were viewed as tattlers, busy-bodies and trouble-makers, and there was a great fear of female misconduct.

The ancients maintained that there could be no true peace in civil society unless there was proper harmony and order in the home. The woman who hosted a church in her home must demonstrate a different set of values from those prevalent in the outside world. Circumspect behavior on the part of a wife demonstrated respect for her husband.

ESTABLISHING A DIFFERENT PATTERN

The houses into which the Christian message of peace came must know another dynamic. The attitudes and activities of the lady of the house were critical to the life and growth of the nascent church. Pagans and

1. Pomeroy, "The Relationship of the Married Woman," 220.
2. Dionysus of Halicarnassus, *Roman Antiquities* 2.25.4.

Christians alike marveled at the character and conduct of Christian women. The philosopher Libanius declared "what women these Christians have!" while the church father Tatian inquired:

> How is it that you are not ashamed to slander the good name of our women—you who have such a large number of vile and useless poetesses, wanton women, and worthless men? . . . Be ashamed, you . . . that you scoff at the women who join us as well at the church who stands by them![3]

The freedom accorded Christian women, in contradistinction to their sometimes sequestered peers, gave rise to concerns of propriety. All believers were enjoined to see that their behavior presented the new faith in a very positive light (1 Pet 2:12, 15). The best defense against the slanders so frequently hurled against them was an irreproachable life, filled with joy and purpose.

The later books of the New Testament contain instructions for family life, especially as it would be observed by those who entered within its doors from the outside. Men, women, children and slaves all are called to demonstrate the love and care of Christ in their daily conduct with one another. Women in particular were advised to make sure that their conduct was beyond reproach. Women, whether by conditioning or by nature, often have more highly developed relational skills, gifts that give a capacity to make others feel welcomed and accepted. In most families inculcating a sense of belonging and solidarity falls to the mother. It is she who contributes most substantively to the contentment of the household. I am always intrigued by the bumper stickers that read "If mama ain't happy, ain't nobody happy."

The directives to women in the so-called Pastoral Epistle ("how to behave in the household of God"—1 Tim 3:15) are surely instructive. Although St. Paul praised the value of the celibate life for women involved in ministry at Corinth (1 Cor 7:34, 39–40), the productivity of women's married lives is emphasized in the Pastorals. Older widows well seasoned in ministry are to be placed on the rolls of the church staff. In their younger years, their contributions to congregational life had included: the raising of children, receiving strangers into their homes, washing the feet of the saints, helping the afflicted, and devoting themselves to doing good in every way (1 Tim 5:10). Younger widows, rather

---

3. Tatian, *Address to the Greeks*, ch. 33–34.

than remaining unmarried, were encouraged to wed, to have children and to rule their household "so as to give the adversary no occasion to revile us" (1 Tim 5:14).

Women were advised to avoid ostentatious and sexually provocative clothing and hairstyles considered an affront to their husbands (1Tim 2:9–10; 1 Pet 3:3). They were to develop an attitude of *hesychia,* often translated as "silence" (1 Tim 2:11, 12; 1 Pet 3–4). Actually, the word more accurately was used to denote peace and tranquility. Plutarch wrote a treatise on *Hesychia* (tranquility) in which he observed that the quality was often in short supply in the women's quarters of many homes. Needless to say, women secluded in their own small quarters often gave vent to their boredom and frustration in unfortunate ways. There were more positive outlets for Christian women.

FEMALE LEADERS OF HOUSE CHURCHES

The role of women leaders of house churches is far more significant than might appear at first glance. In point of fact, we know of more churches that met in the homes of women than of men (Acts 12:12, 16: 13–15, 40; Col 4:15; 1 Cor 1:11; 16:19; Rom 16:3–5; 2 John). We might think of how St. Peter fled to the church that met in the house of Mary the mother of John Mark—only to find the door guarded by a staunch maidservant named Rhoda. There is the elect lady of 2 John whose duty it was to keep the heretics away from her flock. Surely it is significant that "those of Chloe" sent emissaries to ask the Apostle Paul to bring peace between the contentious factions in the Corinthian church (1 Cor 1:11). Most intriguing of all is St. Paul's letter addressed to a family in Colossae: Philemon, Apphia, and Archippus, as well as to the church that meets in their house. He asks for the restoration of a runaway slave who had created a severe household problem before making his escape. It is Apphia who will have to face the task of re-integrating the trouble-maker back into the household, soothing ruffled feelings with an attitude of Christian grace, and creating peace, even as she continues with the responsibility of offering hospitality to the local church.

BUT WE NEED TO TALK ABOUT "SUBMISSION"

How tragic that the scriptural directives to women, intended to further the peaceful objectives of Christ's Kingdom, have in some instances become instruments of oppression. The command to build beauty and meaning into home life has at times been derailed to enforce patterns of abuse. In some unfortunate scenarios, the injunction to Christian wives becomes a tool in the hands of abusers and enablers.[4] They are expected to bow to any and all forms of oppression, humiliation and degradation. Women are viewed as sinfully "unsubmissive" if they offer objection or resistance to abuse.

We cannot help being painfully aware that sometimes the instruction for wifely "submission" becomes a justification for marital abuse. In fact, while the Bible tells children and servants to obey (*hupakouo*), a different verb is used for wives (*hupotasso*). Though frequently interpreted in ways that are at once too simplistic and too legalistic, the term has far broader and grander connotations than we sometimes conceive. It can indeed mean to submit or to place under, but it has a wide range of meanings that may better give us an understanding of the values and potential that a Christian woman may bring to her marriage, her home, the church, and the wider society.

It is significant that when the Greek speaking Fathers of the early church wrote of women, they focused on qualities of attitude and conduct. They understood the apostolic directive as providing a dynamic incentive that would prosper the entire church. Clement of Rome instructed women to demonstrate purity, gentleness, and kindness without favoritism.[5] Polycarp asks that they show faith, love, and purity, while treating their husbands with fondness and fidelity.[6] And younger women were to develop chaste behavior and an unblemished conscience.[7] This would in itself convey an important apologetic to a pagan society which believed that women were devoid of conscience. Ignatius called on wives "to content themselves physically and spiritually with their own husbands,"[8] and the brothers were to love their wives as Christ loves the church.

---

4. See e.g. Johnson and van Vonderen, *The Subtle Power of Spiritual Abuse,* 100.

5. Clement 21, 6–7.

6. Polycarp *to the Philippians* 4.

7. *Ibid,* 5.

8. Ignatius to Polycarp 5, tr. Staniforth, 129.

A SEARCH FOR DEFINITION:
LOOKING AT THE OPPOSITES

"Submission" can denote adherence, loyalty, connection, cooperation, or relating in such a way as to make meaning. A lack of these qualities could create a serious problem. *Atakteo*, the opposite of *hupotasso*, meant to be lawless, to fail to discharge an obligation or to be neglectful of duty.[9] This antonym turns up in 2 Thessalonians 3:7 in the sense of living a disorderly life. The historian Polybius, along with the ancient scientist Ptolemy, used a negativized form of the adjective (*anupotaktos*) to designate concepts or persons who are dissociated from others, confused, or difficult to comprehend - not part of an integrated group.[10] The writer of the Pastoral Epistles applied the term to individuals displaying irresponsibility or lack of accountability (1Tim 1:9; Tit 1:6, 10).

What about the positive?

Hupotasso or its noun form, *hupotage* had many positive meanings (this is called a broad semantic range). One of its senses implies orderliness of conduct and proper responsibility toward others. Similarly Christians were told to comply (*hupotasso*) with the institutions of the state (Rom 13:1; Tit 3:1; 1 Pet 2:13). Never for a moment did they give slavish obedience or compromise themselves when commanded to worship the emperor. The contexts make clear that believers are being asked to exercise the virtues of lawful behavior and good citizenship (See Rom 13:1–7; 1 Per 2:13–15; cf. Jer 29:7).

The ancient translators who produced a Greek version of the Hebrew scriptures (the Septuagint) employed this term at three points in Psalms: 37:7 and 61:1 and 5. They used *hupotasso* to translate a Hebrew word meaning to be ready to receive communication from God and to respond appropriately. The same attitudes of receptivity and response can enormously enrich a marriage.

Paul, in thanking the Corinthians for their generosity to needy saints, says the recipients glorify God because of their "submission" to their profession of the Gospel (2 Cor 9:13). How is one obedient to a profession of the Gospel? In sending their gift to impoverished Christians, the Corinthians had "put their money where their mouth was." We must understand the phrase "submission to the profession" as indicating the

9. Xenophon *Cyropaedia*. 8, 1, 22; *Oecumenicos* 5, 15; Lysander 141, 18.

10. Polybius *Histories* III.36,4; 38.4. V. 21.4. Ptolemy *Tetrabiblios* 61.

consistency with which the Corinthians brought their behavior into a meaningful adherence, identification, association, and integration, with what they had already confessed. Here, as in a number of other places, the sense is one of identifying or connecting with a concept, person, or thing rather than obeying it. The Corinthians had followed through on, aligned, associated, and identified themselves with their profession. They had matched their walk to their talk.

We find broader connotations of *hupotasso* in non-biblical writers as well. Polybius, a military writer of the first century B.C., uses the term sometimes to denote those under the command of a leader and sometimes to mean his adherents, allies or associates, i.e., those aligned with him. More interesting yet, Polybius sometimes used the word to indicate the identification, integration, or association of one person, idea or thing with another in a meaningful relationship. One gains a better understanding of geographic locations, he said, if one associates or identifies those areas (*hupotasso*) with the cardinal directions north, south, east and west.[11] Polybius was not above pigeon-holing. Human behavior, he said, is sometimes easier to analyze if one relates or integrates (*hupotasso*) individuals into a broad general category of persons displaying common certain characteristics.[12] The relationship gives meaning to the individual. I suggest that the concept of relating one person to another in a meaningful fashion is a highly important value.

Stobaeus, writing about 400 A.D., quotes from a multitude of earlier sources, in one of which the term is used repeatedly to indicate the relationship between cardinal virtues and qualities of character appropriately connected with them. Translations of *hupotasso* are italicized.

> Of the virtues, some are primary, others are *related to* the cardinal ones. Four are cardinal: prudence, self control, fortitude and uprightness. . . . Of those *related to* these virtues, some are *associated with* prudence, some with self control, some with manliness, and some with uprightness. Those *associated with* prudence are soundness of judgment, circumspection, sagacity, discretion, ingenuity. Those *connected with* self-control are good discipline, propriety, modesty, restraint. Those *associated with* fortitude are perseverance, daring, high-mindedness, good courage, industry. Those *related to* uprightness are reverence, kindness, congeniality, fair dealing.[13]

11. Polybius, *Histories* III. 36. 6–7.
12. Polybius, *Histories* XVIII.15.4.
13. Stobaeus, Eccl. 2.60, 9W.

The repeated use of *hupotasso* in this discussion of moral values reveals the relational aspect in which the term must be understood.

How does this apply to the conduct of women?

One of the basic values of *hupotasso* is that of attachment. Christian women were encouraged to alter their legal status from that of *sine manu* so that they became attached (fully integrated) into the families of their husbands, to align themselves with household values, sharing in every aspect of life and spiritual practice. They were asked to bestow primary commitment to their husbands rather than their families of origin, and to behave in an orderly and respectful fashion.

They were instructed as to how they might behave not only so as not to bring reproach upon Christ and the Gospel but so that they might be its proclaimers. In no way did this imply submission to wrong doing or agreeing to comply with sinful demands. While all Christians are called to be subject to one another, St. Paul made it very clear that it was not right to yield the slightest submission to an individual whose behavior or communications were wrong (Gal 2:5–6). Still to-day women are asked to bring peace to church, home and society by demonstrating what is right and faithful and just.

On the faculty of Gordon Conwell Seminary there is a couple who propound in their teaching and writing the equality of men and women in church, home and society. They were once contacted by an international student completing a course at another seminary who asked if she might spend a few days in their home before returning to her home country at the end of her academic program. Communication was not optimal due to the language barrier, but the student was immersed with enormous amounts of instructional material that she could process at a pace consistent with her ability.

At dinner on the last day of her visit, she said to the wife "You are so nice to your husband." In surprise, the woman said "But why shouldn't I be? He's nice to me." Only later did the couple realize that essentially the student had come to see what transpired within the everyday home life of those who professed mutuality in marriage. Yes, she was there to observe the private domestic conduct of the wife and to carry the news back to the church in her home country. Women who understand their status in Christ are still major propagators of the gospel as they bring peace and meaningful relationships within the household.

REFERENCES

Clement 21.6–7.

Dionysus of Halicarnassus. *Roman Antiquities* 2.25.4.

Johnson, D., and J. van Vonderen, *The Subtle Power of Spiritual Abuse: Recognizing and Escaping Spiritual Manipulation and False Spiritual Authority*, Minneapolis: Bethany House, 1991.

Lysander. 141, 18.

Oecumenicos 5, 15.

Polybius. *Histories* III.36, 4; 38.4. V. 21.4

Polycarp *to the Philippians* 4.

Pomeroy, Sarah B. "The Relationship of the Married Woman to her Blood Relations in Rome," *Ancient Society* 7:215–22.

Ptolemy. *Tetrabiblios* 61.

Staniforth, Maxwell. tr. *Epistle of Ignatius to Polycarp* 5.

Tatian. *Address to the Greeks.*

7

Calling Couples to Accountability

—*It's in the House*

Jacqueline Dyer

INTRODUCTION

IN THIS CHAPTER I report on selected results of a research project wherein I spoke with Christian couples about how they use their faith during times of conflict and stress. The couples in this research project are African American—all of them are of the African Diaspora and live in the United States. In this research both partners in each couple are African American by birth or immigration, married, Protestant Christian, and living in the northeast United States. Also, in all but two couples both *partners* attend the same church. In order to keep the voices of the couples present as they speak about their relationships, I have shared many quotes.

RESEARCH METHODS

This study was designed to explore the interactional faith processes in Protestant Christian couples through interviews, with additional information obtained through questionnaires. The goal of this study was to explore how faith is used by couples in relatively healthy non-violent relationships to address stress and discord or conflict in their relationship. It is a strengths-based approach to explore use of faith in marital conflict. The study generated information about what aspects of faith are at work in maintaining healthy couples. Basically it answers the question of: what is 'in the house' of faith that can be emphasized in work with Christian couples that cultivates and sustains strong marriages?

Volunteer participants were identified by lay leaders in their churches who thought that particular couples they knew might be interested in the study and thus provided them with informational packets containing contact forms and self addressed stamped envelopes.

Couples where both partners mailed back the forms were contacted by me. I arranged a meeting with these couples to discuss the research, answer their questions, and obtain consent to participate. Each partner first completed a questionnaire separately, and then each was interviewed individually. The individual interviews were taped so they could be transcribed and lasted from between half an hour and 90 minutes. Follow-up meetings occurred about three to four weeks after the initial visit. During the follow-up meetings, the partners together got to review the transcripts of their interviews for accuracy, as well as those of their partners, and the results of the questionnaire. They were then able to have open commentary on the interviews and questionnaire results.

The couples in this study were identified because they appeared to have strong marriages. A screening instrument was also used to determine that there was no intimate partner violence in the relationship after obtaining informed consent but before any other activities of the study were implemented. The couples that participated gave evidence of strong relationships by self report, objective data and through observation. Both partners were equally strong contributors in their relationships in all ways, including emotionally.

While popular belief tends toward men being less expressive emotionally, that was not the case in this study. Gottman (1994) found that in healthy marriages, men and women are equally emotionally mature.[1] The information from this study parallels what Gottman found. The characteristics that stood out across all the couples were the spiritual and emotional maturity of both partners.

Findings

Discussion of the different topics is presented as much through the comments of the participants as through my own. I do this to validate the knowledge gained and the voice of the participants, which is a Womanist approach to presenting this information. Womanist theory—which

---

1. Gottman, "*Why Marriages Fail.*"

emerged out of the African American community—values and validates the experience of community members and recognizes that they are experts in their experience.

The findings discussed in this chapter include the importance of faith for the couples; the role of faith in their marriages and its dictates for relationship responsibility; silence and communication; strategies used during discord; the marital triad; and race-ethnicity, marriage and faith. Additionally help seeking is discussed in relation to clergy and to mental health providers and recommendations for each of these service categories are discussed.

IMPORTANCE OF FAITH

All of the couples talked about faith being of utmost importance in their lives both individually and in their relationships. As evident in the following quotations, couples were able to identify their belief in God as something that provided guidance and stability:

> Dave: I can depend on Him. I can call on Him, and I have faith that He'll answer my prayers or lead me in any direction that I need to be led in.

> Seba: It means my way of life, it means everything to me.

> Boaz: It means a lot to me. It gives me, to begin with, it gives me strength. It gives me hope, and it lets me build a foundation to grow on.

> Ruth: Well, it means that everything that I do, I do with trusting that God will see me through it.

THE ROLE OF FAITH IN MARRIAGE

The role of faith in the relationship of these participants began to emerge as they talked about their lives. Though the questions about their lives together didn't cover every area, the couples attributed most of their life activities to God, including that of finding their mates as they gave testimony about their marriages. Giving testimony is not mentioned here as a religious activity, but as people discussing their lived knowledge in context and in the presence of witnesses. This creates a collective space where the parties "affirm and validate the experience as real."[2] Faith was foundational to the partners in developing their relationships.

2. Taylor, "*Womanism*," 59.

> Jake: If I could give my testimony about my marriage it would be
> that I am completely convinced, comfortable and pleased that I
> found the woman that God sent to me. I know that there was no-
> body else in my life in any of the past relationships that brought the
> spiritual-based principles to the relationship that she has . . . .

> Rach: [Jake] and I met at a time when, at that point, I was just so
> immersed in my faith. I was very serious about it. It was going
> to be an important part of any relationship we were gonna have
> from the beginning. And if he had had any trouble with that,
> then it wouldn't have gone forward.

Relational responsibility

Faith in God did not obscure recognition or acknowledgement of the
difficulties experienced by the couples. Faith delineates for some of the
participants their personal role when tensions exist. Ava's comments appear to express a traditional female perspective and also reflect a tendency
noted in both the women and the male participants not to hold grudges.
Isak finds that his faith encourages him to be responsible when tensions
arise, and Sena reflects on both her faith and that of her husband.

> Ava: I tolerate certain things with him more than I would have
> done before and…there are certain things in my relationship
> with him that I look and say, you know, "if it wasn't the Lord with
> this situation . . ." [Y]our faith in God—it's the basis for success
> in your marriage.

> Isak: Regardless of my wife and I not seeing eye-to-eye on every
> plan, I value her opinion, more than she believes that I do. But,
> I do also understand that ultimately I am accountable for the
> final decision that we as a couple, as a Black couple, as a Black
> Christian couple make. It's my responsibility. I'm never going to
> do what Adam did and say, "well, it's the wife that You gave me,"
> you know, blaming God for this.

> Sena: God bring[s] us through. It's brought us closer and real-
> izing that we need to kind of hold each other up and encourage
> one another and count our blessings.

The matter of submission

Both partners were aware of the faith principle of submission in marriage, but understood its application in healthy relationships. The re-

lationships represented by these couples were partnerships, not power struggles. Understanding that continual power struggles are destructive to the relationship facilitates both a pragmatic and faith orientated perspective about submission:

> Ava: I think you have to have that mutual respect and understanding that he has a point of view, I don't try to beat it down. He doesn't try to beat my point of view down.

> Reba: [T]he mantle that's been put on me [is] as a helpmate, not a leader in my marriage; and I don't mean to be subservient like that, but to know my place. And in God's eyes, that's not a slave… it's an equal banner. Ultimate decision belongs to my husband, a man who's submitted unto God. There's a difference. Now let's get that clear; a man who's submitted unto God.

Silence and communication

One interesting finding was the extent to which silence was used by the partners. As expected, silence occurred in varying degrees when discord existed. One unexpected finding was the pervasive use of silence even when no discord was present. Six couples discussed this use of silence, which I found to be an extended form of communication in the relationships. Silence appeared to be as much a part of communication between the partners as use of words. When there were no relational tensions the use of silence still flowed freely in their interactions and did not indicate some unspoken concern. The comments of Isak, Boaz, and Mo provide a description of elements of the unspoken process amongst the partners:

> Isak: We have touches and looks that are—that kinda transcend just physical intimacy but are more of a spiritual intimacy. . . . I think that language is there or naturally develops if the two people are committed to God in their relationship.

> Boaz: But there's something that developed and we understand each other. . . . I guess it's just instinct on my part or on her part too.

> Mo: [I]t's those kind of nonverbal expressions that are part of the whole mix in terms of how we communicate with each other and relate to each other.

As might be expected, the use of silence tended to increase during times of stress and discord. One of the strategies used by the couples extended the use of silence into moments of discord. The partners recognized the need to disengage from escalating tensions and heated arguments. This was discussed by four couples. Disengaging was frequently done by physical separation, i.e. walking away. However, silence was also a form of disengaging. In one case, that of Isak and Reba, the partners realized they had surpassed their own ability to step out of their argument but describe an experience of God's intervention. Disengaging from rising tensions appeared to be guided by human decision and could also be triggered by Godly action.

After an interval in which each partner had calmed down, action was initiated to re-engage, with an emphasis toward finding common ground. The strategy that frequently accompanied separation, discussed by six couples, is simply identified by the name 'chasing.' The person who initiated actions to re-engage varied based on the couple; one partner reached out to the other or both partners mutually sought out the other.

> Sena: I think we kind of step back and go our separate ways sometimes.
>
> Jose: What we tend to do, sometimes it works for us sometimes it doesn't, but we tend to kinda separate for a little while, and maybe she'll stomp up the stairs [and] I'll go up to the attic and cool off.
>
> Isak I believe that real Divine Intervention [is] God just steps in and says, "Enough! OK you guys! You guys lost it," and, "Let Me!"
>
> Reba: mmhm.
>
> Isak: "Neutral corners. Go, go, go to your corners." That's what that is.
>
> Reba: Exactly.

Disengaging when conflict arose was not designed to disrespect either partner but to provide space as needed by each to de-escalate tensions. It appears that each partner in these healthy couples had implicit permission from his or her partner to use separation strategies to de-escalate discord.

Two verses were identified by the couples: Eph 4:26 (KJV), "Be ye angry, and sin not: let not the sun go down upon your wrath," which was cited by several couples; also Matt 5:24 (KJV), "first be reconciled to thy brother," was cited by one couple. Seven of the couples noted that they actively try to apply their faith during moments of stress or strife. The partners acknowledge that periodically they struggled to apply faith guidelines when they were in the middle of tense moments. However, doing so is a course of action to which they were committed. Importantly, their application of their faith was not dogmatic but was fluidly applied according to the nature of their stress or conflict.

MARITAL TRIAD

A notable manifestation of faith in these healthy marriages is the incorporation of God as a third person in the relationship. God being incorporated into faith-oriented families has been discussed by Griffith, and by Butler and Harper, as the "God-family relationship"[3] and the "Divine triangle."[4] In the marital triad, God is considered a person by the partners. God's incorporation is based on the passage that "a threefold cord is not quickly broken" (Eccl 4:12 KJV). Each partner represents a strand in a three-strand cord, where God is the third strand. God's presence manifests in the lives of these couples according to the many ways individuals can experience God. The ways the partners encountered God individually was also how they experienced God corporately or dyadically via prayer, bible reading, and meditation. Through individual and corporate prayer and meditation the couple converses with God.

> Rach: We really, really, both believe strongly in God's Hand on our lives and—and the ways in which His Hand guides the walk that we have; and so we really believe that it's the three of us.

> Isak: We still just talk about situations and we will come to a point of understanding. And I think the greatest feeling that we have that invokes those kind of situations of connectivity is then we'll hear it in church as a confirmation. We'll say, "yes, we're on the right track." 'Cause we came to that on our o—lemme change that—I'm getting ready to say we came to that on our own. That's not true. The Holy Spirit brought that to us and we came into agreement with the Holy Spirit.

3. Griffith, "*Employing the God-Family Relationship.*"
4. Butler and Harper, "*The Divine Triangle.*"

When the couples experience a stressor, the partners initiate individual and dyadic contact with God for guidance. God may speak to one or both partners and also may intervene with one partner on behalf of the other. The marital triad served the function of being one of the stabilizing forces in the marriages. It could possibly be considered the greatest stabilizing force because of the centrality of God in the lives of the couples.

> Isak: We're free moral agents. However, when we've committed and submitted, now you are a free moral agent that belongs to God and God's going to protect those things that are His.

> Jose: I think when you enter into marriage, I think it's a sacred step. . . . I mean basically [you] have made a promise and a vow to your wife but you also have done the same thing—you've made that same commitment to a Higher Being than your wife. And that's important. See you're accountable, in my opinion.

> Seba: I guess it all comes from the love of Christ and the Christ that's in me that will make me (pause) go that extra mile as far as forgiveness or to soften my heart. Ah, the Lord softens my heart in the next instant so that it's never as bad as it seems. You know?

> Dave: She was not that way before Christ.

RACE/ETHNICITY, MARRIAGE AND FAITH

Research indicates that faith continues to play an important role in the lives of African Americans.[5] Interestingly, six of the participant couples stated that they did not believe race/ethnicity affected their levels of marital stress. However, such statements were contradicted by the results of racial stress questionnaires the couples also completed. The questionnaire results indicated that the couples did experience some stress from cultural racism. Cultural racism is holding the practices and culture of one group superior to that of another. The apparent contradiction between the spoken and written information may be due to the protective effects of faith, documented in research.[6]   Faith may allow the partici-

5. Dyer, *Challenging Assumptions;* Lincoln and Mamiya, *The Black Church;* Waites, *Building on Strength;* Utsey et al., *Cultural, Sociofamilial, and Psychological Resources.*

6. Flannelly et al., *Methodologic Issues ;* Levin and Chatters, *Research on Religion and Mental Health.*

pants to cope with and separate out the negative effects of race-related stress. As a result, the partners are able to counteract much of the race-related stress that could otherwise negatively affect their relationship.

IT'S IN THE HOUSE: EXISTING STRENGTHS THAT SUPPORT HEALTHY RELATIONSHIPS

Couples were asked what they believed contributed to a good marriage. The comments of six couples were replete with the *words trust, committed, compromise, honesty* and *communication*. These were all qualities evidenced in their discussions about each other and about their marriages in both the individual and the paired interviews. This would lead one to consider what elements we need to build strong marriages are 'in the house.' We have accessible faith practices that we can emphasize and blend with other techniques in our efforts to strengthen Christian marriages and eradicate the terrorism of intimate partner violence.

> Boaz: I think marriage for African American couples should be based on, first, communication. And once you have established the communication, then there should be a 100% on each partner's part. Marriage is not a 50–50 thing, so 50% of the house work belongs to me. It's not. We should help each other. That's the only way that we grow with each other, by helping each other. And if you just left the work on one person then that person gets tired, then you don't have—your relationship kinda pulls apart. . . . You cannot withdraw if you haven't deposited anything.

> Dave: [W]e just try to have a mind of Christ; and yeah, it's in us. Another thing is that you have to apply it to your daily life.

> Seba: Basically you just have to be there for one another. . . . So it's a compromise and, well, you just have to be there for one another and do what it takes.

> Adam: Once you know you want your marriage to work, you get down, you read the Word, you pray, you respect each other and you love each other. . . . [Y]ou've got to give yourself time and be sure that the thought of marriage is coming from a mature mind. Not from a mind that just wants to partake in certain privileges . . . then you find that's not how it is . . . and you want to get out now, 'cause it's not what you thought it would be. . . . [S]ome men, some women I have observed, they will—well the wife has no say at all, or the husband has no say.

CONCLUSION

There is much work to be done to eradicate relational violence and increase peace and safety in Christian homes. This chapter focused on how we can re-assert existing strengths to support what is working well. These are aspects of Christian beliefs that can be assessed when stress or discord begin to overwhelm the couple. While some situations may require additional resources to support couples at such times, there are resources primed for use that already exist in the house.

REFERENCES

Butler, M. H., and James M. Harper. The Divine Triangle: God in the Marital System of Religious Couples. *Family Process* (1994) 277–286.

Dyer, Jacqueline T. "Challenging Assumptions: Clergy Perspectives and Practices Regarding Intimate Partner Violence." *Journal of Religion & Spirituality in Social Work: Social Thought* (2010) 33–48.

Flannelly, Ellison, et al. "Methodologic Issues in Research on Religion and Health." *Southern Medical Journal,* (2004) 1231(1211).

Fortune, Anne Marie. *Violence in the Family: A Workshop Curriculum for Clergy and Other Helpers.* Cleveland, OH: The Pilgrim Press, 1991.

Gottman, John M. "Why Marriages Fail." *The Family Therapy Networker* (1994) 40–48.

Griffith, James. L. "Employing the God–Family Relationship in Therapy with Religious Families." *Family Process* (1986) 608–618.

Jalata, Asafa. "Revisiting the Black Struggle: Lesson for the 21st Century." *Journal of Black Studies* (2002) 86–116.

Levin, J. S., and Linda M. Chatters. "Research on Religion and Mental Health: An Overview of Empirical Findings and Theoretical Issues." In *Handbook of Religion and Mental Health,* edited by H. Koenig, 34–47. Burlington, MA: Elsevier Science & Technology Books, 1998.

Lincoln, C. E., and L. H. Mamiya. *The Black Church in the African American Experience.* Durham, NC: Duke University Press, 1990.

Taylor, Janette Y. "Womanism: A Methodologic Framework for African American Women." *Advances in Nursing Science,* (1998) 53.

Utsey, S.O., et al. "Cultural, Sociofamilial, and Psychological Resources That Inhibit Psychological Distress in African Americans Exposed to Stressful Life Events and Race-Related Stress." *Journal of Counseling Psychology* (1998) 49–62.

Waites, C. "Building on Strengths: Intergenerational Practice with African American Families." *Social Work* (2009) 278–287.

PART TWO

Barriers to Peace and Safety

THE ROAD WITHIN

years
of doing
the needed thing
temper
the fire
but do not
extinguish it

now the self burns
at odds
in the confusion
of vanishing boundaries
that served a love
now gone

the habit
of former patterns
persists even
as life deconstructs them

how to live
in this dark interval
where losses spar
with new opportunity

now a glance
once dismissed lingers
on the eye

is this a door
opening through
prevenient grace,

or is it another
threshold of loss
fashioned by some
tormentor's plan

will a new house of belonging
rise between
the cloud
of sensed memories
and emergent hopes

do not be anxious
for the morrow
for the future is found
in no other place
than where you are

within the temple
of your aloneness
below the commerce
of identification
in the hidden gift
you will bear to
another great love

come
take my hand

I remember
Who you will be

ROBERT PYNN

8

Acting Abusively in the Household of Faith

Nancy Nason-Clark and Barbara Fisher-Townsend

THE STORY OF OUR RESEARCH

THE MURIEL McQUEEN FERGUSSON Centre for Family Violence Research was founded in 1992 at the University of New Brunswick, in Eastern Canada.[1] This centre began with five research teams, one of which, the Religion and Violence Research Team, headed by Nancy Nason-Clark, was devoted to understanding domestic violence in Christian churches.[2] Working with many faith traditions, and employing a variety of methodologies, a series of studies done by members of this team in the first ten years of its existence included mailed questionnaires and personal in-depth interviews with clergy, focus groups of church women, telephone surveys of shelter workers and religious leaders, and community.[3] Those early days of collaboration also involved writing that utilized our emerging data combined with religious voices for change.[4] This collaborative work has now been updated with additional materials and resources.[5]

---

1. Stirling et al., *Understanding Abuse.*

2. Nason-Clark, *The Battered Wife.*

3. Beaman-Hall and Nason-Clark, "Partners or Protagonists;" Nason-Clark, "Conservative Protestants;" Religion and Violence;" *The Battered Wife;* "Shattered Silence;" "Making the Sacred Safe;" "The Steeple or the Shelter;" 'Woman Abuse;" "Linking Research."

4. Kroeger and Nason-Clark, *No Place for Abuse.*

5. Kroeger and Nason-Clark, *No Place for Abuse, 2nd Ed.*

More recently, a closed case file analysis of a large faith-based batterer intervention program[6] has been followed by interviews with many of the constituents involved in the community response to domestic violence—parole and probation officers; judges; batterer intervention program facilitators; mental health therapists; community and shelter advocates; and agency staff members, board members, and executive directors. Importantly, we also completed interviews with fifty men individually and fifty men in focus groups who were enrolled in a faith-based batterer intervention program. Follow-up interviews were conducted every five to six months with fifty of these men—many of whom have served time in prison—over an almost five year period.[7]

THE STORY OF CHARLES JONES

Interpersonally warm and comfortable with conversation, Chuck tells us about his life working in maintenance and grounds care on a large university campus, a job he has held for almost twenty years. Chuck found his way to the faith-based batterer intervention group we are studying after he had been accused of cheating on an assignment in another local program. Since he had been mandated by the courts to attend a state-certified program for men who act abusively, Chuck had to either continue in the group or find an alternative program.

So what happened? He talked to his probation officer, heard about the faith-based program and decided to check it out.

Charles Jones arrived at the LEAF [Learning to End Abuse Forever] program full of angst. Never before had he been accused of having a ghost writer, or of failing to take responsibility for a work-related assignment. How could the facilitators make such a claim? Even telling the story to us made him get agitated. As Chuck told of his first experience in a batterer intervention group, it became very clear to us how such a misunderstanding might have taken place.

Charles grew up in an upper-middle class household, with two well educated parents, who held professional positions their entire working lives. As a result of extensive childhood travel and social capital that he had acquired from his father and mother, Chuck was adept at communi-

---

6. Fisher-Townsend et al., "I am Not Violent."

7. Nason-Clark, "Can Hope;" "Christianity and Domestic Violence;" Nason-Clark and Fisher-Townsend, "Gender;" "Seven Christian Myths."

cating his views and experiences. In this way, he stood out from several other men in the group he attended. His written skills might indeed have led a group facilitator to think that someone else had written his assignment for class.

But, in a fashion characteristic of other times in his life, Chuck quits the group—just fails to show up for the next group meeting. No doubt, this confirms in the mind of the leader that indeed he has failed to take responsibility for the letter of responsibility he was supposed to write on his own. While Chuck may be articulate, he is not skilled at defending himself, or dealing with conflict, in ways that are socially acceptable. He becomes angry. He says and does things that result in intense hardship for others and severe consequences for him. That is why—in part—he has been mandated by the criminal justice system to join an intervention group in the aftermath of domestic violence at home.

Underneath the surface of a very pleasant smile and friendly chit-chat, Chuck harboured a great deal of anger. As a teenager, he got into minor scuffles at school. At home, his sister had some health problems, and when Chuck felt deprived of the attention he sought, he would act up. By 13, he was drinking to excess and, as a young teen he was involved in several break-and-enter charges in an attempt to sustain his drinking habit. The downward spiral of the life of Charles Jones was beginning to speed up.

By the time, Chuck reached his twentieth birthday, he was addicted to alcohol. He went through a variety of phases in his drinking career, which he labels as binge drinker, daily drinker, maintenance drinker, workaholic-functioning-with-a-job drinker, and getting ploughed every night kind of drinker. Yet, he maintains steady employment, in part a result of a strong work ethic he inherited from his parents.

Once Chuck becomes a father, he tries to reduce his drinking. But both he and his wife are consuming large quantities of alcohol and doing lots of drugs. The downward spiral now includes them both.

Over the years, Chuck has had a lot of experience with the police, the courts, the jail, and probation. When things do not go his way, he gets angry. He has been angry at neighbours. He has been angry at staff in a government office. And he has been very angry with an intimate partner. One time when a neighbour called the police, Chuck was brandishing a firearm after an argument with his wife over the packing of their car.

Because of an extensive support network, through his family and his employer, Chuck receives almost as many chances as cats have lives. In part, this explains how he has been able to keep his employment, yet continue to have intermittent contact with the criminal justice system for so many years.

Is there any hope he will change? Workers in several agencies believe he has good prospects for living life in a new way. He believes this too. But there is a lot of work to be done—learning to live differently one day at a time.

For many reasons, Chuck really likes coming to LEAF, the program we are studying. He appreciates its focus on "helping you to understand yourself." He likes the group experience, for the most part, though, like others, he is very resistant at the beginning. He really likes the staff at LEAF and feels that they truly want him to succeed in life and in his relationships—with his children and a new partner.

He credits the program for helping him to own his own abusive acts and to see clearly the harm he has caused to others—particularly his ex-wife and his children—and to himself.

Attendance at a prior group was the context through which he interpreted the faith-based intervention program. In the first group he resented the money it cost, resented the mandate to attend, felt he was condemned to be seen as a batterer forever, and felt that nothing he said or did was understood as being "good enough." In essence, in his first experience of a mandated group, Chuck felt trapped in a room with facilitators he neither respected nor trusted.

By contrast, Chuck evaluated the faith-based program like a breath of fresh air. Here he was challenged to try to understand his life, his actions and his past. Why did he behave the way he did? What caused him to resort to violence? What might be added to his personal "toolkit" that would assist him to think and act differently than he did before? He was invited to begin a process of change and he accepted the invitation.

It does not take Charles long to see great improvements in his life.

By our third interview with him, he is talking about getting married to a new partner. Chuck offers us lots of examples of how he is thinking and behaving in a new way. He has learned to listen. He has learned to stop, think, and sometimes extricate himself from a situation that might lead him to behave in a way characteristic of his past. He has been introduced to other *principles of living* by the group facilitators and he is anxious to put these into practice in his home and work life. Chuck's tone has changed when he talks about group: he believes the leaders respect him, want him to learn and ultimately will help him to change his beliefs and his behaviour.

But change is such hard work.

The LEAF program works very diligently and intentionally to gain the men's respect and "buy-in." In essence, it treats them like consumers who are purchasing a product. The facilitators are clear that violence is condemned and the men must own their own abusive behaviour. But their model of operations is focussed on helping the men to see that everyone at the agency *wants them* to succeed and *believes* that change is possible.

Like other men, Chuck likes to arrive early to group, so that he can see a few minutes of the sports channel, available in the group meeting room, via a cable TV that is turned on 30 minutes before group is scheduled to begin. Rather than punishing those who arrive late, group facilitators reward those who come early. And in response most of the men actually come early. For those living in shelter, or without TV or cable, watching thirty minutes of sports is a highlight of the week. And even for Chuck, who has both, watching the playoffs with some other men is a bonus. It sets the tone for the group—we are all working together. The message: you too can be on a winning team!

Since the group is organized with the notion of *consumer choice*, it operates as if it is competing for consumers—as if the men have a choice in terms of their attendance. This does not diminish in any way the content of the program, the competence of the staff to provide it, or the severity of the consequences of non-compliance. But it does impact the environment in several, important ways.

The space, or physical location, of LEAF is pleasant, decorated appropriately, with a large waiting room, comfortable chairs, and a vending machine that sells drinks and snack foods. There is ample privacy in the main waiting area to talk to the administrator about matters of finance, and when her sliding glass window is open, there is no barrier between clients and staff. Fresh flowers, soft music and recent magazines offer an atmosphere conducive to professionalism and warmth. The space sets the tone and encourages client compliance. Outside the building, there is ample parking and a nearby bus stop.

When a man is scheduled to graduate from the program, there is pizza at the last class so that all the men have a chance to celebrate his individual accomplishment. Given that there are new men added to each of the classes on a regular basis, this means that some newcomers observe this *rite of passage* of the seasoned veteran who has been coming for 52 weeks, doing the work and living life in a new way.

The program is child friendly—this can be observed in the number of references to "being a good parent" and also the way that staff remember the names and appropriate details of the children related to the men in group. Enhancing the lives of children who have witnessed (or experienced) abuse is high on the priority list at the agency. Staff attempt to be creative in how they assist the men with the responsibilities of parenting and yet be realistic. In the lives of many men mandated to group attendance, improved relationships with their children is the carrot that keeps them coming—week after week.

Financial stability is a central part of the agency's story. Because of this, LEAF's programs and services are able to engage in longer-term planning and new initiatives without undue concern for financial solvency. In large measure, this is a reflection of those responsible for its creation, development and present direction. It has remained under the leadership of one of its founders who is a member of an influential, wealthy family in the region. Mediated through the agency director, there is a strong social justice imperative and a long history of social and religious activism, coupled with therapeutic engagement. The network of support that this offers the agency and its staff—not to mention its clients—should not be underestimated.

Staff at the agency is trained mostly in social work, with many holding graduate degrees and professional licensure; some are credentialed as licensed mental health counsellors. They represent a variety of faith perspectives and attend various local congregations for worship. Turnover at the agency amongst staff is low, particularly as contrasted with other similar agencies where we have obtained data. This has led to a high degree of solidarity amongst the staff and a thorough knowledge of local programs and resources. It also enhances referrals from staff within the criminal justice system as positive working relations stand the test of time.

The agency director is involved in working within a coordinated community context. This includes a commitment to attend the local domestic violence advocacy council, to show support for the women's shelter and its associated programs, and to ensure that there are intermittent updates of the work of the agency with the directors of other initiatives in the local area. While her personal faith and affluence is known throughout the community, it does not seem to draw either criticism or praise. The result of the agency's work and the director's personal commitment—and skill—in working with families in crisis is what matters most to others in the broader domestic violence community.

While some do not personally endorse the agency's faith-added approach, there was no sense that their work was compromised by religious persuasion, nor any evidence that they were proselytizing clients, or reluctant to accept clients from a variety of faiths, or no expressed beliefs. What was surprising was that several of the men were critical of the agency's reluctance to talk more fully about matters of faith—a failure, from this point of view, to push harder at the spiritual agenda. Yet, other men in the program referred to how well group facilitators were able to call religious men to accountability, particularly by refusing to accept their attempts at justifying abuse using the language of the Scriptures or their individual faith traditions.

The success of the agency in numeric terms alone was a matter of some discussion within the local community. The number of men who attended weekly groups could go as high as 200—and many others in the criminal justice community and within the women's shelter movement wondered how they could engage the men and keep them coming week after week. Informal conversations with professionals in other jurisdictions of the country suggested that this numeric success must be due to a selection bias (working with men accused or charged with less serious offenses). But this explanation was not true. And no one locally ever suggested that the LEAF program drew—or catered to—less serious offenders.

Over time, the other state-certified Batterer Intervention Programs in the local area were in serious numeric crisis, one closed, and it appeared that the other may not be economically viable over the longer term. As the program we were studying was gaining in reputation both within the criminal justice community and amongst the men who were its graduates, this further weakened the remaining alternative. Yet, this was not a cause for any celebration amongst the agency staff. In reality, the LEAF program needed other alternatives in the area as a point of comparison. Men who were disillusioned with other programs became their best "word of mouth" support. This was especially instrumental when men new to the program complained about having been mandated to come. Then, other men, the veterans of the program, would simply challenge them to a reality check of the other available options.

UNDERSTANDING ACCOUNTABILITY

For many years, we have been researching men who act abusively and have been mandated by the criminal justice system, or others, to participate in a program for batterers. Early on in our work, it became apparent to us that it was very difficult to assess whether men were accepting personal responsibility for their violence despite rather heroic efforts on the part of the criminal justice system and therapeutic interventions to assist them to do so. In another publication,[8] we argue that most of the men in the early stages of group attendance—and our first contacts with them in focus groups or personal interviews—reported that *I am not violent*. In large measure, the men use as their frame of reference for situating their own behaviour someone whose violence was greater than their own. They also blame, or explain, the abusive acts as a response to something that happened to them. In this way, they attempt to locate responsibility for the violence on shoulders other than their own.

In a chapter in another publication entitled, *Doing the Work*, we discuss the story of Pete, who remarked in an interview with us how hard it was to be an adult, to take responsibility, to act responsibly and to do so on a regular, ongoing basis.[9] There is ample evidence throughout our fieldwork of how challenging it is for the men to *do the work* that is required of them. Staying clean and sober takes effort, there are setbacks, and the consequences of failed attempts reinforce the belief that a man is a failure, unable to do anything right. It is also a lot of work to learn to think and act in non-abusive ways, to relinquish the desire, need or behaviour of control and to do this on an ongoing, regular basis— when life is going good and especially, when it is not.

Becoming accountable for your actions—whether to a parole or probation officer, to a therapist, to the facilitator of a men's group,

8. Fisher-Townsend et al., "I am not Violent."

9. Nason-Clark and Fisher-Townsend. Book manuscript in progress.

to other men in group, to a judge, to a pastor, to a new intimate partner, to your children, to your broader family network and ultimately to
yourself—takes motivation, skill and assistance. How many are really
able to do this—and keep on doing this?

There is the snapshot approach through which to answer this question, and the video-camera, or longitudinal response. As we interviewed
and re-interviewed Chuck over several years, the evidence of his progress
in becoming accountable changed. During the first two years of contact
with him—punctuated by 6–8 month intervals—it appeared that he was
well on the road to doing the work required of changed thinking and
behaviour. We had observed that he was willing to challenge other men
less engaged with the group, had become aware of some of his own vul-
nerabilities and begun to assemble skills and knowledge from the group
experience of how better to respond to disappointment, frustration and
relationships in his own life. He was consistent in group attendance and
meeting regularly with both his parole officer and a private practice
therapist.

In our fifth meeting with Chuck, almost a year after he was engaged
to a new partner, and several months after he was married to her, his interview was punctuated with more disparaging talk of the relationship.
He appeared to focus much less on his journey, the air of excitement of
the new relationship had evaporated and he seemed resigned to the fact
that his life was not going as good as he had hoped.

When we returned to the agency six months later—and now several
years since Charles had been in the program—for the first time he did
not accept our invitation to be re-interviewed. At the close of our data
gathering, six months after this, once again we met with Chuck but it
was clear that things in his life, from his perspective, were deteriorating
once again.

Learning from Charles' Story

For many years now, we have been attempting to understand various
components of the lives of men who act abusively towards wives and
girlfriends. In the second part of this chapter, we wish to turn our attention to what can be learned from the lives of men like Charles. To do
this, we pose four questions:

1. In what ways is Chuck's story typical of the men we have studied?

2. What are some of the intervention points that a pastor or religious leader has with a man like Charles?

3. What caution does Chuck's story give to a pastor who wants to work with men who act abusively?

4. What are some of the elements of Charles' story that have been impacted by his faith?

Charles' Story: Typical or not?

For the five years that we were collecting data on batterer intervention groups and the men who participate in them, we interviewed and observed many men like Charles. At first they were angry about being mandated to attend a group that would call them to account for their violence and ask them to begin a process of change. They resented the time, resented the money, and resented the hard work that was involved in the process of changed thinking and changed behaviour. Second, like Charles, many of the men did "get with the program," coming week after week, participating when asked to do so, asking a question or two, exchanging pleasantries with the administrative staff and group facilitators, and sometimes speaking voluntarily to other men who would be sitting in the room waiting for group to begin. Third, it was not uncommon for the men to voice high hopes for the future and in fact we asked them each time during the interview setting what they would like to be able to tell us about their lives in six month's time when we returned again for a further interview. Almost without question the men, like Charles, were able to articulate dreams and goals along with some problems they hoped to be resolved when they saw us again. Often they would mention how far along they were with the 12 step plan of "one-day-at-a-time." Most of the men we interviewed moved in and out of relationships with women during the years of our research—in fact, their past history of violence did not appear to be a problem in terms of potential partners.

Notwithstanding these similarities, there were some marked differences in the story of Charles from other men we interviewed personally or in focus groups. First, Charles' family of origin was upper middle class—with successful parents who were able and willing to provide for the material and emotional needs of their children. As an intact family, they offered both stability and rich cultural experiences that enabled Charles to have a broader, more informed view of the world and a network of extended relationships that he was able to harness in times of trouble. He had a very strong work ethic and in fact he was able to keep regular, consistent, adequately-paid employment throughout his life—despite his many arrests and convictions. A final factor that differentiated Charles from some (but not all) of the men we studied was his ability to maintain close relations with his children (grown by the time we interviewed him) throughout his life. When things got too heated at home, they would seek refuge at his parent's home. Charles' extended family support translated into the provision of alternative emotional and physical support for his own children. It did not appear that they ever felt abandoned or were left to "look after themselves," something that many of the other men we interviewed either claimed for themselves as children, or in the lives of their own offspring.

Pastoral Intervention Points

During his interviews with us, Charles would sometimes refer specifically his faith. One time he claimed, "I just know that . . . you move closer to God, God moves closer to you and more will be revealed." This is how Chuck understands his spiritual life and the ongoing struggle to be clean, sober and non-violent. There are a large number of professionals attempting to keep Charles on his journey towards accountability, justice, and healing. Some of these women and men have their own personal faith, some are in faith-enriched environments (where faith is celebrated as being part of the mission of the organization) and others are rather sceptical that religion has anything to offer a man like Chuck. In a coordinated community response team, the religious leader can help Charles keep account of his journey using the language of faith and his spiritual tradition. Working with representatives of the criminal justice system and advocacy community, the religious leader learns how important it is for the faith community to speak out against violence and for the pastor to use his or her moral authority to help a victim or an aggressor see that their walk of faith can help them to achieve therapeutic goals.

Thinking back over the course of his life, there was a time that Charles reconnected with the faith of his grandmother. There was also his time in jail when he had time to think about what was important to him—and to the future. And there was the pain that was experienced by his extended family in trying to make sense of the poor choices Chuck had made—those that led him to alcohol, drugs, violence and trouble with the law. A vibrant church community is what men like Charles need—and what can offer assistance to a family like his. Twice Charles was married—so each time there was the possibility of pre-marital counselling. Chuck needs the friendship of non-violent men to help him stay on course. The support of a men's group in the church, if such were available, would help to reinforce the goals he is starting to claim as his own. In essence, he would benefit from another safe place to be held accountable, using a language, fashioned in a religious tradition, which he appreciates and understands. Of course, none of this offers a guarantee that Charles will continue to make therapeutic progress, or that he will never again engage in violent or abusive acts. But what it does ensure is that there are people in his life that are comfortable harnessing spiritual language for change—a language with which he chooses to understand his life and his journey.

Caution for Pastors and Congregations

Men who act abusively can be very difficult for pastors. And it is not surprising that many religious leaders shy away from offering assistance to abusers and families impacted by domestic violence. Many men like Charles have a hard time thinking of others, even, or perhaps especially, the family members for whom they have caused so much pain and heartache. Wise spiritual counsel can offer hope while never diminishing the reality of the crisis or the long road towards wholeness. As a result, they can expect a lot from the pastor—and often there is little evidence on which to base a positive evaluation of the impact of the time the religious leader has spent with the man who has been, or perhaps still is, abusive. So pastors need to be realistic in their expectations of what they can accomplish. Otherwise it is easy to be manipulated. Or discouraged. Or frustrated.

When religious leaders begin to obtain a greater awareness of the prevalence and severity of abuse in the community and within their church family, it will impact sermons, prayers, Bible reading, premarital counselling, the curriculum of the youth program, and the various types of support groups that are offered during the weekly routine of church life. Of course, one pastor cannot do it all. So sometimes, churches and their leaders will think together about how they can respond to families impacted by domestic violence. Over the period we have been study-ing batterer intervention programs, we have observed many interesting programs offered by congregations, or using church facilities and church volunteers. Many of the best practices we have observed are partnership driven, where there is both secular and sacred input into the content and the structure of what is offered. Referrals between churches and community agencies should be commonplace as should awareness rais-ing amongst volunteers working in any congregational context. In the domestic violence literature on men who batter, the term accountability generally refers to personal and professional monitoring of the person who has been abusive. It includes monitoring strategies from a variety of people, trained in a myriad of disciplines. It also includes the jour-ney towards greater ownership for the wrong that has been committed. Anything that faith leaders and religious communities can do to increase accountability in the life of someone who has been violent in the family context is welcome assistance.

Faith in the Lives of Batterers

At an early stage of our research, we analyzed over 1100 closed case files from a batterer intervention program. Here we learned that men in the faith-based program we were studying were *more* likely than men in secular programs (studied by other researchers) to have witnessed or ex-perienced abuse in their childhood homes. In terms of modelling then, as young boys they had been exposed personally to abuse in the fam-ily context. When we asked those men that we interviewed in another faith-based agency about their personal faith, several told us stories of how they reconnected with their religious tradition during their time in prison or after the downward spiral of their life into abusive behaviour. To us it appeared that such reconnection was a specific form of religious experience—at the point of crisis looking for pieces from your past that might enable you to keep on the road to wholeness.

Further analysis of our data reveals no particular pattern as to which men experienced the reawakening of their spiritual life after judicial sentencing to prison. Catholics, Pentecostals, Baptists, and Methodists alike reported similar stories. For one man it was his place-ment in solitary confinement that led to his request for a Bible to read. For another it was the prison chaplain. And for another it was attend-ing a Bible Study in jail. Yet, in each case, reconnecting with their faith tradition gave the men hope for the future. It offered words for a new start, the reconnection brought hope that fuelled motivation to change and it brought a community of people (a faith family) that embraced the language of change and provided random acts of kindness to those who had stumbled. While the faith-based program, LEAF, which we studied, combined these elements in interesting ways, it was never named as such. Yet, throughout the local domestic violence community professionals understood that LEAF spoke and acted the language of faith, that they maintained hope for change, and that they went to great lengths to offer charity (in terms of kindness and assistance) towards men who had acted in violent ways.

THE ROLE OF HOPE

What role does hope play? Men who have acted abusively in the past, and who are working to change their futures, do rely on hope to guide their journey toward change. However, movement from a lifetime of troubles and despair to a context in which hope prevails is difficult, and for most men we have interviewed their sense of hope is slow to shift into a catalyst for change.

Why might this be so? Beginning in childhood, life for the men we interviewed was difficult—alcoholic and sometimes absent parents, experiencing and witnessing physical violence, involvement in the youth criminal justice system, living on the streets, and an early initiation into drugs, alcohol, and parenthood. For most these factors and others contributed to a downward spiral into a vortex of despair. This despair most often continues into the adult years. The lives of many of the men we interviewed seem truly dismal, with broken family relationships, terrible financial burdens, poor living circumstances, and work that offers little opportunity for advancement or any kind of creativity. Additionally, many men also believed that they had been victimized by the "system" and saw the way back from all of their troubles as arduous and long—if not impossible. As Hodge[10] notes: "In a forest of troubles, clients can lose sight of the spiritual truth that gives them hope and meaning and helps them endure trials and persevere through hardship." A context in which hope is offered and modeled is necessary to assist abusive men on their journeys toward change.

10. Hodge, "Spiritual Lifemaps," 83.

But what is hope, and how does it lead to action? There is a diverse array of definitions, frameworks, models, and characterizations making it difficult to arrive at a concise definition. Yet a common theme that links all of these approaches is that hope is intrinsically adaptive and positive.[11] The word *hope* appears frequently in a spiritual context. It is seen as an abiding Christian characteristic, along with faith and love, in the New Testament.[12]

According to Snyder et al.[13] hope is the belief that one has the means or ways to do what is required to realize one's desired expectations and that one is able to sustain movement along those selected pathways. A slightly different definition is provided by Meadows et al[14] who describe hope as "positive expectations about the future and positive ways of assigning causality to events . . . ." Thus, hope, particularly linked with faith, engenders positive attitudes and serves as a potential protection against despair, giving up, failing to meet goals. Additionally, a person's entire sense of well-being is affected by the ability to perceive positive effects following negative experiences[15]: "If we have our own way of life, hope is not based on a hoped for 'thing,' but rather on a 'state of affairs,' that being the prospect of tomorrow being a better day,' leading to the outcome of change." The "why" leads to the "how."

REFERENCES

Ai, A. L., et al. Hope, Meaning and Growth Following the September 11, 2001, Terrorist Attacks. *Journal of Interpersonal Violence* (2005) 523–548.

Beaman-Hall, L. and N. Nason-Clark. "Partners or Protagonists: Exploring the Relationship between the Transition House Movement and Conservative Churches." *Affilia: Journal of Women and Social Work* (1997) 176–196.

Bergin, L. and S. Walsh. "The Role of Hope in Psychotherapy with Older Adults." *Aging & Mental Health* (2005) 7–15.

Fisher-Townsend, Barbara, et al. "I Am Not Violent: Men's Experiences in Group." In *Beyond Abuse in the Christian Home: Raising Voices for Change*, edited by C. Kroeger et al., 78–99. Eugene, OR: Wipf and Stock, 2008.

Hodge, D. R. "Spiritual Lifemaps: A Client-Centered Pictorial Instrument for Spiritual Assessment, Planning, and Intervention." *Social Work* (2005) 77–87.

11. Bergin and Walsh, "The Role of Hope."

12. Ai et al., "Hope, Meaning."

13. Snyder et al., "The Will and the Ways."

14. Meadows et al., "Protective Factors," 110.

15. Park and Folkman, "Meaning."

Kroeger, Catherine C. and Nancy Nason-Clark. *No Place for Abuse: Biblical and Practical Resources to Counteract Domestic Violence*. Downers Grove, IL: InterVarsity Press, 2001.

_____. *No Place for Abuse: Biblical and Practical Resources to Counteract Domestic Violence*. 2nd ed. Downers Grove, IL: InterVarsity Press, 2010.

_____. "Evangelical Women as Activists: Their Response to Violence against Women." In *Shared Beliefs, Different Lives: Women's Identities in Evangelical Context*, 111–132. St. Louis, MO: Chalice, 1999.

Meadows, L.A., et al. "Protective Factors against Suicide Attempt Risk Among African American Women Experiencing Intimate Partner Violence." *American Journal of Community Psychology* (2005) 109–121.

Nason-Clark, N. "Conservative Protestants and Violence against Women: Exploring the Rhetoric and the Response." In *Sex, Lies and Sanctity: Deviance and Religion in Contemporary America*, edited by Mary Jo Neitz and Marion Goldman, 109–130. Greenwich, Conn.: JAI, 1995.

_____. "Religion and Violence against Women: Exploring the Rhetoric and the Response of Evangelical Churches in Canada." *Social Compass* (1996) 515–36.

_____. *The Battered Wife: How Christian Families Confront Family Violence*. Louisville, KY: Westminster John Knox Press, 1997.

_____. "Shattered Silence or Holy Hush: Emerging Definitions of Violence against Women." *Journal of Family Ministry* 1999 36–56.

_____. "Making the Sacred Safe: Woman Abuse and Communities Of Faith." *Sociology of Religion* (2000a) 349–68.

_____. "The Steeple or the Shelter? Family Violence and Secularization in Contemporary Canada." In *Rethinking Church, State and Modernity: Canada Between Europe and the USA.*, edited by D. Lyon and M. Van Die, 249–62. Toronto, ON: University of Toronto Press, 2000b.

_____. "Woman Abuse and Faith Communities: Religion, Violence and the Provision of Social Welfare." In *Religion and Social Policy*, edited by P. Nesbitt, 128–45. Walnut Creek, CA: Rowman & Littlefield, 2001.

_____. "Linking Research and Social Action: Violence, Religion and the Family. A Case for Public Sociology." *Review of Religious Research* (2005) 221–234.

Nason-Clark, Nancy and Barbara Fisher-Townsend. "Gender." In *Handbook on Sociology of religion and social institutions*, edited by H.R. Ebaugh, 207–223. New York, NY: Plenum Press, 2005.

_____. "Seven Christian Myths about Violence in the Family Context." *Voices: Overcoming the Silence of Domestic Abuse*, (2005a) Third Quarter 4–5.

Nason-Clark, Nancy and Catherine C. Kroeger. *Refuge from Abuse: Hope and Healing for Abused Christian Women*. Downers Grove, IL: InterVarsity Press, 2004.

Park, C.L. and S. Folkman. "Meaning in the context of stress and coping." *Review of General Psychology* (1997) 115–144.

Snyder, C.R., et al. "The Will and the Ways: Development and Validity of Individual Differences Measure of Hope." *Journal of Personality and Social Psychology* (1991) 570–585.

Stirling, M.L., et al., eds. *Woman Abuse: Partnering for Change*. Toronto, ON: University of Toronto Press, 2004.

9

The Needs of Immigrant Families

Victoria Fahlberg and Anjuli Ferreira-Fahlberg

INTRODUCTION

MANY OF US TAKE for granted being safe in our own homes, fearing only the stranger looming in a dark alley at night. We know, however, that millions of women and children[1] are hurt every day, not by a man with a mask, but by a boyfriend or husband who was supposed to protect them. The betrayal and fear associated with domestic violence is often coupled with dependence and isolation which prevent many victims from seeking safety and pursuing justice.

In immigrant communities, the threat of domestic violence is just as severe, yet the barriers to seeking help are so great that few immigrant women are able to successfully leave an abusive relationship and rebuild their lives without fear of abuse, poverty, or social isolation. While many individuals and agencies have reached out to help victims in these unique situations, the lack of understanding and resources results in the continued abuse, and sometimes death, of immigrant women and children. Change will only come through raising both awareness of the barriers that face immigrant families living with abuse, and the potential for individuals and organizations to make a significant impact in the lives of these families.

1. The authors recognize that domestic violence occurs against women, men, and people who identify as transgender, and that these communities are impacted in both American and immigrant populations. This paper focuses on the male-female dynamics most frequently found in abusive immigrant homes and refers to perpetrators as male and victims as female.

Prevalence of Domestic Violence in Immigrant Communities

It is often difficult to accurately identify and study the prevalence of domestic violence among women from different immigrant groups, but
it is clear that abuse is a serious issue within every community in the
United States. According to the National Violence Against Women survey[2] of 8000 women and 8000 men, one in four women and 7.5 percent
of surveyed men reported being raped and/or physically assaulted by
an intimate partner at some time in their life. This same survey found
that Asian/Pacific Islander women reported significantly fewer intimate
partner physical assaults than other women and Hispanic women reported significantly more intimate partner rapes than non-Hispanic
women. These differences may be due to reporting practices that differ
among the racial and ethnic groups.

In 2002, Brownridge and Halli found that immigrant women from
developing countries had higher rates of domestic violence than other
immigrant women, which the authors attributed to the more sexually
proprietary behavior exhibited by partners of the women from these
countries.[3] Raj (2003), in a study of 160 South Asian women, found that
spousal abuse among the Indian immigrants living in the United States
was higher than that reported for women living in India.[4] A total of 40
percent of all Indian women interviewed had experienced physical or
sexual abuse in their current relationship. Of those women, 90 percent
had been abused within the past year. Another study of South Asian
women living in the Greater Boston area, where 87.5 percent were born
outside the United States, found that 40.8% reported intimate partner
violence in their current relationship.[5] Finally, a multi-year review of
homicides in New York City from 1995 to 2002 found that 57 percent
of foreign born female homicides were victims of intimate femicide.[6]
Studies confirm the prevalence of domestic violence in immigrant communities, although it remains unclear if immigrant women are in fact
more susceptible to being victimized than North American women.
However, it is quite clear that immigrant women face many challenges
in seeking and receiving help. This chapter will explore some of these

2. Tjaden and Thoennes, *Extent, Nature, and Consequences.*

3. Brownridge and Halli, "Double Jeopardy?" 455–471.

4. Raj and Silverman, "Immigrant South Asian Women," 435–437.

5. Ibid.

6. NYC Department of Health, *Femicide in New York City.*

challenges, as well as how immigrant women, in spite of all odds, are finding ways to survive, to find safety, and to persevere.

THE CHALLENGES OF ACCULTURATION

Acculturation is the process that all immigrants go through in adapting to their new surroundings. The adaptations can seem endless, from things as simple as learning how to order food in a restaurant to those as complicated as learning a new language. When immigrants first arrive in a new culture they must learn how to obtain immediate necessities such as food and shelter. This requires learning how to rent a home, pay bills, get a driver's license, use public transportation, buy groceries, and more. Once situated with a place to live, newcomers must learn how to use the health care system, the educational system, the banking system, and the job search process. While many immigrants engaged in these activities in their native country, they often function so differently in the new country that a re-education process is necessary.

As time passes, well adapted newcomers will make the adjustments necessary to the new culture. However, as newcomers master the American way of doing things, they are simultaneously confronted with differences in values and attitudes, such as those related to dating and child rearing, that can challenge their cultural identity. All of these challenges in the new culture can feel overwhelming. Eventually, those immigrants who choose to remain in their new country usually learn how to live adequately, or even thrive, in the new culture. Failure to adapt can lead to poor outcomes for the family, and in some cases newcomers may even return to the home country, even though it offers fewer opportunities. Throughout the years of adaptation, individuals can feel unable to manage so many challenges simultaneously, which can lead to feeling powerless and unable to control one's life. In an effort to regain a sense of power and control, immigrants may resort to controlling and abusing their families.[7] Immigrant women whose partners already have controlling tendencies therefore become more vulnerable to abuse upon arrival in the United States.

---

7. Tran and Des Jardins. "Domestic Violence," 71–96.

Prior Trauma

Certain groups of newcomers experience additional challenges in adapting to the new culture. Many newcomers to the United States are refugees who have fled hostile situations. Since 1980, the United States has taken in hundreds of thousands of refugees from countries like Cambodia, Rwanda, Somalia, Cuba, Haiti, Hmong from Laos, Vietnam, and, most recently, from Iraq, Nepal, and Burma. Refugees often spend years in camps, where their access to work and school is limited. Some, like the Cambodians and Rwandans, have been through genocides that have left them fighting mental illnesses such as depression and post traumatic stress disorder. Immigrant families whose primary provider is struggling with a mental illness may become susceptible to abuse because, although mental illness does not cause a person to be abusive, it can sometimes exacerbate tension in a relationship, which can lead to abuse.

Other refugee groups, like the Hmong, come from agrarian cultures and have never experienced modern society where education, banking, and healthcare are formally organized and dependent upon new technologies. The transition for these groups is fraught with hardship, stress, misunderstandings, and sadness. Unlike immigrants, who leave their home countries in search of a better life for themselves and their children, many refugees were forced to leave their homes due to war or political persecution. They are less prepared to take on the many challenges of acculturation. Both men and women from these communities struggle with communicating their needs to the broader community and accessing much-needed resources that might help address violence in the home.

Poverty

Many newcomers who arrive in the United States start their lives here living in low-income neighborhoods which are often characterized by high crime and neglect. Sometimes immigrant families find themselves isolated, without a support system of friends, relatives, or neighbors to help out during times of need. Other times, they may move to a specific neighborhood where others from their home country have settled, as a means to surround themselves with support and a sense of the familiar. Unfortunately, these neighborhoods are often marginalized by the mainstream community, show low engagement with the larger community, and have higher crime rates than surrounding neighborhoods. This can augment a sense of insecurity and fear that is a natural result of living in a place where so much is new and unfamiliar. It can be particularly stressful for those coming from situations of war or genocide, where a sense of loss and insecurity has become a permanent fixture in their lives.

Additionally, poverty increases the risk of escalated abuse when already abusive men turn to violence in an attempt to regain control of their lives. Women and their children, who may be financially dependent on the abusive husband or boyfriend, have few resources with which to escape. Immigrant women, who may not have the legal status or relevant skills to get a job, are frequently unable to survive on their own without the support of their church, friends, or family. Access to resources, such as financial assistance and social service agencies, is limited in low-income neighborhoods, so victims who do not have community support may find it challenging to find that help elsewhere.

Family Dynamics

Family life often suffers when immigrant families arrive in the United States. Changes in family dynamics and roles are often required in order to survive and adapt in a new country. For example, in many developing countries women work in the home, caring for the children and keeping the home running smoothly. However, most immigrant families in the United States find it necessary for both husband and wife to work outside the home in order to make ends meet. Women are required to learn to drive, to acquire job skills, and to find child care that was not needed back home when the wife was not in the workplace.

While many men are willing, if not eager, to see their wives gain independence and earn an income, abusive men who are used to maintaining power and control in the home are often reluctant, if not prohibitive, of their wives working outside the home. These men may fear that their wife will tell her friends about the abuse, or that she will gain the knowledge and means to leave him. The more insecure the abusive partner feels, the more control he will exert over his partner. Additionally, because the American economic situation requires both parents to work, it is not uncommon that wives can earn more than their husbands. This shift in economic power may be new to both husband and wife and can also cause friction in a marriage.

Children's roles in the family may change drastically as well. Children are often the first to master the English language, and so parents begin to use them as translators and interpreters. The more that children are used in this way by their parents, the more power the children hold in the family. Children can be called upon to administer family finances, to mediate between the school and the home, and to be the bridge between health care providers and parents. This can lead to poor academic results for children, who are able to mislead their parents regarding their success in school. It can also lead to teens rebelling against the authority of their parents because in so many ways the parents have relinquished control to them as a result of not knowing the language or culture. Sometimes parents will attempt to regain control during the teen years when American dating norms and behavior begin to diverge steeply from those of the home culture. The more control exerted by the parents at this point can lead to even more out-of-control behavior by the teen. This becomes another source of stress in the family and can make parents feel, in yet another way, that they have little power or control over their lives. Whenever an individual feels a loss of power and control, they are at an increased risk of using violence as a means to dominate another in their attempt to regain what they have lost.

Anti-Immigrant Attitudes

Since September 11, 2001, foreigners have found life in the United States to be particularly stressful. At that time foreign terrorists committed the greatest act of terrorism in the history of the United States, and since then, a general anti-immigrant sentiment has settled across the country. This has resulted in the dismantling of bilingual education programs, a stereotyping of immigrants as those who take American jobs and use American benefits which are not deserved, the conflating of immigrants with terrorists, and the rounding up and deportation of thousands of undocumented workers through a series of workplace raids by the Immigration and Customs Enforcement police (ICE). Beyond the general stress and anxiety caused by these raids and deportations, they have also led to great fear of government authorities in most immigrant communities. Immigrant women, who may already distrust police because these authorities are harsh and corrupt in their home country, are even less likely to call for help when they fear that they will be imprisoned and deported rather than protected against an abusive partner.

Because immigration laws, regulations, and procedures for obtaining visas, permanent residency, and citizenship are so complicated and difficult to obtain, immigrant households often include a mix of those who have no visa or documented status, a current visa, permanent residency, and even citizenship. Prior to 9-11, Americans did not focus much on an immigrant's legal status and therefore, legal status was not as powerful a weapon to use against those without status as it is now. Since 9-11, it has become easier for an abusive husband with legal status to control his wife when her status is dependent upon his or she has no documented status at all. In abusive homes, a husband with greater legal status than his wife can control her by threatening to have her deported or denying her economic support if she is disobedient or tries to leave him.

In the past, stress related to moving to a foreign culture was called "culture shock" and described all of the stresses that can overwhelm newcomers. For some, it takes an entire life time to adjust and sometimes a newcomer is never able to make a healthy integration into a new culture. This extra stress that exists in immigrant and refugee families as they adjust and adapt can increase family breakdown and especially increase one's need to feel in control of one's life when so much around him/her feels like it is out of control, which in turn can lead to abuse and violence.

BARRIERS TO SEEKING HELP

The Role of Culture

Cultural norms can play a role in increasing domestic violence as well as preventing battered immigrant women from accessing services.[8] Conceptual constructs of rape and domestic violence can be culture specific and affect issues related to marriage and divorce, paternal rights over children, rights of a husband over his wife, and the social stigmatization of being a single woman.[9] These issues can influence a woman's decision to leave an abusive partner. For example, Latino women appear to be impacted by gender roles[10] [11] such as those determined by their church leaders.[12] Some pastors and priests preach that men have

8. Huisman, "Wife Battering," 260–283.

9. Fahlberg, *Supervising and Supporting*.

10. Perilla et al., "Culture and Domestic Violence," 325–339.

11. Perilla, "Domestic Violence as a Human Rights Issue," 107–133.

12. West et al., "Sociodemographic Predictors," 361–375.

the dominant role in the family and that divorce is unacceptable by the Church, which makes immigrant women vulnerable to tolerating abusive relationships.

For Asian women, norms around shame and honor can prevent them from leaving an abusive relationship.[13] Supriya (1996), reporting on an ethnographic inquiry at a shelter for Asian immigrant women, found that women constructed identities as "shameless wives."[14] As one woman commented, "See, I should not be here without husband . . . must look after him, that's what a good wife does."[15] Other traditional Asian values such as privacy, honor, self-restraint, harmony, order, and family cohesion may prevent a battered woman from seeking outside help.[16][17][18] Many Asian people reportedly have a reluctance to discuss issues publicly.[19] As one Cambodian man commented, "Our people are not aggressive, we keep quiet and are passive until you block our way entirely. If there is still some room to get around you, we will keep quiet. You have to block the whole way. Our nature is soft."[20] Raj and Silverman (2003) found that 19 percent of 160 Asian women interviewed had witnessed physical violence between their parents while growing up and 40 percent had witnessed emotional abuse.[21] For some, violence as a norm had been internalized, as 17 percent of those surveyed felt that some women deserved abuse and 4 percent felt that they sometimes deserved to be abused.

One domestic violence advocate who worked with Cambodian women and was herself Cambodian was frequently demoralized by the lack of anger and resentment that her clients felt towards being abused. While the advocate was appalled by the way many Cambodian men demeaned and abused their wives, the victims themselves were frequently accepting of, or at least resigned to, the fact that abuse was part of marriage.[22] While no woman wants to be abused by her partner, many cultures teach women that their role is to support their husbands no matter

13. Narayan, "Mail-order Brides," 104–116.

14. Supriya, "Confessionals, Testimonials," 92–106.

15. Ibid., 96.

16. Chan and Leong, "Chinese Families in Transition," 263–281.

17. Hofstede, "The Cultural Relativity of the Quality of Life Concept," 389–398.

18. Friedman, "Rape and Domestic Violence," 65–78.

19. Rimonte, "A Question of Culture," 1311.

20. Fahlberg, Barriers Faced by Immigrants.

21. Raj and Silverman, "Immigrant South Asian Women," 435–37.

22. Personal interview with the author, November, 2007.

how they treat their wives, and that to leave an abusive husband would bring dishonor to the family.

Isolation

Isolation is a serious barrier to seeking help for any victim, but is an even greater challenge for immigrant women. Since many immigrants come to this country with only their nuclear family or even on their own, they must adapt to their new community without the support of an extended network of family and friends. Without their support system, immigrant women can be isolated from their local community,[23] [24] and may not have anyone to turn to when they need help. For example, Adriana was a young Brazilian woman who decided to leave her American boyfriend when he began to abuse her and their one-year-old daughter. She wanted desperately to return to Brazil, where her family and friends could provide her with a home and safety. Without the consent of her child's father, however, Adriana was unable to take her child back to Brazil. Without family or friends, Adriana relied on members of her local church and local rape crisis agency for support. They were able to help her leave the abusive relationship before it became lethal, and she was able to use this support system to secure a job, find legal resources, and permanently separate from her abuser. Without the support of her church, however, Adriana would have had nowhere to turn and may not have successfully found a means to escape.

One report found that lack of transportation was also a major barrier to immigrant integration because of its isolating effects.[25] Through a series of focus groups with battered immigrant women conducted through the National Institute of Justice, it was found that many women felt isolated because they could not drive.[26] In many immigrant families, it is frequently the men who learn how to drive, and in cases where neither partner has a legal driver's license, men are often more willing to take the chance of driving without a license. Because men can drive and women are limited to using public transportation, female victims have less access to support services and are not easily able to escape a threatening situation.

23. Abraham, "Speaking the Unspeakable," 215–241.
24. Menjivar, "Immigrant Women," 898–920.
25. Fahlberg, *Barriers Faced by Immigrants.*
26. Senturia et al., *Cultural Issues.*

Lack of Community Support

Isolation of battered immigrant women can be further exacerbated when victims feel like their local community supports the abuser. Abusers are characteristically charming, and often are described as having two personalities: the kind, helpful, respectful man who treats friends and extended family members well, and the controlling and abusive man who hurts his partner and children behind closed doors.[27] When a victim speaks out about the abuse, she may not be believed by those who have only witnessed the nice side of her partner. In addition, men have greater social standing than women in some cultures and are more connected within the ethnic communities. Because of this, members within the ethnic community are unlikely to assist a wife against her husband and may refuse to get involved, believing that abuse is a private family matter.

In the case of Laura, a woman from Uruguay who had moved to the United States with her boyfriend, roommates were unwilling to stand up to her abusive boyfriend, for fear that it would cause tension in the house and might draw the attention of the police. Laura was frequently abused by her boyfriend in their apartment, which they shared with other people who rented the other rooms. While her roommates were aware of the abuse and could often hear her cry and get pushed against the walls, no one was willing to intervene on her behalf. Laura was only helped to safety when her daughter's preschool teacher reported the child's stories about the abuse at home and the Department of Child and Family Services intervened and helped her get to a shelter.

In some ethnic communities, people will completely deny that intimate partner violence exists, due to a belief in male dominance and in the rights of a husband to treat his wife however he wants. This denial works to silence victims, who fail to report abuse out of respect for their community and its values. This makes it difficult to create community services that help victims,[28] particularly when these services may appear to contradict cultural values and promote American beliefs about family roles. Domestic violence advocates, who are usually trained to put the victim's physical safety first, may be quick to advocate for interventions such as divorce, pressing legal charges against the abuser, attaining financial independence for the victim, and procuring mental health services that address common emotional side effects of trauma. While some

27. Enander, "Leaving Jekyll and Hyde."
28. Narayan, "Mail-order Brides," 104–116.

agencies and advocates believe that taking these steps is the best way of dealing with an abusive relationship, the insistence on this method my alienate immigrant victims who do not want to pursue this route. Common family values of unity, lifelong commitment to spouses, and making personal sacrifices for the wellbeing of the children leave little room for considering the more radical option of leaving. Furthermore, the stigma attached to seeking mental health services is prevalent in many immigrant communities, and the insistence by advocates for victims to get therapy or take medications may push the victim away from getting the help she needs.

Some agencies have recognized that suggesting only one set of options to victims does not allow for the empowerment of victims to make their own decisions, and is also not sensitive to the fact that leaving an abuser may not be the best choice. Many agencies will now offer a variety of options, which may include leaving the abuser, but also includes finding ways to stay with him safely if that is what the victim decides. Keeping an open mind and allowing the victim to control her own destiny is the most effective way of supporting immigrant victims. Once the victim feels trust for her advocate, she will seek out help in the future if that is warranted.

Legal Status

The disempowerment that many immigrant victims suffer is exacerbated for victims who are undocumented. Undocumented immigrants often live secret lives in which they literally have no identity and few, if any, ties to social services, friends, or family.[29] One study of undocumented immigrants found that for 64 percent of Latinas, a primary barrier to seeking social services is the fear of deportation.[30] Although many immigrants suffer from isolation, battered women's isolation can be enforced by the batterer, who often determines his wife's legal status.[31] [32] For example, when an immigrant woman accompanies her husband to this country on his temporary work visa, she is prohibited by law from working here. This inability to work not only isolates her from others, but prevents her from having any kind of economic freedom that would

29. Tiede, "Battered Immigrant Women," 21–22.
30. Anderson, "A License to Abuse," 102(6).
31. Abraham, "Speaking the Unspeakable," 215–241.
32. Tiede, "Battered Immigrant Women," 21–22.

be necessary to live apart from her husband. Her immigration status is completely dependent upon her husband, who can decide whether to apply for her temporary visa and also whether to cancel it.

Sometimes an immigrant woman is married to an American, who refuses to apply for her permanent residency status. In situations where a wife's legal status is dependent upon her husband's status, it becomes a powerful weapon that he can use to control his wife's behavior. Besides threatening to report her to Immigration and Custom Enforcement (ICE) for deportation, he can also report her for working "under the table" if she is working, or hide or destroy her documents such as her passport, permanent residency card, or health insurance card. Undocumented women may be so fearful of deportation that they will not call the police when being beaten or raped by her partner. According to Dasgupta (1998), the United States immigration and welfare policies confer greater power and control to the male head of the household and are very dangerous for women.[33]

The Case of Anna Lucia

Anna Lucia arrived in the United States in 1980 at the age of 18. Her mother and sister had been living here for many years and were naturalized American citizens. She secured a tourist visa, but after six months it ran out and Anna Lucia became undocumented. However, in the 1980s those without documents were not being actively hunted or deported, so Anna Lucia did not let her status dissuade her. In 1989 she married an American citizen and a year later they had a son. They were married in her husband's American church, the same church where he had grown up. He'd known many of the people in the church most of his life.

Even before their baby was born, Anna Lucia's husband began to abuse her. At first the abuse was verbal, but over time it became physical as well. One way that he controlled Anna Lucia was to threaten her with being deported. He also refused to apply for her citizenship. As long as she was undocumented, he could use the threat of deportation as a means of control. Not knowing where else to turn, Anna Lucia went to see their pastor. Her English was broken and she had found that most of the people at the church did not have the patience to listen carefully and help her express what she needed to say. Her visit with her pastor was brief. She left the church thinking that he had not understood what she

33. Dasgupta, "Women's Realities," 209–219.

was saying nor how desperate she was. He suggested that she enroll in an English class in order to better communicate with her husband. He also called Anna Lucia's husband and told him about the visit.

After that, life went from bad to worse for Anna Lucia, with the physical abuse and terror becoming so severe that even the threat of deportation was not enough to keep her living with her husband. One day, while he was at work, her mother and sister brought a truck over to the house, loaded up Anna Lucia's belongings, and moved her and her son, by then two years old, out of the house.

Anna Lucia's husband made good on his threat to call the immigration authorities. She was summoned to court and began a round of court appearances that started in 1992 and ended with her deportation in 2005, a week before Christmas. During that time, Anna Lucia had attempted to gain legal status by applying for a green card via the special legislation in the 1994 Violence Against Women Act (VAWA) for women in her situation. Anna Lucia's first letter indicating a court appearance, however, arrived at her husband's address, which he withheld. Her second letter arrived when she was in the hospital having surgery for thyroid cancer, and so she missed her second court date as well and was not able to secure legal status.

After her recovery from cancer, Anna Lucia entered into a court process against her husband for failing to provide child support. His back payments amounted to more than $20,000. Her husband again contacted immigration authorities to let them know where they could find her, which led to Anna Lucia's arrest in September of 2005. Her son was put into his father's custody, even though they had not lived together since he was two, and he was not allowed to see his mother during her detention, that lasted until the end of December. In fact, neither her sister nor friends had any contact with her after she was arrested, as they were told that she had left the country. For Anna Lucia, who had made this country her home for twenty-six years and had not been to her home country even once during that time, she was not even allowed to say "goodbye" to her son.

Language Barriers

Language barriers prevent immigrants from easily integrating into mainstream life. For the battered woman, linguistic barriers prevent her from accessing information that would increase her understanding and awareness of domestic violence as well as assist her in reporting the abuse to authorities. Erez (2000) noted that investigating police officers will gather information from the batterer, his extended family, or the victim's children when other interpreters are not available and when the victim cannot speak English.[34] This can lead to distorted information that favors the perpetrator. Immigrant victims often do not know that police protection is available. However, even when a victim may be aware of police help, if she cannot speak English she cannot make the phone call necessary to get help.

Not knowing the language also prevents victims from knowing what services are available and how to access those services. In some communities, agencies that work with domestic violence victims offer multiple language services that are also culturally appropriate. While these agencies are usually staffed by women from similar cultures, it is still necessary that the victim know of the existence of these agencies. Multicultural domestic violence agencies rarely have funding for outreach and many women fail to take advantage of these services because they do not know they exist. One study found that of 40 percent of South Asian women who reported domestic violence, only half of these women knew how to obtain services for countering domestic violence and only 11 percent had sought counseling.[35] Immigrant women are sometimes afraid to use these agencies because ethnic communities are small and they worry that others, including their batterer, will find out that they have sought services.

Cultural Sensitivity

Services that provide support for immigrant victims of domestic violence may lack cultural sensitivity. These can include the legal system,[36] the health care system, and other mainstream service agencies. Mainstream agencies often lack the linguistic and cultural competency necessary to be utilized by immigrants. They often do not understand the complications that arise from legal status issues and therefore are not able to address significant concerns for battered immigrant women. However, one study consistently recorded the voices of battered immigrant women

34. Erez, "Immigration," 27–36.
35. Raj, Immigrant South Asian Women," 435–437.
36. Coto, "The Struggle for Life," 749–759.

stating how significant it is to have an advocate from the same language and cultural group as the battered woman.[37] Some battered women's shelters will not house undocumented women or women with temporary visas, or will not shelter women who do not speak English.[38]

Mainstream agencies may not be able to provide the support needed without a bi-cultural, bi-lingual advocate because they do not understand the complexity of the situation. On the other hand, immigrant advocates have high visibility within their ethnic communities, which can put them at risk of violence by their clients' partners. The immigrant advocate may also be held accountable by her ethnic community to be available and competent, but can also be seen or accused of being Americanized, which can compromise her ability to effectively relate to her community. Her high visibility can affect her home life as well, as it is difficult to maintain a professional distance in a small community, especially when professional boundaries are viewed as incompatible with the culture. For employers, it can be difficult to hire an immigrant advocate since she must be adept at cultural switching – using language and culture rules equally well in both the mainstream community and the immigrant community. In addition, the immigrant advocate is often the only bridge between her clients and other services due to the lack of linguistic capacity of the other systems such as the courts, immigration, and the police.

THE ROLE OF RELIGIOUS ORGANIZATIONS IN THE LIVES OF IMMIGRANTS

Immigrants and refugees who have entered this country in the last twenty years belong to a wide variety of religions, including Catholicism, Islam, Buddhism, Hinduism, and Evangelical Christianity. Religious communities can provide a wealth of support for new arrivals and are usually the first place that immigrants seek guidance on how to navigate the new country. Immigrants often attend religious services in congregations with people from their communities, and services are provided in the language of the home country. Leaders in immigrant congregations are called upon in much the same way as mainstream religious leaders—with the addition of helping their congregants, many of whom

37. Senturia et al., *Cultural Issues.*
38. Volpp, "Feminism," 101.

are non-English speaking, with the many issues related to settling in a new country and learning a new culture and language. While an American pastor may be asked to visit someone recovering in the hospital, an immigrant pastor familiar with American systems may be asked to accompany a church member to an immigration appointment or to resolve an issue with their landlord. It is not uncommon that pastors are even called upon to help the newcomer get a cell phone plan or set up a plan for cable TV or the internet. Those simple activities become great challenges when one cannot speak the language or does not know who to call.

In general, many of the religions to which newly arrived immigrants belong are socially conservative. Several promote hierarchy in marriage and assign the wife the role of family caregiver. Divorce is frowned upon, and in some cases prohibited, unless initiated by the husband. Religious leaders from developing countries generally have not been trained in understanding domestic violence and may underestimate the grave level of harm being suffered by the wife. In addition, ethnic communities often feel they are under scrutiny by the mainstream community, and can have difficulty addressing the issue of domestic violence within their walls. It can appear easier and even safer for their survival as a community to deny its existence.

However, religious leaders are often the first people sought out by a victim when she is seeking help. Because these leaders are respected in the community and are seen as wise, adept in the new culture, and well-connected, resolutions dictated by religious leaders have the potential to remedy the problem without isolating the victim. Yet priests, pastors, and imams may be more harmful than helpful in responding to a member's request for help. They may arrange a meeting to discuss marital issues with both husband and wife, which is both dangerous for the victim and usually unproductive since abusers often do not admit to the abuse to others or consider changing their behavior. Other leaders may encourage the victim to attend church more often, join a women's prayer group, or come to confession. Several women have been told to pray to God and ask for His guidance, which was suggested as an alternative to finding an immediate solution or helping the victim find safety.[39]

It can be challenging for church leaders or members to support a victim if the abuser is also a member of the congregation. Any pub-

39. Personal interviews by author with multiple victims.

lic support of the wife can cause tension and division, and can lead a fragile community to quickly turn against those supporting the victim. Furthermore, recognizing that there are abusers among the congregation could make immigrant leaders feel vulnerable to negative publicity from mainstream media and communities. Finally, some members may feel it is unsafe to help the victim, as it might jeopardize the safety of their own families as well.

When a leader or church member does step up to help a victim, however, the impact is tremendous. For example, Maria was an Ecuadorian woman who found herself in an abusive relationship when her husband returned from serving in the army in Iraq. He had been diagnosed with PTSD and demonstrated abusive tendencies. She belonged to an Evangelical Christian church and asked the women in her Bible study for help. They found her a bedroom that she could rent cheaply far away from her abuser, helped her get a job cleaning houses, and accompanied her to the attorney's office, where she was able to apply for a green card through the Violence Against Women Act (VAWA). Even while she suffered the loss of her relationship and many of her belongings, she was not forced to choose between her safety and her religious community. In fact, "my sisters," she said, "saved my life. Without their help, I wouldn't be here."[40]

Congregations or individuals may feel that they are not equipped to help a victim, particularly if they are not well-informed about domestic violence or believe that the abuser is very dangerous. Many religious leaders and members have assisted instead by referring and linking victims to domestic violence agencies that specialize in working with that community. Once victims begin working with community agencies, friends from their religious community may still help out by donating clothes and food, providing emotional support, and affirming for the victim that she made the right choice in leaving. It may not seem like much, but supportive members of a religious community who believe the victim and support her decision to seek safety are an integral component for her long-term success and healing.

Finally, it should be noted that prior to 9-11, undocumented Christians were not as concerned about their legal status as they are today. Since 9-11, many see themselves in a morally untenable situation, being forced to choose between staying in this country, where they often

40. Personal interview by author with victim.

have deep roots and know they can adequately provide for their family, or leaving for a home they no longer know and where the language and culture is unknown to their American born children. Immigrant pastors of congregations that include undocumented immigrants have additional stressors—not only must they provide spiritual guidance and counsel in these situations, but most are eligible for visas specifically for pastors while no visas are available to their congregants. This creates a situation in which the pastor does not share in the suffering of his flock, and for some pastors this can become a moral dilemma.

HOPE AND CONCERNS FOR IMMIGRANT VICTIMS OF DOMESTIC VIOLENCE

In the last twenty years many positive legal, societal, and political changes have taken place to assist immigrant victims in seeking and maintaining safety. Many mainstream social justice agencies who serve domestic violence victims are hiring bilingual staff and providing cross cultural training to American staff so that they can appropriately assist immigrant victims. Certain state funded programs, such as the Refugee and Immigrant Safety and Empowerment program (RISE) that is administered through the Department of Public Health in Massachusetts was created specifically to fund agencies doing multicultural prevention and advocacy work. Agencies that specialize in other services, such as legal assistance, health care, day care, family services, mental health, and others, are also working to better serve abuse victims from immigrant communities.

In many states, domestic violence hotlines are now able to serve callers in other languages, and often are connected to local agencies with that language capacity. Many hospitals now provide domestic violence advocates who can work with patients who have been raped and abused and in some places these advocates are bilingual and bicultural. There is also a push among agencies that primarily serve immigrants to learn more about family violence and to provide support to potential victims.

The law has also changed in the last two decades to enhance assistance to immigrant victims of domestic violence. In 1994, the federal government passed the *Violence Against Women Act* (VAWA), which, among other things, created a process by which immigrant wives of abusive citizens can apply for a green card independent from the abuser. This allows immigrant women who were threatened by their abusive husbands with denial of status or deportation to leave their abusers without losing their legal status. VAWA also created the U-Visa, which was defined and regulated in 2000. The U-Visa grants a temporary visa to undocumented people who are witnesses to a crime in a criminal process. Frequently, undocumented immigrants who were victims of a violent attack and are willing to testify against the abuser can qualify for this visa. Less frequently, some abuse victims have also qualified for asylum when the abuse occurred in the home country and the victim fled to this country for reasons of safety. To obtain asylum, the victim must prove that the abuser still poses a threat to her if she returns to the home country.

While there is a movement afoot to provide more rights and services to immigrant victims, there are still very few resources available compared to the number of women and children who are in need of help. Domestic violence shelters in Massachusetts, for instance, turn down an average of 162 callers a day who need a safe place to stay.[41] Many immigrant women are still not aware of or connected to bilingual domestic violence services, and even those who are find enormous legal and financial barriers to leaving their abuser. Cultural and religious beliefs that put family unity above a woman's safety continue to play an important role in the life of many immigrant families, causing isolation and shame for women who may want to leave. And even those churches that are willing to stand up for victims of abuse often lack the network of social services necessary for caring for a victim of domestic violence.

Finally, the general anti-immigrant sentiment prevalent in this country, along with the frequent ICE raids and deportations, has caused immigrant victims of abuse to isolate even more. Fear of the police and immigration may be so great that the fear of their abuser may not seem as bad in comparison. This fear of government, combined with the lack of information regarding services available to immigrant families, results in many victims of domestic violence feeling that that the dangers outside their homes are greater than that within.

In spite of all odds, however, immigrant victims of abuse are persevering and finding their way to safety and independence. Every year more and more immigrant women reach out to social service agencies, the police, and their communities for help. New programs are educating immigrant communities about the prevalence of abuse and helping

41. NNEDV, "2009 Domestic Violence Counts," 1.

friends and family find ways to support those who may be suffering abuse. Church leaders are finding ways, both from the pulpit and in individual conversations, to educate their congregations about the existence of domestic violence and to condemn this behavior. And they are reaching out to members who show signs of being victimized. Bilingual advocates are continuously swamped with cases of immigrant women seeking help, which is both a sign of the continued need for services, but also that immigrant victims are actually reaching out. The more people find resources and share that information with others, the more people will seek safety and support.

The challenges for immigrants, even in the best of situations, can at times feel overwhelming. For immigrants facing violence in their own homes, the challenge is even greater. Immigrant victims of abuse will only seek help and safety when they believe that they can make it on their own, that they won't be deported, that they are not risking the well-being of their children, and when they know that their ethnic and religious communities will not abandon them. What she needs is the outstretched hand that lets her know that her human condition is more important than any barriers of language or culture or status in this new place she now calls home.

REFERENCES

Abraham, M. "Speaking the Unspeakable: Marital Violence against South Asian Immigrant Women in the United States." *Indian Journal of Gender Studies* (1998) 215–241.

Anderson, M.J. "A License to Abuse: The Impact of Conditional Status on Female Immigrants." *Yale Law Journal* (1993) 102(6).

Brownridge, D. A., and S. S. Halli. "Double Jeopardy?: Violence against Immigrant Women in Canada." *Violence and Victims* (2002) 455–471.

Chan, S., and C. W. Leong. "Chinese families in Transition: Cultural Conflicts and Adjustment Problems." *Journal of Social Distress and the Homeless* (1994) 263–281.

Coto, V.P. "The Struggle for Life: Legal Services for Battered Immigrant Women." *University of Miami Law Review* (1999) 749–759.

Dasgupta, D. S. "Women's Realities: Defining Violence against Women by Immigration, Race, and Class." In *Issues in Intimate Violence*, edited by R.K. Bergin, 209–19. Thousand Oaks, CA: Sage, 1998.

Enander, V. Leaving Jekyll and Hyde: Emotion work in the context of intimate partner violence. Submitted manuscript, (2009).

Erez, E. "Immigration, Culture Conflict and Domestic Violence/Woman Battering." *Crime, Prevention, and Community Safety: An International Journal* (2000) 27–36.

Fahlberg, V. Barriers Faced by Immigrants and Refugees Residing in the City Of Lowell, Massachusetts. Unpublished report by the One Lowell Coalition, Nov. 8, 2001.

————. Supervising and Supporting Bi-lingual/Bi-cultural Domestic Violence Advocates. Immigrant and Refugee Conference: Learning as we Grow. Northeastern U. May 22. Sponsored by Jane Doe, Inc, 2002.

Friedman, A. R. "Rape and Domestic Violence: The Experience of Refugee Women." In *Refugee Women and their Mental Health: Shattered Societies, Shattered Lives*, edited by E. Cole et al., 65–78. New York: Haworth Press, 1992.

Hofstede, G. "The Cultural Relativity of the Quality of Life Concept." *Academy of Management Review* (1984) 389–398.

Huisman, K.A. "Wife Battering in Asian American Communities. Identifying the Service Needs of an Overlooked Segment of the U.S. Population." *Violence against Women* (1996) 260–283.

Menjivar, C. "Immigrant Women and Domestic Violence: Common Experiences in Different Countries." *Gender and Society* (2002) 898–920.

Narayan, U. "Mail-order Brides: Immigrant Women, Domestic Violence and Immigration Law." *Hypatia* (1995) 104–116.

National Network to End Domestic Violence. "2009 Domestic Violence Counts: A 24-Hour Census of Domestic Violence Shelters and Services." (2009) 1. Online: http://Janedoe.org/know.

New York City Department of Health Bureau of Injury Epidemiology. *Femicide in New York City: 1995 - 2002*. No pages. Online: http://www.nyc.gov/html/doh/downloads/pdf/ip/femicide/1995-2002_report.pdf.

Perilla, J.L., et al. "Culture and Domestic Violence: The Ecology of Abused Latinas." *Violence and Victims* (1994) 325–339.

————. "Domestic Violence as a Human Rights Issue: The Case of Immigrant Latinos." *Hispanic Journal of Behavioral Sciences* (1999) 107–133.

Raj, A., and J. Silverman. "Immigrant South Asian Women at Greater Risk for Injury from Intimate Partner Violence in the Pacific-Asian Community and the Cultural Defense." *American Journal of Public Health* (2003) 435–37.

Rimonte, N. A. "A Question of Culture: Cultural Approval of Violence Against Women in the Pacific-Asian Community and the Cultural Defense." *Stanford Law Review* (1991) 1311.

Senturia, K., et al. *Cultural issues affecting domestic violence service utilization in ethnic and hard to reach populations. NIJ Final Report*, US Department of Justice, NCJ #98-WT-VX-0025, 2000.

Supriya, K.E. "Confessionals, Testimonials: Women's Speech in/and Contexts of Violence." *Hypatia* (1996) 92–106.

Tiede, L.B. "Battered Immigrant Women and Immigrant Remedies: Are the Standards Too High?" *Human Rights* (2001) 21–22.

Tjaden, P., and N. Thoennes. *Extent, Nature, and Consequences of Intimate Partner Violence: Findings from the National Violence Against Women Survey*. National Institute of Justice and the Centers for Disease Control and Prevention, NCJ #181867, 2000.

Tran, C. G., and K. Des Jardins. "Domestic Violence in Vietnamese Refugee and Korean Immigrant Communities." In *Relationships among Asian American Women*, edited by J. L. Chin, ch.5. American Psychological Association, 2000.

Volpp, I. "Feminism versus multiculturalism." *Columbia Law Review* (2001) 101.

West, C.M., et al. "Sociodemographic Predictors and Cultural Barriers to Help-Seeking Behavior by Latina and Anglo American Battered Women." *Violence and Victims* (1998) 361–375.

10

Notes from the Pastor's Office

Terry Atkinson and Steve McMullin

STEVE MCMULLIN'S EXPERIENCE AND ADVICE

WHEN A DEVOUT PROFESSIONAL woman in my congregation requested an appointment to see me, I had seen no signs that she was a victim of domestic abuse. Although she attended church services faithfully, her husband attended only on rare occasions, but he appeared to treat her well whenever I saw them together. I had also visited the home on two occasions, and in my presence he had been the model husband. But in my office, she told me a very different story of control, manipulation, anger, and fear.

The occasion for her visit to my office was a recent episode when her husband had lost his temper, called her a whore, and slapped her across the face. For a woman who faithfully lived out her Christian commitment and took her marriage vows seriously, such a label was particularly devastating. Although being slapped was the first and only incidence of physical violence, she was wise enough to recognize that the abuse was escalating to the point where she was in greater danger than had been the case previously. The first person to whom she turned was her pastor.

As she told me about her home situation, I learned for the first time that she had endured several years of unwarranted control by her husband. She had a very responsible job, but he made her give him her paycheque each week and he then provided her with an unreasonably small allowance to pay for all of the household and personal expenses. He did not allow her to talk on the telephone unless he was in the room to monitor the conversation. He limited or prevented her contacts with members of her family, and did not want them visiting their home. Although the couple could certainly afford one, his refusal to purchase a car prevented her from visiting family members and friends and made life difficult for her by socially isolating her.

In my office she made it clear to me that she loved her husband very much and wanted him to find help, but she knew that she had to leave their home until it was safe to return. Over the next few days she was able to find a relative who was willing to provide her with shelter. Once she had left the home she asked me to contact her husband in the hope that he would meet with me, recognize the problem and express a willingness to seek help.

Over the next two months I met with her several times, and had two separate meetings with her husband. Although he was certainly upset that she had left and at first expressed his desire and determination to change, he was unwilling to accept any responsibility for his actions. He freely admitted to me that he had slapped his wife and called her a whore, but he seemed not to think that was sufficient reason for a wife to leave home. In fact, he laughed and said to me, "You know what women are like." He hoped that I could talk some sense into her. As we talked, I discovered that he was filled with anger not only toward his wife, but toward much of the world. I made it clear that he needed to be willing to get help, but he took no steps toward making any real change. He made an appointment for a third meeting with me, but did not show up and did not answer the phone when I called. Finally, with her husband showing no signs of remorse and no willingness to change, his wife reluctantly made the decision to end the marriage.

The Pastor's Role in Responding to Domestic Violence

This experience, along with others like it, has emphasized to me the important role that pastors can play in the response to domestic violence. First, for a woman of devout faith, the pastor may be the most likely person to whom she will disclose what is happening at home. Because of the commitment of a Christian woman to the marriage vows she made before God, the pastor is in an important spiritual position to provide permission to an abused woman in a time of crisis to find temporary shelter and seek immediate help and personal safety. In a sense, this abused woman was looking for me to confirm that she was in an abusive relationship and needed help—something which I readily did.

Second, unlike others who may respond to the needs of a victim of abuse, the pastor is usually in the position of ministering to both the victim and the perpetrator. Abused wives love their husbands and are concerned that the perpetrator is given an opportunity to find help. Although it is important that pastors meet with each person individually and not disclose to the other anything that is said in the privacy of the pastor's study, it brings comfort to the abused spouse to know that someone who shares her faith perspective and her concern for her husband is talking with him and attempting to ascertain whether there is a possibility of real change. Because I knew this woman's husband, he was willing to meet with me. When meeting with him I was able to make clear to him that the abuse was unacceptable, and I was also able to pray with him and encourage him to deal with the anger that was so evident in his soul. I was able to show from scripture why violence is wrong while offering him hope that with help, support, and accountability he could change. I was also able to assure him that if the marriage ended as a result of the abuse, I would remain willing to provide spiritual guidance to him, as would others in the faith community.

Third, I was able to provide the victim with spiritual counsel. I talked to her about what the Bible says about violence, I prayed with her, and I was able to affirm her as a valued member of our congregation. It is important that survivors of abuse are not made to feel like second-class citizens in the church, and the pastor is in the best position to make it clear both to victims and to the congregation that being a survivor of abuse does not diminish a person's status in the congregation.

Fourth, a well-designed pastor's office can provide a safe environment for a Christian woman to disclose abuse. In the office suite at our church, all office doors have large windows facing the outer office, so nothing in the pastor's study is secretive, yet the offices are quite soundproof so conversations can be kept confidential. When a woman who is being abused by a man wishes to disclose abuse to a pastor who is also a man, such considerations take on added importance.

Fifth, the pastor is able to provide faith-based resources that affirm the woman's religious commitment while guiding her through the journey to healing and wholeness. The RAVE website, the PASCH website, and many excellent books and materials from a Christian perspective are a reminder that many women of devout faith and commitment are victims. An abused Christian woman need not feel alone on her journey to healing and wholeness. The pastor may also know of women in the congregation, or in a nearby congregation, who have themselves experienced abuse but have with God's help been able to find healing for themselves and offer support to others. Such people are an invaluable resource. Pastors need to be wise enough to discern that not every survivor of abuse in the congregation will be helpful to other victims. Some survivors are still in the midst of the healing process and are too angry or broken to be of help to others. Pastors may also recognize women in the congregation who have not themselves been victims, but who are able and willing to empathize and reach out to those who are broken and need Christian nurture and support through the healing process. Some women are particularly gifted for ministry to those who have experienced abuse.

Sixth, the pastor can refer victims to community-based agencies who are equipped to provide both crisis care and long-term support and who will respect and affirm the woman's Christian faith. Ideally, the pastor should have made contact with the local battered women's shelter and should be aware of community services offered both to victims and perpetrators. It is especially helpful if the pastor knows personally some of the staff at the local shelters and those who might be helpful as counsellors and victims' advocates. If the pastor is part of the community partnership to respond to domestic violence, it will be much easier to refer people confidently to the help they need and it will also be easier for community agencies to work along with the pastor so that spiritual care and guidance for the victim can be provided during the process of healing.

Seventh, through preaching and teaching ministries, the pastor is able gently but clearly to inform victims of abuse that the church is a safe place to disclose that one needs help. By addressing domestic violence from the pulpit on occasion, by affirming that homes are to be free of violence and manipulation, by expressing a willingness to listen without judging, and by encouraging victims to find help, a pastor can provide important signals to victims who suffer in silence that there is hope and help.

Finally, the pastor can make sure that she or he is well prepared to respond to the needs of victims of abuse. By having information about women's shelters and community resources, by having contacts with advocates and agencies, and by knowing how to respond appropriately, the pastor can make appropriate referrals that will ensure that abused women know that they have options. I would have to say that my seminary training for responding to victims of domestic violence was woefully inadequate, but through years of pastoral ministry I have found information and community resources—sometimes through a process of trial and error—that have made me better prepared.

Premarital Counselling

Premarital counselling provides pastors with a strategic opportunity to address the issue of domestic violence with those who are considering marriage. Pastors can include some basic information about domestic violence—what abuse is and is not, the prevalence of domestic violence in society and among people of faith, what to do if the marriage shows signs of being abusive, and how to find help. The pastor can guide the couple through scripture passages that address violence and can refute misinterpretations of scripture that may be used to justify abuse and control. It would be quite naïve for a pastor to think that the brief time available for addressing domestic violence during a few premarital counselling sessions will prevent any abuse from happening in every marriage. What is more likely is that if the pastor has addressed the issue clearly before marriage, the couple will know that they can come to the pastor for help should the relationship begin to be abusive, and it is likely that they will seek help far sooner than they would have had it not been addressed.

When addressing the issue of domestic violence, couples can be introduced to the RAVE website as a potential source for guidance and information. They can be assured that if they need help they can call the pastor. They can be provided with information about community agencies that can help in the event of domestic violence. Rather than making violence the focus of the counselling sessions, such information can be provided in the context of providing information about a variety of agencies that may be helpful to married couples.

During premarital counselling, there is also the opportunity to ascertain whether either or both of the persons preparing for marriage have themselves been victims of domestic violence or if they have witnessed abuse in the homes in which they were raised. In many cases, such violence has never been addressed or discussed with anyone, including the person they are planning to marry. It is important that the premarital counselling allows the issue to be addressed and discussed in ways that deal with the fears of the person who has experienced or witnessed family violence and that inform the person who may not have ever had that experience.

People who have grown up in a violent home and who are preparing for marriage may be fearful that they will be violent or that their spouse will become violent. They may have unhealthy understandings of the marriage relationship that need to be challenged and corrected. They may feel shame or embarrassment about their past, and that shame may negatively affect their future marriage if it is not addressed. If past experiences are not addressed, in their marriage they may express anger in inappropriate ways, or they may suppress their anger instead of dealing with issues in their own lives or in their marriage. They may find it difficult to express emotion and love, or may do so inappropriately, because of the experiences they have had in their own home. These are issues that a wise pastor can talk about during premarital counselling; the pastor can then refer the couple to someone who is particularly qualified to help individuals work through such issues.

Affirming Victims in Congregational Life

Because our congregation provided a support group for people who were separated or divorced, and several of those people had been victims of domestic violence, we often have had survivors from other congregations come to us for help and support. Sometimes they come bruised and confused because of the ways that their pastor or their congregation or even their close Christian friends have responded to the disclosure of the abuse they have suffered. For example, one very devout woman who came to our support group told me that she had endured beatings from her husband for several years, because she thought it was her Christian duty to honor her marriage vows. Eventually her husband began beating their two very young children, and when that happened, she left with her children and the marriage ended. She told me that in her congregation, her pastor had said to her that it was acceptable for her to remain a member of the congregation, but that she should "keep a low profile." In other words, because of her past the congregation did not want her involved in ministry or in leadership. For many years she faithfully continued to attend her church on Sundays, speaking to few people and feeling like an outcast.

In the support group at our church she began to think about the grace of God. She learned that Biblical forgiveness did not mean that what her husband had done to her and her children was acceptable, but that it meant that she could let go of the hurt and the pain that had been so personally debilitating for so long. As she began attending our congregation, we urged her to become involved in ministry. We affirmed her as a full member of our congregation, dependent on God's grace as we all are regardless of our pasts.

With my support, another woman who had been the victim of horrific abuse at the hands of a violent husband was elected to the governing board of our church. It not only affirmed her, but I discovered that it also made a very important statement to other people in our congregation who have been victims of abuse. It was a very practical demonstration that the congregation does not marginalize those whose marriages have ended because they were victims of abuse, and it provided encouragement and hope to survivors.

TERRY ATKINSON'S EXPERIENCE AND ADVICE

As a social worker for ten years I saw my share of domestic violence. Doing child protection for eight of those ten years exposed me to the ills in our society and the cruelty directed especially at women and children. When I shifted careers and entered the ministry, I left my government job, went back to school and trained for three years at seminary. Although there were courses offered in the counselling area, most seminaries do not equip clergy to handle the challenges when an abused person comes to the church office seeking one's advice. I am thankful for my social work training, but I know I am in the minority when it comes to clergy feeling equipped to handle such situations.

Having been exposed to domestic violence alerted me to the fact that churches are not exempt from this problem. I am well aware that violence is occurring in homes of people within my congregation. I also realize that it is often well hidden and we must do what we can to ensure that people who are members of the church will feel safe when these situations come to light. I am convinced that pastors are gate-keepers; and they set the tone for the level of freedom or lack thereof in a church setting when it comes to speaking about sensitive issues like domestic violence. Therefore it behoves us as clergy to be informed on this issue and be prepared to speak on it from the pulpit, in Bible studies, through groups such as social action committees, and with the rest of the leadership team.

As clergy we are in a unique position because people often come to us with their problems and we need to be cautious in reassuring people that sharing such deep secrets will not be carelessly tossed aside. It takes great courage to come forward when one finds oneself in an abusive situation; it is imperative that clergy listen well and not pass judgment, but accept that person and share God's love and grace, even to the perpetrator.

Here are a few things that clergy can and should do to address this issue in our society and especially in our churches . . .

- First, education is key for clergy and for congregations. As a pastor, if you have had little or no exposure to this social ill, you need to read, search the internet, and talk to other pastors who are better trained in this area. Don't play ostrich and "hide your head in the sand." This is a real issue in which a person must be educated.

Then, take positive steps to educate your congregation. As mentioned earlier, preach on this and other social topics that need to be addressed. Provide literature in ladies' washrooms, your church library, or at the church office. (Several great pamphlets are put out by the RAVE project, two of which are "Christian Love Shouldn't Hurt: Support for Women" and "Love One Another: Dating Violence and Christianity").

Because violence is often passed on from one generation to the next, it is imperative that youth pastors and youth leaders talk openly about this topic with our teens. Youth pastors/leaders are also in a very unique position when they can have such a positive impact on teens and teach them about healthy and unhealthy relationships.

- Second, I believe it is also important for every pastor, when he or she settles into a new church and a new community, to learn of the resources that are available—such as shelters, secular and/ or Christian counsellors, government agencies, etc. We need to see ourselves as a referral source. Yes, we can assess a situation, we can support and encourage the victim, and sometimes even the perpetrator, but ultimately we need to work in collaboration with other community resources. Do not try the "lone ranger" approach. It is a complex issue and we need all the help we can get.

- Third, we need to model what we preach. We need to ensure that church is a safe place for everyone. This means having police checks done on children and youth workers. It means that adults, youth and children are always safe on the church premises. Too often, abuse (physical, sexual, emotional or spiritual) has occurred in our churches by so-called "trusted" leaders. We need to ensure that this *is* a safe place which will then allow people to more readily open up if problems arise in the home.

- Fourth, we are in a good position to connect victims with other survivors within the congregation. Obtain permission first and then introduce people to one another. This can be a tremendous support and help victims see that as Christians, our God is a God who can rescue, restore and heal individuals and families. Ministries such as Divorce Care are wonderful tools that can be used to address and deal with situations of abuse.

There is much to be done in raising the awareness of this serious problem within our churches. As pastors, we play a key role. Let's get educated and then address this in a caring, Christ-like manner.

11

Notes from the Shelter

Julie A. Owens

Y EARS AGO WHEN I was working in a secular shelter for battered
women, I received a frantic call from a co-worker on my day off.
"Several boxes of Bibles were just donated and the manager put them out
on the curb with the trash. They're getting rained on and ruined! What
are we going to do? Some of our women want one!" she said through
her tears. She explained that the manager had told her that the agency
would risk losing its government funding if it "violated the separation
of church and state" by allowing Bibles into the shelter. I was frustrated
and saddened by a shelter manager's obvious unawareness, particularly
about the needs of women who have been so broken, physically, emotionally, and spiritually. Scripture, although often used as another tool of
abuse by batterers, frequently becomes the very healing balm that brings
comfort and peace at last to victims who have suffered unimaginable
chaos and terror.

Later, when I was managing the transitional shelter for battered
women and their children that my church had started, I received a call
from a woman in distress who, along with her four children, was a current shelter guest. She was in a panic after leaving an unscheduled counselling session that her pastor had requested. Sobbing, she explained
that when she'd arrived at his office, she had unexpectedly found herself
face-to-face with her estranged husband, a heavy drug user who had
brutalized her and her children for years. Not only was she terrified by
his presence, she had been told in no uncertain terms by the state Child
Protective Services team that if she ever violated the mandated protective
order, her children would be removed immediately. She fled the church,

feeling "set up" and utterly betrayed by the pastor she had once trusted. Again, I was frustrated and saddened—this time by a pastor's obvious ignorance about the safety and support needs of battered women and their children.

These unfortunate situations illustrate the historical disconnect between the church and domestic violence shelters, born of a mutual suspicion and lack of trust. It's not hard to figure out how and why this tension originated, but I believe it emanates essentially from a genuine ignorance on both sides. I believe this because I walk with a foot in both worlds. I am a survivor of domestic violence who has worked simultaneously in both secular and faith-based domestic violence programs for over twenty years. In my current position I oversee more than thirty domestic violence and sexual assault programs throughout seventeen counties for the state in which I live. During the week I consult with these programs, providing technical assistance and training. The weekends often find me teaching church leaders about the issue of violence against women. I hear the bitter comments of domestic violence advocates who have had terrible experiences trying to keep safe victims who are threatened with excommunication if they don't reconcile with an abusive husband. I have attended countless domestic violence events for the clergy, only to be terribly disappointed at the abysmal turnout.

Numerous myths perpetuate and exacerbate the ignorance that pervades both camps. They are all rooted in misunderstanding and sometimes they are the result of unfortunate experiences that have created a fear-based bias which has generalized to "the other." Pastors may fear that shelter workers will encourage victims to divorce, while advocates may fear that pastors will insist on reconciliation, resulting in further abuse or worse. Until clergy and domestic violence advocates understand each other and put to rest the many myths and misconceptions that separate them, there is precious little hope for the coordinated response that can make a difference.

An advocate's work is draining and often thankless. It is exhausting and frustrating to operate within multiple systems (i.e. legal, criminal justice, child protection, faith communities) that consistently re-victimize battered women. Day in and day out, the advocate may be the only person who stands with a victim in her pain, saying, "I believe you. You don't deserve it. It's not your fault," while others doubt the veracity of her story, blame her for the problem, or make excuses for her abuser's behavior. While fighting for justice on behalf of crime victims, she is also often treated poorly and disrespectfully by persons in these same systems.

Shelter workers are changed by the difficult work they do. It is not a neutral job that one can just leave at the end of the day. Often advocates are on 24-hour call. Even when they are not, the faces and stories of all the women and children they have served go home with them. These lay heavy on their hearts every waking moment and permeate their dreams at night. Victim advocacy is much like working as an EMT, always dealing with people in crisis—people who are wounded and bleeding, confused, and terrified. It changes a person.

Terri Spahn Nelson explains this well:

> We bear witness to their victimization. We listen, we support and we validate their feelings and their experience. We offer them the opportunity to let go of some of their burden. As witnesses and healers, we can't help but to take in some of the emotional pain they have left with us. As the victim releases some of their pain, we take it in. By the end of the day, we've collected bits and pieces of accounts of trauma. We may have pictures in our mind or intense feelings running through our body. We've become a witness to rape, child abuse, domestic violence, and death . . . .[1]

At the same time, advocates walk through the world all day, every day, steeped in the internalized, discouraging reality of global violence against women. That truth can be overwhelming, almost too much to bear, leading to a sense of futility and hopelessness at the seemingly endless stream of victims needing help. They know what most of the world doesn't—that one out three women is battered, that domestic violence is the most common cause of injury to women, that most women killed are murdered by their husbands or boyfriends, and that the time of separation is the most lethal.[2] They see abused women everywhere, because they are everywhere. Their friends and families become weary of the weight their loved ones carry, and want them to go back to being the person they were before they carried this weight. Once a feeling person

1. Nelson, *Vicarious Trauma*.

2. Men are battered, too, of course, as are individuals in same-sex relationships. When this occurs in a consistent pattern and meets the definition of domestic violence, it is equally lethal. Since the vast majority of victims are female, however, I will be focusing on violence against women for the purposes of this article.

has taken the ugly truth into her consciousness though, there is simply no going back. The ubiquity, the enormity, and the appalling commonality of the violence women suffer are "in her face" all the time. It's no wonder that advocates may seem abrupt or have little patience for the untrained but well-meaning pastor who wants to do couples counselling with a batterer and his victim. It's exhausting and frustrating to feel the responsibility for educating all the professionals she comes in contact with, especially the ones who act as if they already know it all, but who clearly are ill-informed.

Shelter workers interact with faith leaders as a necessary part of the advocacy and outreach work they do. When this occurs, it is not unusual for them to be met with cool resistance or outright suspicion. Additionally, they are mentored by older seasoned advocates who have worked in the field for years; women who have "seen it all" and who may have grown cynical when it comes to the role of religion in the lives of survivors.

Domestic violence advocates, of course, have their own spiritual and religious beliefs that permeated their thinking and influenced them long before they worked in the field. Once firmly ensconced as a part of the "battered women's movement," they have multiple experiences with victims whose faith has influenced their decisions, often resulting in their return to an abuser and an almost certain escalation of the violence.

Ultimately, shelter workers tend to lean one of two ways when it comes to issues of faith, depending in part on their work experiences and the tenor of their interactions with the faith community. They might find themselves totally "turned off" by religion, having seen victim after victim trapped and re-abused because of misguided teachings or a misinterpretation of scriptures. They may, however, experience a spiritual awakening or a deepening of their faith, having worked with numerous victims whose survival seems nothing short of miraculous. I have known many victim advocates who have come to believe strongly that they were called by God to their work. Those who find their personal beliefs strengthened often refer to their work as a ministry rather than a job. When this is the case, their mindset is not unlike that of a missionary. I frequently encounter shelter advocates who are very comfortable talking with victims about matters of the spirit, and I have met multiple survivors who have found this to be their greatest source of healing and hope.

On the other hand, I have known numerous other advocates who strongly feel that it is inappropriate to discuss religion or spirituality with victims. Sometimes these shelter workers are believers and sometimes they are not. Most very experienced advocates will honor a victim's belief system even if it differs widely from her own. She will maintain an appropriate boundary, being careful not push her own beliefs onto a vulnerable victim, while validating the woman's need for spiritual direction and support. Whenever possible, the well trained advocate will try to find and make a referral to a local faith leader with training in domestic violence who is from the victim's own religion or denomination. In recent years, many secular programs have come to understand and promote the necessity of a comprehensive and holistic approach to advocacy that acknowledges domestic violence victims as multi-faceted human beings with a variety of needs. Recognising and validating an individual's spiritual needs and desires when expressed, along with her physical and psychological ones, is gradually coming to be considered a best practice in the field of victim services.

The primary reason that shelter workers may have a general mistrust of the clergy and the faith community is the fact that, unfortunately, domestic violence situations are mishandled by them more often than not. This may be hard to hear, but it is in fact true. Every shelter worker can cite many, many examples of incidences when battered women have been told by their pastors or church leaders, "Go home. Pray harder," "God hates divorce," "Be a better wife," "Stop making him so mad!" or "You must stand by him. He is sick. He needs your support."

Just a few days ago I was contacted by a woman who has been battered for thirty years by her police officer husband. I was only the second person she had ever told about the abuse. Her husband was finally arrested last weekend but is now stalking her, has cut off her telephone, emptied their bank account, and is refusing to turn in his guns as ordered by the judge. She is terrified and could not stop crying as we talked. The first person she had contacted? Her minister. His advice? "Come in for marriage counselling."

Last night I was speaking with a frustrated advocate who met with a victim in court just yesterday. What had her pastor told her? "You must submit to your husband." Many, many women have been severely beaten or even killed after following similar advice dispensed by well-meaning faith leaders. Advocates know this and are understandably wary.

Sometimes clergy may not know about domestic violence agencies, what they do, or why their services are critically important. Others who are familiar with them may simply be reluctant to work as partners with secular advocates because they believe that the church is the best place to deal with "marriage problems" and that involving secular counsellors might complicate matters. Still others may feel a sense of embarrassment or inadequacy. If a pastor has not received any formal training in the area, he or she may be in the uncomfortable position of feeling ill-prepared to deal with such a complex issue. After all, it is only very recently that seminaries have begun to incorporate curricula about family violence. These pastors will necessarily approach victims with a counselling perspective that has been formed primarily by their own life experiences and no doubt by the many common societal misunderstandings that exist regarding domestic violence. For example, a minister who was raised in a family where the mother was not treated with respect may feel little empathy for another a woman in a similar situation, perhaps because he or she grew up identifying with a father who often stated that "she asked for it." Or, as many children of mistreated mothers have come believe, "She was weak and didn't protect us." Still another clergy member who grew up with a parent who had a drinking problem may think, "I have to get this poor woman to Al-anon so she can stop enabling him." Abuse may not be the counselling focus at all. Another pastor may believe, "If I directly confront him, he might stop abusing her." All of these approaches, while understandable, are misguided, and could easily escalate the violence.

It must be said that there is another group of ministers that is not just reluctant but in fact actively resistant to working with shelters and victim advocates. These individuals may have internalized common myths such as the classic, "Domestic violence advocates are feminists, and all feminists are man-haters." Another is, "Shelters cause divorces." (I've always liked something I heard said once in reference to the latter myth, "Shelters don't cause divorces any more than emergency rooms cause car wrecks!") Whatever the cause of such resistance, when victims worship in churches led by clergy members operating under regrettable, fear-based assumptions that disallow referrals to the safety resources, it is unlikely they will receive appropriate counsel and support. These unfortunate parishioners end up being forced to choose between their safety and continuing as a member of their faith community. It is tragic indeed when a victim who has already been stripped by an abuser of nearly everything meaningful to her—her safety, her support system, her freedom, her home, her self-esteem, her privacy, her reputation, and perhaps even her children—must then forfeit her church because of a pastor's unwillingness to partner with secular resources that could help her tremendously.

It is probably safe to say that anyone who is still reading this chapter is likely doing so because of a genuine concern about, and desire to respond appropriately to, victims. If this is the case, congratulations! You may be ready to take advantage of the expertise and resources available within the secular domestic violence agencies. But you may also be wondering where to start or how to begin building a bridge between your church and the local shelter. Below are some suggestions to help you break the ice and get started:

1. If possible, join the local domestic violence coalition or task force and build relationships there. They are eager to include concerned representatives of the faith community;

2. Call the local domestic violence program or shelter. Ask for a face-to-face meeting with key staff when possible (program director, shelter manager and lead advocate). If you are a male, you want to consider taking a female staff member or lay leader with you to the meeting. A survivor of domestic violence would be ideal;

3. Acknowledge that you are not an expert in the area but that you are eager to learn and partner with them. Let them know that your priorities are safety and confidentiality for the victims and accountability for perpetrators. That fact that you have read books such as this will impress them and demonstrate your sincerity; [3]

4. Be prepared for lots of questions. Don't be surprised if they seem cautious or suspicious. Be patient. When they learn that you understand the dangers associated with domestic violence and are not a clergy person who believes in "saving a marriage at all costs," they will be happy to work with you. Remember, they need people like you to make referrals to!;

3. See the Christian resources listed elsewhere in this book. In addition to these materials, I strongly recommend that you read secular works. Among my favorites are *When Loves goes Wrong* by Ann Jones and Susan Schechter, *Why Does He Do That?* by Lundy Bancroft, and *Trauma and Recovery* by Judith Herman, MD.

5. Tell them that you need and desire training. Ask if they can help you with this, or refer you somewhere for some training;[4]

6. Demonstrate respect for their expertise and their own religious beliefs;

7. Offer to partner with them and assist them in some way, perhaps with consultation, support, or joint programming. Give them a copy of your denomination's domestic violence statement or policy, if one exists. A really wonderful way to show support is to let them know you would like to include their agency in your local mission budget. Just offering a free space for victim support groups to meet (especially if a childcare room is available as well) will speak volumes, even if they do not currently need a meeting place.

8. Be sure that you make it clear that your/your church's partnership with them comes with "no strings attached." They need to know that their staff members' and clients' religious backgrounds or beliefs will not be questioned or be an "issue" in this partnership. They must know that the relationship will be one of mutual respect. It should not be viewed as an avenue for proselytizing, although you may find that survivors will start attending your church once they know that you "get it" about domestic violence and do not place demands on them. That was our experience at the church my father pastored.

If you have already made initial inroads within your local violence against women community, then you may be ready for next steps. Once you feel you have achieved a comfortable level of mutual understanding and trust with the secular agencies, you can greatly enhance the coordinated community response to domestic violence in your community by helping to establish a faith task force on violence against women. The possibilities for such a group are endless. For instance, such a group might collect and distribute domestic violence and sexual assault policies, pro-

---

4. One of the best places to receive training is your state's domestic violence coalition. Training is provided by experienced advocates who can assist with best practices information and materials. You might also inquire about other faith leaders who are already working on the issue in your state. A map of all state coalitions in the US is available (with a hot link to each corresponding website) can be found on the RAVE website. www.theraveproject.com. Additionally, PASCH offers training and conferences specifically designed for Christian pastors and lay leaders www.peaceandsafety.com.

tocols, and educational materials appropriate to specific denominations or faith traditions.[5] A consortium of churches can also work together to help fund programs that assist victims. This is a wonderful way to demonstrate your understanding of the importance of such programs and your eagerness to partner with them.

Before my father retired we lived in Hawaii, a very multi-cultural state. There he and I were instrumental in founding an interfaith task force against domestic violence that included Catholic, Jewish and Buddhist representatives, as well as Protestant Christian leaders. This group became a respected entity amongst the local shelters and secular agencies and was routinely invited to participate in various endeavors, including memorial vigils.

Our faith task force eventually decided to offer actively a direct service to victims, in addition to providing training for clergy, fundraising for shelters, and promoting awareness in our houses of faith. We began providing quarterly free Saturday "mini-retreats" for survivors, offering holistic spiritual healing workshops, childcare, inspirational tokens, and a simple luncheon. What a gift this was to beleaguered mothers and their children.

A survivor activist group that I co-led at the time also began an annual event that a faith task force could easily replicate. We decided to honor some hardworking advocates during October, national Domestic Violence Awareness Month. We accepted nominations and selected individuals to receive an "Unsung Hero" or "Unsung Sheroe" award, which was presented with much fanfare, to the delight of these individuals who had gone above and beyond the call of duty to assist victims in our community. These efforts were all accomplished by a relatively small group of dedicated volunteers who solicited donations to cover any modest costs involved. They meant a great deal to the secular advocates and community programs that typically work in isolation with very limited resources and time to undertake special events such as these.

A local committee that I helped establish in the city where I now live sponsors annual domestic violence memorial candlelight vigils. Each year a different house of faith opens its doors to host an interfaith service where victims who have died that year are remembered, and survivors are celebrated. Childcare is provided and the community

5. FaithTrust Institute's website lists a number of links to denominational policies and protocols related to domestic violence and sexual abuse. www.faithtrustinstotute.org.

is invited. Residents of the local shelters and members of victim support groups are invited. Law enforcement officers provide security. A simple reception follows and resource literature from local programs is displayed and offered.

If you decide to reach out to shelters and advocacy groups within your community, and particularly if you offer to assist them in some way, I believe that you will be doing one of the most important things you could ever do for victims of domestic violence. You will be demonstrating to those within your own congregation that you understand their need for the personal advocacy, support groups, and legal assistance that only these resources can provide. By reaching out, you will also be demonstrating to the secular agencies the unconditional love and acceptance that Jesus himself would offer them and the victims they work so hard to protect. When they see by your actions that you truly seek to "act justly and to love mercy and to walk humbly with your God" (Mic 6:8) they will almost certainly be eager to partner with you in a way that will enhance safety for victims in your community and hold abusers living there accountable for their actions. By putting your faith into action in such a way, both survivors and advocates will come to see that the church is not an obstacle to be overcome but a valuable ally to be embraced.

PART THREE

Removing the Barriers and Bringing Peace

STAINED GLASS

Life can shatter
like glass,
sending shards
of broken promises
into the flesh,
severing the self,
bleeding the soul.

The smooth
transparency of yesterday's
assumptions
can spill blindly
onto an inner ground that folds
in upon itself.

And yet
a beauty
emerges
from the jagged disarray

Light
that will not leave us
illuminates colours
and hues not seen before,
fusing the senseless debris
into a story of emerging wholeness.

Press the glass—
it will speak
in images of wisdom and hope.
No pain is denied,
no truth distorted,
no love bound
in the stained glass story
of our true salvation.

ROBERT PYNN

12

Peace, Peace When There is no peace

—Looking Past Flimsy Whitewashed Walls

Catherine Clark Kroeger

THE VIEW OF JERUSALEM FROM EXILE

EVEN AT A DISTANCE, the prophet Ezekiel was aware that Jerusalem and its king were being lulled into a dangerous complacency. There were plans for a revolt, and danger was hanging in the air. Using a distortion of God's promises, religious charlatans held out a guarantee of safety that only heightened the peril.

> These evil prophets deceive my people by saying 'All is peaceful' when there is no peace at all! It's as if the people have built a flimsy wall, and these prophets are trying to hold it together by covering it with whitewash! (Ezek 13:10)

The whitewash to which the prophet referred was clay that was daubed over poorly built walls in order to conceal their shoddy construction. A torrential downpour could sweep away not only the clay but also the shaky walls that it had covered. Proper plaster required the use of slaked lime, but the clay was cheaper and had superficial cosmetic value. Just so flimsy a system had been patched together to enclose the lives and minds of those who ought to have known better (see Ezek 22; 28). Often we hear the phrase "peace peace when there is no peace" quoted (see it repeated in Jer 6:14 and 8:11; Ezek 13:16) but we do not know its context as the saying of false prophets.

Already the city had fallen once to the forces of the Babylonian Nebuchadnezzar. In 597 BC, after only three months as king, Jehoiachin had surrendered to Nebuchadnezzar, thereby avoiding destruction of the city. The royal court, along with Ezekiel and thousands of the land's most capable citizens were led into exile. Jerusalem had been despoiled of its treasures, but the city still stood. Even though the gold utensils had been removed, the bronze vessels remained in use, and there were still services of worship in the temple (Jer 27:6–9).

By 593 BC, having endured five years as a captive on enemy soil, Ezekiel understood only too well the power and cruelty of Babylonia. Any effort at resistance would bring further disaster. Babylon maintained its empire not by stationing armies of occupation in conquered lands but by inflicting terrible retaliation for any who tried to break away.

From afar, Ezekiel sensed what was in the minds of those still remaining in the city. After Jerusalem's fall in 597 BC, the Babylonian conquerors had extracted a promise of tribute from Judah and left it a vassal state with a new king, Zedekiah, half brother of Jehoiachin, on the throne. Of course he had been made to vow loyalty to Nebuchadnezzar. Yet Jerusalem still had its own king, its own worship and its own system of government. The Babylonians moved on to new fields of conquest, and now Zedekiah sought to escape from under Babylon's heel.

In this the king had the backing of would-be prophets and power-seeking politicians. God intended Jerusalem to be free of foreign dominion, they insisted, and its safety had been guaranteed by the Lord's promises to David. There was nothing to fear in pursuing their God-given destiny. Like many others, these theologians centered on the promises of the covenant that guaranteed divine favor but forgot their call to serve the true and living God. The promise to Solomon, David's son, had been that if the people worshiped other deities, "I will sweep Israel off the land which I gave them; I will reject the house which I have consecrated to my name" (1Kings 9:7). The onslaught of the Babylonians was inevitable as kingdom after kingdom fell before them, and Jerusalem must answer for its rebellion.

There were serious flaws in the thinking of those who encouraged a rosy view of Jerusalem's political aspirations and her right to divine protection. The people in David's time to whom the promise was given were those committed to serve God alone. Now the city and its temple were given over to idolatrous shrines and iniquitous practices. This was not the city that God had vowed to keep safe. It is very hard sometimes to admit the terrible harm that has been created by human sin.

The earlier defeat had already demonstrated a critical inability to defend the city. Now that the city had been emptied of "all the able men, to the number of seven thousand—all of them warriors, trained for battle—and a thousand craftsmen and smiths" (2 Kings 24:16), there was even less reason to expect a successful outcome.

The deluded prophets simply refused to accept the harsh military reality or to assess the horrendous vengeance that the Babylonians wreaked upon those who attempted revolt. Under the pretense of certain peace hid certain destruction. Truly, Jerusalem's citizens dwelt within an enclosure of flimsy walls, constructed of false premises and white-washed so that they could not see the truth. Like the window dressing of cheap clay, the words of the false prophets were enormously persuasive, concealing the deadly reality. What was hidden at home was chillingly clear to Ezekiel at a distance:

> Therefore this is what the sovereign Lord says: I will sweep away your whitewashed wall with a storm of indignation, with a great flood of anger and with hailstones of fury. . . At last my anger against the wall and those who covered it with whitewash will be satisfied. Then I will say to you "the wall and those who white-washed it are both gone"... They were lying prophets who claimed peace would come to Jerusalem when there was no peace. I, the Sovereign Lord, have spoken (Ezek 13:10, 16).

The exiled Ezekiel sent this message to his fellow countrymen, but most paid no heed. The reassuring message of peace was more attractive. The temple was its guarantee, or so they had supposed. But the prophetic vision of Ezekiel saw the violation of the holy place, the idols, the worship directed toward other gods, the corruption (Ezek 8:1–18). As he watched, the glory of God moved out of the gate of the sanctuary and returned to heaven (Ezek 10:18). Bereft of the divine presence that had settled on its dedication (1 Kings 8:10–2), the temple had become only a massive and meaningless piece of real estate.

Encouraged by the ill-advised prophets, King Zedekiah looked forward to the overthrow of Babylon's hold upon his city and the enjoyment of national peace and prosperity. Surely it lay within his grasp. With revolt in mind, he formed a coalition with Edom, Moab, Ammon and the Phoenician cities of Tyre and Sidon. This was a clear breach of the covenant that the king had made with the clever Nebuchadnezzar, who had thus ensured that "only by keeping her treaty with Babylon could

Israel maintain her national identity" (Ezek 17:14). Ezekiel perceived that Zedekiah had "despised the solemn oath made in the name of God" (v.19). How sad are the consequences when covenants made before God are disregarded, especially those vowed at the altar to love and to cherish, even in adversity.

In 589/8 Nebuchadnezzar set out to quell the revolt and to punish Zedekiah. The former allies were soon crushed, while only two cities beside Jerusalem still held out in Judah. And the prophets still maintained their invincibility. But Ezekiel was not the only prophet who understood the danger of proclaiming "peace, peace when there was no peace."

JEREMIAH

The View from Inside Jerusalem

Though they are not arranged in chronological order, the prophecies of Jeremiah give us an intimate view of the political, psychological, and spiritual transactions within the besieged city. Eerily, as the invading armies came ever closer, the prophet Jeremiah likened the doomed city to an abused woman. Frequently concealed in modern translations, Hebrew poetry often uses the term "daughter of my people" as can be seen most clearly in the King James Version. With tears, Jeremiah bemoans the fate of daughter Jerusalem.

> Shout to Jerusalem and to all Judah! Tell them to sound the alarm throughout the land "Run for your lives! Warn everyone that a powerful army is coming from the north to destroy this nation. O Jerusalem, you are my beautiful and delicate daughter" (Jer 4:5, 6:1–2).

But daughter Jerusalem had made some very wrong choices and must now face the consequences. She too was suffering at the hands of her former partners.

> Your lovers despise you. They seek your life. I hear a voice of one in travail. Anguish as of a woman bearing her first child, the voice of Fair Zion panting, stretching out her hands: "Alas for me! I faint before the killers!" (Jer 4:31)

The killers indeed were at hand. On January 15, 588, the siege army set up its position around Jerusalem. The city was doubly enclosed, both by an invincible siege machine and by a circle of mistaken conviction and complacency. When in actuality the city was ringed by a hostile army, the citizenry were being led to believe that they were secure. They did not understand their own danger.

> Yes, even my prophets and priests are like that. They are all frauds. They offer superficial treatments, for the daughter of my people's mortal wound. They give assurance of peace when there is not peace (Jer 8:10b–11. For other peace passages see Jer 27–28; 23:9–40; 29:20–28).

Jeremiah's desperation increased

> Do not listen to what the prophets are prophesying to you; they fill you with false hopes. They speak visions from their own minds, not from the mouth of the Lord. They keep saying to those who despise me 'The Lord says: you will have peace.' And to all who follow the stubbornness of their hearts they say, 'No harm will come to you.'(Jer 23:16–17).

Beware a bum steer: Easy answers and pat solutions

How very similar this is to some of the "peace, peace" professions that we hear today! The ugly truth of domestic abuse is so often whitewashed. We receive many distress calls describing life-threatening situations. Religious groups and authorities sometimes insist upon dangerous courses of non-action because they are confident that God will prevent anything terrible from happening in Christian homes.

Over the years, here are some of the stories that have been told to me:

- A woman whose husband chokes her into unconsciousness at least once a month, while her Christian friends tell her that she must not seek a safe environment;

- An angry husband who cleans his shotgun while warning his wife that her life is in danger; but she has been taught that she may not leave him under any circumstances;

- A priest who tells his parishioner that she must return to an abusive home situation. If her husband kills her, she will simply be a martyr in heaven;

- A pastor who insists that unless a woman returns home from a battered women's shelter, she will be excommunicated.

The discovery of her abusive husband's adultery led one woman to decide to leave a twenty-three year marriage filled with many acts of violence.[1] The police had paid scores of visits to her home, always bringing at least two cruisers to control the violence, sometimes using mace and billy clubs to subdue the offender. After committing repeated assaults, he was adjudicated a "felon for life." This classification meant he was no longer permitted to vote, to possess firearms, or to leave the country. The victim's church reproached her constantly and maintained that her husband's misconduct was not valid reason for seeking a divorce.

In a very small community, the woman found herself trapped within the flimsy whitewashed walls. The pastor continually badgered her to reconcile, demanding "peace, peace" when there was no peace to be had. She was publicly condemned by the church leadership. The members spoke to her only to rebuke her, and thoughts of suicide have crossed her mind. The church council simply refused to look at the thick pile of police reports, the court documents, or a physician's report of the permanent disability resulting from the repeated injuries that she had sustained. Far worse than her wounds was the trauma inflicted by the church. A neighboring pastor wrote in protest:

> Our concern to preserve the bonds of marriage and to discourage divorce does not mean that we should force the issue when there are biblical grounds for divorce and any putative reconciliation could amount to a death sentence. I believe that you mean well, but I can't tell you how disappointed I am at the way that this has been handled. It all seems to play into the typical media caricature of evangelicals. None of you were willing to speak to those who witnessed what took place over the course of the marriage.[2]

A victim needs to be able to view realistically both the existing danger and also the condition of a marital relationship where there is no longer trust, respect, or integrity. Just as Jerusalem presented a false image of being a holy city, so a marriage can be only a sham within which danger may lurk. Just as the inhabitants of Jerusalem were deceived, the victim may be deceived into believing false promises that do not look honestly at the havoc wreaked by sinful conduct. Accepting the reality can be incredibly difficult, especially the concession that the home is no longer a peaceful place. It is particularly heart-wrenching when Christian instruction has presented the home as an ideal and sacred haven.

1. As told to Catherine Kroeger by the victim.
2. Used with permission of writer.

Face the hard facts

Jeremiah, an acute military and political observer, was not willing to accept platitudes of peace, even from those who supposed themselves to be prophets. He argued that it was essential to view the ugly realities—the king had endangered the city by his unwise conduct, and an overpowering military might was now arrayed against them. It was futile to expect divine intervention when the city, and even the temple, were filled with pagan shrines and practices. The key lay in a return to God and in obedient adherence to the words of a faithful prophet.

It was very unsafe to listen to a false hope, especially to put it in a religious context. Scripture misinterpreted can become very dangerous indeed.

> How can you say "we are wise because we have the word of the Lord" when your teachers have twisted it by writing lies? These wise teachers will fall into the trap of their own foolishness, for they have rejected the word of the Lord. Are they so wise after all? (Jer 8:8–9)

Twisted theology could not change the hard facts. Nor was it right to deflect those who needed to pursue a genuine path toward peace. Even today many a victim is turned from the path that might lead to peace and induced to ignore the obvious danger signals. They hope so desperately for the perfect marriage that they cannot see the actual danger signs. One permanently maimed victim declared:

> I believe that domestic violence is an issue that is where breast cancer was 15 years ago. It's an issue that most people know little about. And it's an issue where much of the impact can be dealt with if you learn the signs and intervene early.[3]

Reality can be very hard to face, even in the midst of danger, whether in the present or in times gone by. For over two years the city had held out against the siege, as Jeremiah argued that both the temple and the holy city had become a travesty. Idols had been placed in the sacred place, and heathen gods were openly reverenced throughout the city. The law of God was flouted at every turn. Gone were all the values on which temple and city had been established, gone was the determination to exalt God by faithful lives and worship, to demonstrate the will

---

3. Walker, "After Abuse," B1.

of God as a dedicated people. Jeremiah denounced the sham and called for realism.

> Do not trust in deceptive words and say, 'This is the temple of the Lord, the temple of the Lord, the temple of the lord!' . . . look, you are trusting in deceptive words that are worthless. Will you steal and murder and commit adultery and perjury, burn incense to Baal and follow other gods you have not known, and then come and stand before me in this house, which bears my Name and say, 'We are safe'—safe to do all these detestable things. Has this house, which bears my Name, become a den of robbers to you? But I have been watching! declares the Lord (7:3–11).

THE UNACCEPTABLE PATH TO PEACE

There was no reason for God to provide the city with a miraculous deliverance as He had in the days of Isaiah. Jeremiah, the faithful prophet, advocated going out to those who did not know God, who did not follow His ways nor call upon His name. The unfamiliar and unsanctified constituted the path to peace.

> The Lord God Almighty, the God of Israel says: If you but surrender to Babylon, you and your family will live. And the city will not be burned. But if you refuse to surrender, you will not escape! The city will be handed over to the Babylonians, and they will burn it to the ground (Jer 38:17–18).

His advice meant leaving behind a city and a sanctuary that were supposedly steeped in divine approbation and protection – but it meant viewing things in a clear light. In the same way, an endangered woman may best be kept safe in a community shelter, even if it does not provide a distinctively Christian context. God's paths to safety are not always easy to understand.

Jeremiah's warnings earned him fierce resistance and imprisonment. The ultimate ignominy came when he was thrust down a cistern in the middle of the palace courtyard. In vain did he argue for a negotiated settlement while there was still time. The odds, he said, were insurmountable and needed to be dealt with realistically. The way to preserve the city lay in suing for peace. It was of such situations that Jesus counseled making peace when the enemy was still at a distance (Luke 14:31–32).

Individuals might save their lives by leaving the city and appealing to the Babylonians for clemency. The king could prevent the destruction of the city by acknowledging his guilt and seeking the best terms possible for the population. Clearly there would be a heavy price to pay, but Jerusalem would remain standing. He needed to settle for a less than perfect solution.

In a secret meeting with Jeremiah, Zedekiah did indeed consider this option but decided against it because he feared the derision of those who had already defected to the Babylonians (Jer 38:19). He did not want to admit that he had been wrong. It was so hard to give up the beautiful dream.

How often this very consideration causes women to hold back from entering a shelter where they might be kept safe –it just doesn't feel like what they had been led to expect of marriage. Recently I pled with a woman not to return home to the Bible-reading husband who had come very close to murdering her. She had been warned by the child protection agency that she would lose custody of her baby if she brought him back into so dangerous an environment.[4] Nevertheless, she insisted that they must be together as a happy Christian family— even though she knew it meant the loss of her child.

For many godly folk there must sometimes be an agonizing evaluation. A Christian woman, as well as her pastor, may have a struggle to think that the best course for safety may lie outside the household of faith. Nevertheless those best equipped to provide protection, shelter, and safety counseling, are usually to be found in community agencies rather than within the doors of the church. Those who invest extensive time and effort in developing pragmatic strategies for safety, for keeping women free from danger, are not necessarily persons of faith.

It is very hard to admit that the sacred bonds of marriage are not always protective of human life and welfare. We who have invested so very much in efforts to bring about strong, meaningful marriages find it very hard to acknowledge defeat.

A TALE OF TWO TEMPLES

On July 18, 586 BC the wall of the city was breached, and the flimsy whitewash of rhetoric could no longer cover up the reality. Fighting continued in the city with great loss of human life. On August 14 the

---

4. Told to Catherine Kroeger by the victim and the frustrated shelter worker.

temple and the royal palace were burned and the inhabitants marched away into exile. Over six hundred years later, Jerusalem's second temple was also destroyed by the Romans on the same day of the year, August 14, AD 70.[5]

In Jewish tradition, the loss of the two temples is commemorated with fasting every year on the ninth of Av. But every day the lament of Jeremiah can be heard throughout the world:

> Is there no balm in Gilead? Is there no physician there? Why then has the health of the daughter of my people not been restored? O that my head were water and my eyes a fountain of tears! Then I would weep day and night for the slain of the daughter of my people (Jer 8:22–23).

His image is a powerful one, as is that of Ezekiel's cheap white-washed walls. Do not look for peace where there is no peace. Rather let us look to God for the paths of peace that are provided for those in danger.

REFERENCES

Walker, Adrian. "After Abuse, A Life Renewed." *Boston Globe.* Tuesday, October 13, 2009, B1.

5. For Jesus' prediction of the event, see Matt 24:1–2; Mark 13;1–2; Luke19:41–44; 21:5–6.

13

Finding their Voices and Speaking Out
—Research amongst Women of Faith
in Western Canada

Irene Sevcik, Nancy Nason-Clark,
Michael Rothery and Robert Pynn

A BUSE IN THE FAMILY context is pervasive.[1] This truth is borne out by research, clinical experience, and the testimony of victims and those who assist them. It is also true that abuse occurs within religious communities. Sometimes religious voices have been silenced or sidelined in the response of advocates and community-based agencies to condemn violence in the family and to provide safety and resources in its aftermath. Yet, religious voices must be raised within the broader community, within those agencies that seek to provide services to women, children and men impacted by abusive acts, and within religious communities. Sometimes the secular community does not know how to respond to the specific spiritual needs of victims.[2] Sometimes the religious community does not know how to respond to the specific practical needs of women whose lives have been marred by domestic violence.[3] Almost always there are challenges to be overcome in collaborative ventures. Working between—and within—secular agencies and religious communities takes skill, tact, and passion borne out of professional competence. It is no small feat to work together to end domestic violence and to respond compassionately, and with best practices, to those whose lives have been impacted by it.

1. Statistics Canada, *Family Violence.*
2. Whipple, "Counseling battered women," 251–258.
3. Kroeger et al., *Beyond Abuse.*

The collaborative research described in this chapter began with a conversation over a meal—where each of us shared our desire to understand more fully how women from various faith traditions could be offered a context where they could speak freely and openly about how their communities of faith were responding to domestic violence. Together we represent various faith traditions, work contexts and professional credentials. All of us are deeply committed to understanding how the journey of faith and the experience of domestic violence intertwine.

While our interests can sometimes be defined by theoretical, or theological, or therapeutic concerns, all of us want to be agents of change—impacting the world that we study by evidence-based propositions and illustrations. Challenging faith communities to take violence seriously and challenging secular advocates to offer spiritually sensitive resources is part of our response. As you consider the voices of the women who are part of this research endeavour, we challenge you—the reader—to think about the many and varied ways that you too can speak out against violence and ensure that your voice is heard, by religious and secular communities alike.

DESCRIPTION OF THE RESEARCH PROJECT

In order to gain an understanding of how women experienced their spiritual/religious community's response to the issue of family violence, one project within a larger research initiative[4] was designed to listen intently to what women in three particular communities of faith had to say. A total of 85 women participated in this study: 44 from various Christian denominations, six from the Khmer-Canadian community and 35 from the Jewish community. Women were recruited through personal contacts with the research team and advertisements in churches and community centres. Data was collected through focus groups, small group interviews and individual interviews. All interviews and focus groups were led by FaithLink[5] staff members, each holding professional

4. The research was a collaborative venture between RESOLVE Alberta (a regional research network involving the three Canadian prairie provinces supporting projects which have in common the active participation of community- and university-based researchers and a commitment to provide results that are useful in policy and practice development as well as useful in academic settings), Nancy Nason-Clark, and FaithLink.

5. FaithLink is a community based network of faith-based organizations and secular service providers focussing on issues of domestic and sexual violence. For more infor-

credentials. Each, including the translator for the participants from the Khmer-Canadian community, was familiar with the issue of domestic violence and the respective religious traditions. Data were collected during the spring of 2006.

The research site was a large Western Canadian city, where the population is reflective of the multi-cultural nature of contemporary Canada. The three religious/ethno-cultural communities chosen for the project all have established connections with FaithLink. The Jewish community numbers around 8000 and includes Reform, Conservative and Orthodox congregations. The Khmer-Canadian community is small, around 2000 people, and is comprised of men and women who came as refugees in the 1980s, more recent immigrants and some second generation children. It is primarily Buddhist in term of religious tradition.

The focus group discussions and interviews were conducted in an informal manner, with a series of questions designed to stimulate discussion. They were tape-recorded and transcribed and then analyzed to identify themes and commonalities within and across religious/ethno-cultural constituencies.

In this chapter, we will explore four particular themes that were raised by the women participants in our research on faith and domestic violence: reconciling theology with the reality of abuse; spirituality as a source of strength; the culture of religious communities; and the role of personal experiences. Our focus here will be on the participants who were Christian, though, at some points, we will make reference to both the Jewish and Khmer-Canadian respondents as well.

RECONCILING THEOLOGY WITH THE REALITY OF ABUSE

Women in this research who identified themselves as belonging to evangelical Christian congregations discussed, in detail, how the perspectives regarding marriage, relationship roles, the application of teaching regarding forgiveness and the redemptive role of the Church have impacted their lives as women—especially for those women who experience abuse within their intimate relationships. Evangelical women expressed the need for a broadened interpretation of Scripture regarding marriage and the role of women. They spoke of the lack of congruency between the ideal of the theology that is preached and their daily life experiences.

---

mation on the work and structure of the FaithLink program, visit www.endviolence.ca and follow the links. See also, Sevcik et al., 2008.

This chasm put many women in a difficult situation: accept the teachings, but deny the reality of their personal lives; or embrace the reality of their lives over the religious teachings. Other researchers have noted that the religious teachings on forgiveness, in particular, are often imposed upon victims and survivors as part of the repertoire of spiritual helps.[6]

For the evangelical women in our study, one way to reconcile the theology with the reality of abuse was to view marriage and divorce within a broader perspective. In particular, they made reference to the need to ensure that the teachings on submission be understood as a mutual act between partners. Only then, claimed the women, could safety in marriage be ensured. Some women spoke of the "covenant to love and protect" and noted that in an abusive relationship, that covenant has already been broken.[7]

As one woman explains:

> We forget in situations in marriage that it is a contract and that . . . it's a covenant to love and protect and honour each other. And when one party is not living up to that, I believe that the other party is released and that's how I've reconciled it theologically. That if there's violence, verbal, emotional, sexual, financial, etcetera, then . . . and . . . the party [who is practicing the abuse] is not willing to change, then much better to spare the souls, the relationships with the Lord, the development of the children and the spouse who is being abused . . . to spare their lives than have the whole ship sink.

For women of deep religious faith, reconciling the experience of abuse with their theological beliefs is extremely important. It can—and does—lead to conflict between religious rhetoric and lived reality. Focus group members spoke of having a secular self and a theological self. Some noted that they had to emphasize the *secular* and suppress the *religious* in order to maintain their personal sanity. Not surprisingly, this impacts a survivor's spiritual journey, even as it affects her self-worth. As one participant succinctly stated, *victims of abuse don't want to hear Scriptures, they want someone to listen to them, to validate their experience.*

Religious leaders need to understand the *spiritual* struggle of a committed Christian woman who has been abused by an intimate part-

6. Fortune, *Violence in the Family;* Kroeger and Nason-Clark, *No Place for Abuse,* 2nd Edition.

7. Fortune, *Violence in the Family.*

ner. To be sure, there are many safety issues and practical problems to be addressed. But there are also issues of an explicitly spiritual nature that surface when abuse strikes the religious home. It is critical that someone with spiritual credentials, either a faith-enriched therapist, or a pastor, or a lay-leader within the church, walk alongside someone struggling to make sense of the abuse within the framework of religious beliefs that may hold the intact family as God's ideal and consider divorce wrong.[8] In fact, the celebration of family values as a central component in many church circles leaves those who experience abuse in intimate relationships feeling special shame, guilt, embarrassment and even abandoned by God.[9]

Another struggle that the evangelical women noted in the response of spiritual leaders to domestic violence involved the difficult choices they believe pastors are faced with when congregants disclose abuse. In the focus groups and interviews, women alluded to the option of emphasizing redemption or accountability towards the person who was abusive. From the women's vantage point, by taking a redemptive stance with the abusive partner, in what they called a "*spirit of grace*," the victim's experience can be minimized. One participant articulated the struggle this way:

> I think one of the reasons that . . . violence is more of an issue and harder . . . to combat within the faith community as opposed to a secular community is because we struggle with wanting to be redemptive as opposed to [holding people accountable]. So [the question becomes] where's the role of redemption and grace for the offender in accountability? So that's why I think that when an issue comes up and you maybe know the family, you're scared to put into action . . . the processes, follow-up that would be justified and that someone outside the church would basically . . . have no problems [with] knowing what they did was wrong. Christians [minimize the abuser's behaviour]—they didn't mean to, it was kind of a one time thing, this is gonna mark [his] whole life forever. . . . It's not that you want to spare [the abuser] the consequences, but you [question] that if it goes down this road is there any hope for redemption? . . . so you enable . . . the abuse. . . . As a result] victims . . . may be made to feel like further victims by the church because we're afraid to . . . validate what they're say-

8. Nason-Clark, "Christianity and the Experience of Domestic Violence."
9. Nason-Clark and Kroeger, *Refuge from Abuse*.

ing because to really validate someone, you have to call out the offender and call what it is what it is. But we want to . . . have the spirit of grace for the offender.

Both Dan Allender and Al Miles[10] comment on the discomfort of church leaders in responding to domestic violence incidences within their own congregations. Kroeger and Nason-Clark[11] see the need for Christian leaders to not only increase their awareness of domestic violence—which they believe will reduce their levels of discomfort—but also to grapple with some of the theological questions which arise because of it: "the Biblical paradigm is not to conceal abuse but to deal with it. . . . Often we find it easier to deny, ignore, silence or minimize than to address the reality" (p. 120).

Other participants voiced agreement with these sentiments, noting that there is, in reality, no conflict between taking a redemptive stance and holding someone accountable for their actions. Facing the truth of domestic violence is difficult—for religious leaders and for congregations. There are difficult choices in facing the truth and then walking with men and women in their "*brokenness*"—whether they are a victim or an abuser. The church is not being loving or redemptive if it opts to avoid the truth of abuse out of a primary concern for the abuser's feelings.

It is interesting to ponder why religious leaders appear to avoid speaking the truth on domestic violence. As Steve Tracy argues in another chapter in this book, calling the Evangelical Church to truth is exactly what is needed. But truth can be painful.

In their analysis of religious leaders' responses to men who act abusively, Nancy Nason-Clark and Barbara Fisher-Townsend have argued that there is a very important role for pastors in helping men learn to be accountable for their actions and to walk with them on their journey towards greater accountability and evidence of changed behaviour.[12] Yet, when clergy are involved with the criminal justice process, it is often counterproductive. For example, these researchers have interviewed judges who claim that in cases of domestic violence, when pastors come to the courtroom, it is always in support of the abusive man, while the

10. Allender, "Raping Eve," 24–35; Miles, "Calling the Pastor," 35–46.

11. Kroeger and Nason-Clark, *No Place for Abuse*.

12. Nason-Clark, "When Terror Strikes," 303–310; Fisher-Townsend et al., "I am Not Violent," 78–99.

victimized woman sits alone with a court-appointed advocate. The message—whether intended or not—is that the church sides with the abuser.[13]

Within focus groups and interview settings, the topic of forgiveness was also raised by evangelical women. Here, they expressed concern that the application of a theology mandating premature forgiveness of the abuser further victimizes the survivor. They labelled this as abusive behaviour on the part of the religious leader. As one woman said:

> For people who have been gravely offended . . . gravely violated, we can re-victimize them by saying, 'You know, you need to forgive and you need to do it now. Because if you don't, on the basis of Matthew 6:14. . . .

According to Heggen,[14] many evangelical victims report feeling "reprimanded by Christian professionals for their inability to promptly forgive and forget."

As Christian women discussed the concept of forgiveness, they noted that it is a free act on the part of the victim, part of the healing process. And it occurs when the victim realizes her own power to act. It is not forgetting or excusing the abusive acts, nor does it mean reconciliation of the relationship. It can only be reached within the context of safety. As many writers have noted, forgiveness is a long process, often requiring therapeutic or spiritual support.[15] One woman in this study spoke from her own experience of the healing process and the peace that can result when forgiveness is freely offered. She noted that when a victim gets to a place in the healing process where she no longer acts on behalf of the painful, destructive memories, she can forgive. This does not mean that she forgets, however. What it does mean is that the memories of abuse are no longer motivating her actions or controlling her waking moments. The experience—the memory of abuse—no longer has power over her.

13. Nason-Clark, "Christianity," 379–393.

14. Heggen, *Sexual Abuse*, 122–123.

15. Fortune, *Violence in the Family*; Kroeger and Nason-Clark, *No Place for Abuse, 2nd Edition*.

SPIRITUALITY AS A SOURCE OF STRENGTH

For many women, spirituality provides the context within which to place the experience of abuse. As a result, spirituality can be harnessed as a source of strength for women during both difficult times and the long healing process that occurs in the aftermath. In focus groups and interviews, women acknowledged the deep spiritual wounding they experienced from the trauma of violence and noted the fact that healing can take a very long time. Referring to that part of a woman that connects to the Divine, one woman said:

> [our spirit] reminds us that our lives matter . . . when we are abused and when we are exploited and when we are oppressed or controlled, the spirit within us rebels [and cried for justice] . . . there is something within us that say, 'My life somehow matters, so this isn't right. . . .'

Spirituality provided a context in which to see their experience. Several women spoke of finding that meaning through helping others and in realizing their own increased personal strength.

In their book, *Refuge from Abuse,* Nason-Clark and Kroeger talk about the many spiritual questions that surface at the time a religious woman is experiencing abuse. Questions such as: Where is God in the midst of my suffering? What did I do to deserve this? Has God abandoned me? These are extremely important questions—questions that normally are not addressed by those without spiritual insight themselves. For most women, it is not comfortable to ask these questions in a secular community-based context. That is why it is so important for faith communities to build bridges to secular community-based agencies.[16]

THE CULTURE OF EVANGELICAL CHRISTIANITY

Interwoven throughout their discussions, focus group participants identified specific cultural norms which they believe impacted them as individuals and the way that domestic violence is viewed and addressed within their specific faith community. Those within the evangelical tradition spoke of the ambiguous nature of a pastor's relationships within the congregation. From their perspective, some of a pastor's relationships are based on a professional, formal role as spiritual leader, while

---

16. Sevcik et al., "Building Bridges"; Nason-Clark, "Making the Sacred Safe," 349–368; Nason-Clark, "The RAVE Project," 1–11; Stirling et al., *Understanding Abuse.*

others are rooted in personal, informal relationships with individual congregants. If a congregant, whom the pastor knows on a social basis and/or considers a friend, is accused of abusive behaviour, it can compromise the response, as the following illustrates:

> And so they feel in a very ambiguous position. And to take a firm stand . . . feels like they're violating the friendship part of their role. And that can be a difficult thing.

Further difficulties are faced if the alleged abuser holds an important position within the congregation or is a strong financial supporter of the church. In these cases, according to the evangelical women in our study, the response of the pastor may be to protect the reputation of the individual. Yet, by addressing the truth, our participants went on to add, the individuals directly involved can receive the help they need to change their circumstances and the congregation can be set free to fulfil its calling.

Across the focus groups, we asked women to discuss the current resources they saw as being available to address family violence both within their religious tradition, or congregation, and in the broader community. We were also interested in knowing their experiences and thoughts about how these resources were accessed. Some evangelical participants questioned the capability of their pastors to respond appropriately to disclosures of abuse, while others spoke of the positive response they had received from their spiritual leaders, as the following words make clear:

> . . . I was lucky. [My spiritual leader] was very open to anything I said and he had both of us to contend with. As you would have never known that he was dealing . . . like he talked to me like [my partner] didn't even exist. . . .

Other participants spoke of the importance of being accepted and respected as person, of their situation being taken seriously, and for the concern expressed about their safety. One woman expresses these sentiments in the following words:

> He [the spiritual leader] doesn't kind of rush in and fix your problem. He sits and listens to you and . . . would say, 'If you need to just talk, call me.' I had his phone numbers . . . I could get hold of [him] if I needed to . . . and if he thought I was in danger, he

would suggest to do this or to do that to make sure that I stayed safe.

Some women noted that while they were confident that pastors would listen to victims, they were fearful that these pastors might not have the knowledge of how to help, or even know about other referral options.

Such reservations are well founded. In a study of clergy in eastern Canada, it was found that only eight percent of religious leaders felt well prepared to respond to situations involving violence in the family context. Interestingly, those clergy who felt least well prepared to assist victims and their families were the ones who were most reluctant to refer those seeking their help to other community-based or faith-based resources. Thus, where referrals were most critical (from pastors who claimed to be ill-equipped to respond) they were most unlikely to occur.[17] In this volume, several authors talk about how important it is for clergy to be aware of community-based resources that can assist victims, abusers and their families on the journey towards, healing, accountability and wholeness in the aftermath of domestic violence[18]

Within the Christian communities in our current study, participants identified other congregant women as a primary source of support. From the perspective of women in our focus groups, women offer non-judgmental support to other women within congregations. Often that support is extended through in-congregational women's groups where trust between group members is strengthened, providing opportunities for disclosures.

From her research involving 27 focus groups in Atlantic Canada, Nason-Clark argues that one of the best kept secrets of congregational life is the informal source of support that one woman of faith offers another women when violence strikes the family context. Sometimes that support is practical—like caring for the children while the woman goes to an appointment with a social worker or a lawyer. Sometimes that support is spiritual—like praying together. But the single most important ingredient, according to victims and survivors, is when another woman

---

17. Nason-Clark, *The Battered Wife.*

18. Nason-Clark et al., "Building Bridges"; Fahlberg and Ferreira-Fahlberg, "The Needs of Immigrant Families"; Owens, "Notes from the Shelter"; Owens, "A Survivor Looks Back," 1–23.

offers her a *listening ear.*[19] Other researchers too have suggested that spiritual or religious beliefs can be beneficial.[20]

Yet, women across faith communities in the current research noted that there were barriers to accessing resources within their own communities after someone's life had been impacted by domestic violence. Confidentiality was a big concern. As a result, some women identified a preference for accessing resources external to their faith community in a desire to maintain their anonymity. Others noted that the invitation for victims to come forward is lacking. And still others noted the potentially multi-layered repercussions within the community for a victim deciding whether or not to access services—such as, would it bring any type of reprisal, or added embarrassment?[21] As one Jewish respondent noted: *You know, nice Jewish families aren't supposed to have [abuse].*

When referring to resources external to their communities of faith, some participants in our research in western Canada said that while they were aware of resources within the broader community, they did not know how to access them. Others spoke of learning about what services are available from their own experience. Throughout this book, several authors mention how important it is that religious leaders become aware of the resources available in their own community. Sometimes that information can be in part gleaned from the internet (using resources like the RAVE Project website www.theraveproject.org, or FaithLink www.endviolence.ca, but ideally, the best way to begin building bridges to community resources is to meet the providers, learn of their expertise, and take advantage of local training opportunities.[22] Sometimes one phone call can begin a process of connecting churches to the domestic violence service community, what Nason-Clark calls paving the pathway between "the steeple and the shelter."

When women were asked the question of what might make it difficult for women experiencing abuse to find help, focus group participants and interviewees identified a range of impediments and challenges. Evangelical Christian participants spoke of the implications of particu-

19. Nason-Clark, "Making the Sacred Safe," 349–368; Beaman-Hall and Nason-Clark, "Partners or Protagonists," 176–196; Beaman-Hall and Nason-Clark, "Translating Spiritual Commitment," 58–61.

20. O'Hanlon, *Pathways*; Beaulaurier et al., "External Barriers," 747–755.

21. cf. Hathaway et al., "Listening to Survivors' Voices," 687–719.

22. Nason-Clark, "The RAVE Project," 1–11.

lar theological teachings. They identified the teaching of the submission of wives to their husbands as not only reducing their sense of personal agency, but of increasing their individual accountability. The sentiment expressed here was that just because the husband may *be sinning* by being abusive to her, does not give license to the woman to *sin* by not being submissive. Focus group participants felt that this position is reinforced when leaders do not place the safety of the victim and her children as the first priority in abusive situations.

Evangelical participants also spoke of the shame and guilt that victims of abuse feel when there is a clash between the theological expectation that *Christians don't have problems* runs counter to their personal reality of abuse. Feeling the social pressure to live up to the expectation, they maintain *face* within the congregation, as the following comment illustrates: *I still think there's the pressure of we're in the church and everything's supposed to be okay.* Others noted a different form of pressure: *It's hard to reconcile theology with reality.*

Participants from different Christian denominations spoke of the implications of a theology which downplays our humanness. If expectations are that within a faith community everyone *loves one another*, or that Christians *handle life better*, or are expected to be *happy people*, acknowledging any type of brokenness places the individual in a position of identifying a spiritual deficit. Within this context, there is a fear that the admission of human failings will be met with spiritual condemnation, leading congregants to keep their problems and weaknesses to themselves. Abuse then remains a hidden issue—a holy hush permeates.[23]

To be sure, many participants also noted that the expectations to handle one's life effectively is also reinforced by the mainstream culture, with its emphasis on individualism, strength, self-reliance, competency and successfully managing one's life. As one participant notes:

> We're taught not to ask for help, really. Like, you're supposed to be strong. . . . In the church, we're supposed to be the helpers . . . you don't want to need the help.

Not only are pastors reluctant to preach against domestic violence, but many women participants mentioned that they felt that congregations want to hear a *feel good* message. The women recounted stories of pastors who took a public stand in raising awareness about domestic

23. Nason-Clark, "Shattered Silence," 39–56.

abuse and were criticized as a result. Not surprisingly, the focus group participants applauded these religious leaders and noted that abused women in congregations led by such pastors would be in a better position to come forward and ask for help. All of these sentiments led to the belief that the congregation *needs to work hard at being a safe place for people to reveal their weaknesses.*

Another impediment raised by research participants was related to the low level of awareness within congregations about abuse coupled with the limited capacity of pastors to respond to such disclosures. They noted that without awareness, victims do not have the language to name their experience or the knowledge of how to seek help in its aftermath. Focus group participants claimed that congregant women have less awareness of the issue of domestic violence than women within the general population. The fear that confidentiality within the faith community might not be maintained was highlighted as some participants articulated consequences that a breach of confidentiality could cause— embarrassment, the unwanted pity of others, and the possible consequences of their own or their children's thwarted future opportunities. This has led some researchers to talk about the specific vulnerability of highly religious women who are victims of abuse.[24] These authors claim that it is not that highly religious women are more violated, but that once violated, they are more vulnerable.

An additional complexity is added when both the victim and the perpetrator attend the same congregation. Many focus group participants noted that in these contexts, disclosures of abuse may result in shock, denial, conflicting loyalties and attempts to shield the alleged abuser from any impact upon his reputation and status within the congregation. Noting that women often prefer to disclose their abuse to other women, participants mentioned that it is often men in positions of authority (e.g., police officers, spiritual leaders) who victims encounter when faced with the decision to report domestic violence. This alone is a deterrent to disclosure. Not only may a female victim be hesitant to approach a man for assistance when experiencing abuse from her husband, the relationship a spiritual leader has with other male congregants may be viewed, by the victim, as placing the leader in a position where

---

24. Nason-Clark, "Religion and Violence," 515–536; Giesbrecht and Sevcik, "The Process," 229–248; Drumm and Popescu, "Religion," 375–378; Halsey, *Abuse in the Family;* Horton and Williamson, *Abuse and Religion.*

he lacks objectivity. Interestingly, some women participants talked about the fear of being referred outside of the faith community for help.

Not only did participants identify impediments which were community and culturally based, they spoke with awareness and compassion of the personal challenges women face in disclosing abuse and leaving abusive relationships. Across focus groups and interviews, participants identified the emotional and mental impact of experiencing abuse within one's family: the shame; the self-appropriation of blame for the abuse; the fear; and the sense of failure. This latter impact is heightened for a Jewish woman by her responsibility to keep Shalom [peace] in the home and for keeping the family together. Jewish participants noted that when abuse is present within the relationship, it is not possible to establish peace in the home. They advised that the woman needs to leave the relationship in order to establish peace for her children. Overcoming fear was identified as a significant challenge for victims in making the decision to disclose and/or leave an abusive relationship.[25]

The effects of the abuse on a victim's emotional and mental functioning also impact her presentation and thereby create barriers to her disclosure of abuse.[26] Isolation, resulting from the control exercised and threats made by the abusing partner, distances victims from family and friends who may be able to offer support. The fear that she would not be believed if she were to disclose her situation is often reinforced by the abusing partner. A victim may also fear that if she were to disclose, she would be unable to carry out the advice received in the aftermath of disclosure. Depending upon the person to whom she discloses, the advice given might be either to remain or to leave the relationship. According to our research participants, either option may seem overwhelming to an abused woman at her point of disclosure. Considering what is best for herself and her children, knowing what resources are available and how best to access them, as well as establishing financial stability—all of these are real challenges to be faced. They may seem insurmountable challenges to a woman who has been told by her abusive partner that she can do nothing right.[27]

Given that the effects of abuse lessen the victim's sense of personal agency, she may also be immobilized by the need to take charge of her

---

25. Rothery et al., "Tough Choices," 5–18; DeKeseredy and MacLeod, *Woman Abuse*.

26. *Ibid.;* Beaulaurier et al., "External Barriers," 747–755.

27. Nason-Clark and Kroeger, *Refuge from Abuse*.

situation, and may question her ability to manage all of the varying and complex resources she will need, including shelter, legal assistance, financial and employment services and child-care. There is also the need to trust that others will be supportive and helpful. And sometimes, there is also pressure from extended family to stay in the relationship. If the emotional abuse includes a denigrating of her parenting abilities, she may not believe that she could, or should, take on the role of being a single parent to her children. All of these effects of abuse, then, conspire to lessen the likelihood that it will be disclosed.

Here is where the practical advice and support of a spiritual leader can be so critical. Although focus group participants noted that it is vital that they be encouraged to make their own decisions and plot their own course of action in the aftermath of violence, others spoke of how overwhelming it can be and the way that assistance from a pastor was a central ingredient on the road to recovery. And at one point I said to this person,

> "You have to be my brain for me because . . . all I can think of is
> . . . what do I do next?" And the kids, my mortgage, my job, my.
> . . . I was just so overwhelmed with . . . taking responsibility and
> actually taking hold of the situation. . . . There was no way I could
> have handled doing that. I had no one to turn to.

While it is beyond the scope of this chapter to discuss in any degree of detail the results of interviews with the Khmer-Canadian community, suffice it to note that the predicament of recent immigrant women in that community is even more daunting.[28] Divorce is viewed, culturally, as being detrimental to children. Community awareness of the abuse brings shame to family members. The prospect of leaving an abusive partner, as well as being a single parent and the sole breadwinner for their family, is both foreign within a cultural context and close to emotionally, physically and fiscally impossible. Victims can be immobilized by fear and a lack of hope. Opportunities for employment are often limited to low paying and physically demanding jobs. Reliance upon public transport coupled with long working hours lessens time and energy available to care for children. If extended family members are not available to assist with child care, children may be left on their own, placing them at risk of involvement in dangerous situations and/or apprehension by Child Welfare authorities. With limited awareness of the resources available

28. Menjivar and Salcido, "Immigrant Women," 898–920.

within the external community, and the need for the help of a translator to access these, as well as not understanding the legal and judicial systems, and a fear that contacting the police will not be helpful, women often lose hope that any change is possible. Facing these multiple barriers, it is not surprising that many of these women either stay in abusive relationships, or, if they do leave, return within a short period of time (see also Fahlberg's chapter in this volume).

The complexity of leaving was a theme that ran through the focus groups and interviews as women participants discussed the personal challenges facing victims of domestic violence. Fearing that the future may be worse than the present, victims may choose *the devil they know rather than the devil they don't*. In their book, *Refuge From Abuse*, Nason-Clark and Kroeger (2004) note that the fear that the future may be worse than the present is one of the obstacles to be overcome in the journey towards healing and wholeness for women victims. Spiritual leaders are well positioned to help in this regard if they are knowledgeable about the dynamics of abuse and well acquainted with community-based resources and personnel to assist in the aftermath of violence in the home. Most women will not seek help if they do not believe the future can look brighter, and be safer, than the present. Using a safety plan (like the one available free of charge on the RAVE website by following the links to resources at www.theraveproject.org), religious leaders can help a woman see that she is able to exercise a degree of personal agency in her attempt to experience a better tomorrow, one where her emotional and physical safety will not be at risk.

In sum, across all three constituent groups (Christian, Jewish and Khmer-Canadian) in our research in a western Canadian city, we found the following themes raised about domestic violence:

- The need to acknowledge that family violence occurs in all communities;

- The importance of understanding that abusive behaviours are culturally and religiously defined;

- That marriage and family is an important cultural and religious tenet which has significant influence in how women view themselves and the decisions they make in the face of abuse from a marital partner;

- Patriarchal structures place women in submissive and dependent positions and influence a religious community's acknowledgement of, and response to, domestic violence and the support offered to victims;

- That abuse often impacts every aspect of a victim's life including her spirituality, increasing the difficulty of extricating herself from the abusive situation; and

- Regardless of a woman's cultural or religious beliefs, and sometimes because of them, the complexities and consequences of leaving an abusive marital relationship can seem daunting.

Some findings were specific to the Christian women participants of this research.

- For evangelical women, since the Christian community is diverse and widespread within a large city, women victims can choose to join another congregation if they feel to do so. Forgiveness, repentance, redemption and accountability were all theological tenets that evangelical women felt needed to be interpreted and applied carefully in the context of working with an abused woman of faith;

- Christian women from more liberal traditions identified the important role of the Church in adopting a social justice agenda;

- All Christian women in the research identified the strength that can be drawn from their own spirituality at the time of crisis.

The struggle evangelical women participants identified with the practical application and implications of specific belief tenets is supported by a number of contemporary authors writing from a perspective informed by Christianity. Collectively these writers argue that:

1. the personal safety and integrity of family members is a higher value than the preservation of the marriage relationship;

2. "quick forgiveness" is counter-productive for both the victim and the offender; repentance implies accountability-taking on the part of the offending partner; and

3. reconciliation is multi-dimensional and does not necessarily result in the restoration of a broken relationship.

An important finding to emerge from this study of women in western Canada is the expectation amongst Christian and Jewish women that assistance for women and families impacted by domestic violence be made available within their specific religious communities. Although religious women identify the specific limitations and constraints in accessing either resources within their religious community, or broader community-based resources, there is a shared expectation that such will be available to them. Their suggestions of how resources could be enhanced and action they could take to develop needed resources speak to a worldview which values achievement through personal and collective responsibility, as well as affecting societal change through collection action. Religious women have a long-standing interest in offering support for other women,[29] even though it is sometimes misunderstood by those outside the community of faith. A coordinated community response—something that FaithLink has been instrumental in helping to establish in the western Canadian city where we have collected this data—is part of the story of how churches are able to put into practice what they believe. Drawing from their experience with the FaithLink program, Sevcik et al.[30] offer evidence that collaboration between secularly-based service providers and religious/ethno-cultural communities is not only desirable, but possible. They note that through joint efforts those affected by domestic abuse can "access both the deep resources inherent within the spiritual and the expertise that is vested within the domestic violence service sector" (p. 13). There is strength in collective action and religious women, in particular, seem to understand the power and potential of working together.

From this research project, we have learned that religious beliefs, cultural norms and perspectives and historical events provide an interwoven framework in which life's meaning is determined. This context also influences how domestic violence is defined, whether it is acknowledged or denied, and the importance placed on marriage and family. As Carolyn Heggen[31] argues, beliefs matter, as a challenge to victim's agency or a misguided justification for abuser's behaviour.[32] The

---

29. Nason-Clark, "Conservative Protestants," 109–130.

30. Sevcik et al., "Building Bridges."

31. Heggen, *Sexual Abuse.*

32. cf. Fisher-Townsend et al., "I am Not Violent," 78–99; Livingston, *Healing Violent Men.*

constraints imposed on those who seek to end their marriages and the forms of support offered to victims are also impacted by the religious community. As Sevcik et al. conclude, the ties that provide meaning, support and connection can also bind. Addressing family violence in congregational life requires the faith community to be interconnected with various community agencies and services. It cannot be approached from a one-dimensional perspective. Churches and their leaders who are well established in a community are well positioned to be part of a collaborative community response to violence in the family context. They recognize the benefits of working together for a common purpose and in pooling resources to combat the evil of abuse.

Always, in any response, the safety of victims and their children must take priority. Safety must trump gender-based beliefs whether or not those are religious or cultural in ideology or practice. Safety must be the guiding principle on which needed resources are developed and upon which existing resources are evaluated. Incorporating religiously and culturally sensitive services within the entire community should be on everyone's radar screen. Churches and their leaders are a vital component of ensuring that every community is a safe one for women, men and children.

Religious communities often claim that family life is very important: by their actions, they need to show support that this is true. For actions always speak louder than words.

REFERENCES

Allender, Dan. "Raping Eve: Facing the Unrelenting Fury of Adam." In *Beyond Abuse in the Christian Home: Raising Voices for Change,* edited by Catherine Kroeger, et al., 24–35. Eugene, OR: Wipf and Stock, 2008.

Beaman-Hall, L., and N. Nason-Clark. "Partners or Protagonists? The Transition House Movement and Conservative Churches." *Affilia: Journal of Women and Social Work,* (1997a) 176–196.

_____. (1997b). "Translating Spiritual Commitment into Service: The Response of Evangelical Women to Wife Abuse." *Canadian Women Studies* (1997b) 58–61.

Beaulaurier, R. L. et al. "External Barriers to Help Seeking for Older Women Who Experience Intimate Partner Violence." *Journal of Family Violence* (2007) 747–755.

_____. "External Barriers to Help Seeking for Older Women Who Experience Intimate Partner Violence." *Journal of Elder Abuse & Neglect* (2005) 53–74.

Brown, J., and C. Bohn (Eds.). *Christianity, Patriarchy and Abuse: A Feminist Critique.* Cleveland, OH: The Pilgrim Press, 1989.

Clarke, R. L. *Pastoral Care of Battered Women.* Philadelphia, PA: Westminster Press, 1986.

DeKeseredy, W., & L. MacLeod. *Woman Abuse: A Sociological Story.* Toronto, ON: Harcourt Brace, 1998.

Dobash, R. P., & R. E. Dobash. *Violence against Wives: A Case against the Patriarchy.* New York: Free Press, 1979.

Drumm, René, and Marciana Popescu. "Religion, Faith Communities, and Intimate Partner Violence." *Social Work and Christianity* (2009) 375–378.

Fiorenza, E. S., & M. S. Copeland (Eds.). *Violence against Women.* London: SCM Press, 1994.

Fisher-Townsend, B. (2008). "Searching for the Missing Puzzle Piece: The Potential of Faith in Changing Violent Behavior." In *Beyond Abuse in the Christian Home: Raising Voices for Change,* edited by Catherine Kroeger, et al., 100–120. Eugene, OR: Wipf and Stock, 2008.

Fisher-Townsend, B., et al. "I am Not Violent: Men's Experience in Group." In *Beyond Abuse in the Christian Home: Raising Voices for Change,* edited by Catherine Kroeger et al., 78–99. Eugene, OR: Wipf and Stock, 2008.

Fortune, M. *Violence in the Family: A Workshop Curriculum for Clergy and Other Helpers.* Cleveland, OH: The Pilgrim Press, 1991.

Giesbrecht, N., and I. Sevcik. (2000). "The Process of Recovery and Rebuilding Among Abused Women in Conservative Evangelical Subculture." *Journal of Family Violence* (2000) 229–248.

Halsey, P. *Abuse in the Family: Breaking the Church's Silence*: Office of Ministries with Women in Crisis, General Board of Global Ministries, United Methodist Church, 1984.

Hathaway, Jeanne E., et al. "Listening to Survivors' Voices." *Violence against Women* (2006) 687–719.

Heggen, Carolyn Holderbread, *Sexual Abuse in Christian Homes and Churches,* Scottsdale, AZ: Herald Press, 1993.

Hodge, David. "Constructing Spiritually Modified Interventions: Cognitive Therapy with Diverse Populations." *International Social Work* (2008) 178–192.

Horton, A., and J. Williamson. *Abuse and Religion: When Praying Isn't Enough.* New York, NY: D.C. Heath and Company, 1988.

Kroeger, C., and N. Nason-Clark. *No Place for Abuse: Biblical and Practical Resources to Counteract Domestic Violence.* Downers Grove, IL: InterVarsity Press, 2004.

_____. *No Place for Abuse: Biblical and Practical Resources to Counteract Domestic Violence.* Second Edition. Downers Grove, IL: InterVarsity Press, 2010.

Kroeger, C., et al. (Eds.). *Beyond Abuse in the Christian Home: Raising Voices for Change.* Eugene, OR: Wipf and Stock, 2008.

Livingston, David J. *Healing Violent Men: A Model for Christian Communities.* Minneapolis, MN: Fortress Press, 2002.

Menjivar, Cecilia and Olivia Salcido. "Immigrant Women and Domestic Violence: Common Experiences in Different Countries." *Gender & Society* (2002) 898–920.

Miles, Al. "Calling the Pastor." In *Beyond Abuse in the Christian Home: Raising Voices for Change,* edited by Catherine Kroeger, et al., 35–46. Eugene, OR: Wipf and Stock, 2008

Nason-Clark, N. "Conservative Protestants and Violence Against Women: Exploring the Rhetoric and the Response." In *Sex, Lies and Sanctity: Religion and Deviance in Modern America,* edited by M. J. Neitz & M. Goldman, 109–130. Greenwich, CT: JAI Press, 1995.

_____. "Religion and Violence against Women: Exploring the Rhetoric and the Response of Evangelical Churches in Canada." *Social Compass* (1996) 515–536.

_____. *The Battered Wife: How Christians Confront Family Violence.* Louisville, KY: Westminster John Knox Press, 1997.

_____. "Shattered Silence or Holy Hush: Emerging Definitions of Violence against Women." *Journal of Family Ministry* (1999) 39–56.

_____. "Making the Sacred Safe: Woman Abuse and Communities of Faith." *Sociology of Religion* (2000) 349–368.

_____. "When Terror Strikes at Home: The Interface Between Religion and Domestic Violence." *Journal for the Scientific Study of Religion* (2004) 303–310.

_____. "Christianity and the Experience of Domestic Violence: What Does Faith Have To Do With It?" *Christianity and Social Work* (2009a) 379–393.

_____. "The RAVE Project: Developing Web-Based Religious Resources for Social Action on Domestic Violence." *Critical Social Work* (2009b) 1–11. Available online.

Nason-Clark, N., and C. C. Kroeger. *Refuge from Abuse: Hope and Healing for Abused Christian Women.* Downers Grove, IL: InterVarsity Press, 2004.

Nason-Clark, N., et al. "Clergy Referrals in Cases of Domestic Violence." *Family and Community Ministries* (2010) 50–60.

O'Hanlon, Bill. *Pathways to Spirituality: Connection, Wholeness and Possibility for Therapist and Client.* New York: W.W. Norton & Company, 2006.

Owens, J. (2008). "A Survivor Looks Back: What I Wish Pastors had Known When I was Looking for Help." In *Beyond Abuse in the Christian Home: Raising Voices for Change*, edited by Catherine Kroeger, et al., 1–23. Eugene, OR: Wipf and Stock, 2008.

Rothery, Michael, et al. "Tough Choices: Women, Abusive Partners, and the Ecology of Decision-Making." *Canadian Journal of Community Mental Health* (1999) 5–18.

Sevcik, Irene, et al. "Building Bridges of Collaboration: How Religious/Spiritual Communities and Service Providers Came Together to Address Issues of Family and Sexual Abuse." Calgary, AB: FaithLink (2008). On-line: http://www.endviolence.ca/resources-faith-spirituality-based

Statistics Canada. *Family Violence in Canada: A Statistical Profile 2008.* Ottawa: Canadian Center for Justice Statistics, 2008.

Stirling, M. L., et al. (Eds.). *Understanding Abuse: Partnering for Change.* Toronto: University of Toronto Press, 2004.

Weaver, A. J. "Psychological Trauma: What Clergy Need to Know." *Pastoral Psychology* (1993) 385–408.

Whipple, V. "Counseling Battered Women from Fundamentalist Churches." *Journal for Marital and Family Therapy* (1987) 251–258.

14

Learning from Victim Voices
—Defining the Church
as a "Safe" Place for Abuse Response

René Drumm, Marciana Popescu, and Laurie Cooper

*It's not only what that man can take out of us,
it's what the church can take out of us.*

(Rita,[1] a victim-survivor of two abusive marriages,
both of them to ministers)

INDIVIDUALS WHO ARE VICTIMS of domestic violence often find themselves facing significant barriers as they seek a way out of the abuse
in their lives. For Christians, the church can be a source of meaningful
fellowship and corporate worship with like-minded believers—as well as
a support system during times of trouble. Yet, women who are abused by
their partners often experience a different kind of response from their
faith communities. What do abuse victims need from the church? Could
the church itself sometimes be a barrier to changing abusive circumstances? If so, what can remove barriers found in the church?

A SAFE PLACE

Over and over, the women we interviewed described their desire for the
church to be a "safe" place to address the issue of spouse abuse. As they
reflected on their experiences as abuse victims who were members of a
church community, they were able to imagine the type of environment

1. All names used in this chapter are pseudonyms, to protect the identities of the
women who shared their stories with us.

that would be conducive to disclosure, support, and healing. In addition
to their characterizations of an ideal church milieu, they gave very specific suggestions for a range of services that the church could provide to
abused members. Interestingly, there was a strong connection between
their suggestions for services and their depiction of the safe and caring
place that they wanted the church to be. The descriptions of their desired
church environment included listing the programs that would naturally
be present in that environment.

ATTITUDES AND BELIEFS
THAT DEFINE A "SAFE" CHURCH

The list of defining characteristics of a safe church, gathered from our
conversations with Adventist Christian survivors of abuse, begins with
several pervasive themes associated with attitudes and beliefs within a
church's cultural context.

A church is a safe place when it is willing to admit that abuse happens in its midst.

> I think our church needs to be a safe place for people to be able to
> come and say, 'I have a problem.' (Amy)

A church is a safe place when it has an attitude of believing abuse
disclosure.

> Believe them, you know, instead of treating them like, 'How
> could you be such a sinner and talk and spread gossip about that
> good man!' (Judy)

A church is a safe place when it recognizes that God condemns all
abuse.

> I'm like, 'Wow, I don't have to hate God anymore. He doesn't re-
> ally want me to live like this.' And that gave me the courage to
> leave. (Diane)

A church is a safe place when it values social ministry in addition to
evangelism.

> Prophecy and stuff have their place, but I think we also need to
> share the practical things. (Darlene)

PROGRAMS AND SERVICES
THAT DEFINE A "SAFE" CHURCH

The Adventist women who shared their experiences with us collectively offered recommendations for a broad range of church-based services and programming that could be part of an effective abuse prevention and response strategy. These suggestions for resources in a continuum of care were very often associated with their desire for a healthy, caring church environment, and further define the concept of a safe place for domestic violence response.

A church is a safe place when it has awareness and educational programming about abuse for pastors and for members of all ages.

> When I happened to confide in someone, they were real supportive, but people really don't know how to help you. (Sandy)

A church is a safe place when it has sermons about abuse.

> How often have you heard anybody talk about abuse from the pulpit? I don't ever recall and I've been in the church for 51 years. (Sarah)

A church is a safe place when it has members who are willing to get involved in abuse response.

> I would like to see churches have a healthy, core group of people who want to learn . . . to understand what really goes on in families and churches. (Joanne)

> Is there a place where I can go to get retooled? Is there a place I can go to get recharged? (Nila)

A church is a safe place when it provides a budget for ministry to abused members.

> You have to have some kind of financial backing to support those people because they don't have anything. (Sarah)

IS MY CHURCH A SAFE PLACE?

We have heard the individual and combined voices of forty Adventist Christian women who shared out of their first-hand experiences what they would like to see their denominational leadership and local congregations do about the problem of spouse abuse among church members. Their discussions with us reveal a pervasive theme: the church is a barrier to helping victims of domestic violence when it lacks environmental factors and services that define it as a safe place for abuse response. Victims of ongoing partner violence live in a state of fear, not safe in their own homes. It is natural, then, for them to desire safety in their church "family."

REFERENCES

Drumm, R. D., et al. "Intimate Partner Violence in a Conservative Christian Denomination: Prevalence and Types." *Social Work and Christianity* (2006) 233–251.

Nason-Clark, N. "Shattered Silence or Holy Hush? Emerging Definitions of Violence against Women in Sacred and Secular Contexts." *Journal of Family Ministry* (1999) 39–56.

Popescu, M., et al. "'Because of My Beliefs that I Had Acquired from the Church . . .' Religious Belief-Based Barriers for Adventist Women in Domestic Violence Relationships." *Social Work and Christianity* (2009) 394–414.

APPENDIX

How Safe is My Church Congregation?

This informal self-assessment is intended to be a conversation starter by providing a simple diagnosis of a congregation's "safe church" condition for abuse response.

1. _____ To what extent does my church acknowledge that social/emotional problems (such as spouse abuse) exist and often touch church member's lives?

   0. Generally in denial about social problems in the church

   1. Seldom acknowledges social problems

   2. Sometimes acknowledges social problems

   3. Regularly talks about or has programs to address social problems

2. _____ How would you characterize your church's theological "climate" regarding interpretation of Biblical passages that address marriage, divorce, and gender roles?

   0. Interpretation is rigidly literal; discussion of other views is frowned upon

   1. A few "liberal" members ask questions occasionally but there is generally a literal stance in the church

   2. The church is divided about marriage and gender role theology

   3. Theological issues such as marriage and gender roles are thoughtfully discussed, and members seek to find interpretations that are in harmony with other Biblical principles

3. _____ How would you characterize the "average" church member in your congregation regarding spouse abuse disclosure from a fellow church member?

   0. The majority would most likely not believe the victim

   1. Some members would believe the victim while many would not

   2. Many members would probably believe the victim, but it depends on if the abuser was someone they knew and trusted

   3. The majority of church members would most likely believe the disclosure

4. _____ How would you characterize how fellow church members relate to each other regarding personal or private issues?

   0. There are few or no secrets in our congregation. If one person knows of a personal situation, it's often told throughout the congregation

   1. If I share something private or personal with someone in our congregation there is a 50/50 chance of it being told around the church

   2. There are a few pockets of individuals who gossip in our congregation, but many church members will hold confidences appropriately

3. Members can feel free to share personal information with other members knowing that their personal information will be kept confidential

5. _____ How would you gauge your church's budget for outreach in terms of money allotted to evangelism versus the allotment for social ministry (services to hurting people in and out of the congregation)?

0. Don't know or 90–100% of outreach budget for evangelism; 10% social ministry

1. Outreach budget approximately 80% evangelism; 20% social ministry

2. Outreach budget approximately 60 –80% evangelism; 40 –30% social ministry

3. Outreach budget is evenly split between evangelism and social ministry

6. _____ To what extent does my church promote awareness of abuse dynamics to members (through seminars, bulletin inserts or newsletter articles, posters, etc.)?

0. No promotion of abuse awareness

1. Minimal abuse information offered, mostly posters or some pamphlets

2. Occasional information on abuse awareness, including church publications

3. Regular and intentional programming to members on abuse dynamics, including seminars

7. _____ To what extent does my church actively take a role in educating young people on the elements of healthy relationships?

0. No church programming on healthy relationships apart from basic Bible lessons

1. Infrequent programming on healthy relationships

2. Regular programming on healthy relationships

3. Frequent and intentional programming to young people on the elements of healthy relationships

8. _____ How trained and prepared do I perceive my pastoral staff to be when dealing with spouse abuse in my congregation?

   0. Don't Know

   1. Minimally prepared

   2. Somewhat prepared

   3. Trained and ready

9. _____ How would you describe the treatment of the topic of spouse abuse in your congregation from the pulpit?

   0. I have never heard the topic addressed from the pulpit

   1. Spouse abuse has been mentioned without specifically addressing what could or should be done in the church

   2. Spouse abuse has been the topic in at least one sermon and the abuse was deemed unacceptable

   3. Addressing spouse abuse is an expected (annual or bi-annually) topic which clearly sets abuse as unacceptable in Christian marriage

10. _____ In terms of church members' response to spouse abuse, which would best describe your congregation?

   0. No official or organized plan to respond to abuse in the congregation

   1. Informal and/or uneven response to abuse in the congregation

   2. Identified people in the congregation to respond to abuse in the congregation

   3. Appropriately trained church members are readily identified as competent helpers in the case of spouse abuse in the congregation

11. _____ To what extent does my church take a proactive stance to reach out to marginalized or missing members?

    0. Has no organized program of outreach to marginalized or missing members

    1. Occasionally seeks out marginalized or missing members to offer support

    2. Regularly seeks out marginalized or missing members to offer support

    3. Provides an organized, intentional approach to reaching out to marginalized and missing members to offer support

12. _____ My church provides the following resources especially targeted to victims of abuse. For each item give your congregation 1 point:

    _____Food

    _____Emergency shelter

    _____Money for stated needs

    _____Child care

    _____Legal fees

    _____Transportation

    _____Help with transitional employment

    _____Books on healthy relationships

    _____Books specifically on abuse

    _____Information on local services for victims

    _____Information on services for abusive spouses

    _____Support groups for victims (or referral to community support groups)

    _____Healing seminars or retreats for victims of abuse

Something to think about:

36–46	An Exemplar of Safety
25–35	Caring and Growing in Safety
14–24	Getting on Track to Safety
0–13	Time to Get Moving towards Safety

15

Resources for Pastors and Church People

—The RAVE Project

Cathy Holtmann and Barbara Fisher-Townsend

IN HER 2004 PRESIDENTIAL Address to the Religious Research Association, Nancy Nason-Clark (2005) made the statement that "social action requires partnerships nourished over time by mutual respect."[1] That statement succinctly articulates the focus of our RAVE [Religion and Violence e-Learning] project, which has been about building bridges of collaborative partnerships to effect change. The information and resources made available on the RAVE website are the result of over twenty years of academically directed, data-based sociological research examining domestic violence in communities of faith. These materials are made available in ways that are both practical and accessible to the community and sensitive to the unique needs of people of faith.

The website was conceived of and developed largely in response to the candid admission by hundreds of clergy who were surveyed that they are unprepared to respond to incidents of domestic violence. With only eight percent of clergy indicating that they are well-prepared to respond to abusive situations,[2] the RAVE team has made it a priority to include effective online training that provides opportunities for religious leaders to become familiar with data about domestic violence, to understand what domestic violence is and how it affects victims and families, and to help them learn how to respond effectively and appropriately, especially in times of crisis. We believe it is imperative that religious leaders know

---

1. Nason-Clark, "Linking Research," 221–234.
2. Nason-Clark, *The Battered Wife.*

how to respond because research data does indicate that many victims go to their pastor first for help when confronted with abusive behavior[3] and men who have acted abusively clearly identify the need for assistance from their faith communities.

In this article, we describe an on-line initiative designed to equip religious leaders to be part of the coordinated community response to domestic violence—in effect to assist in building bridges between *the steeple and the shelter*.[4] Funded by the Lilly Endowment, the RAVE Project offers a plethora of information and resources originating from a variety of perspectives within the DV community—victim/survivors, clergy members, biblical scholars, therapists, advocates, shelter workers, probation and parole officers, judges, police officers, and researchers.

THE IMPORTANCE OF FAITH-BASED RESOURCES

People of faith do have unique needs that might best be met in a religious context – for them what might serve as a "haven." Stone et al.[5] argue that religion serves as a crisis buffer on two levels. Applying their argument to the crisis of domestic violence, belonging to a community of faith provides a sense of belonging and support. Additionally, religious beliefs and values can offer a framework for understanding and evaluating the situation.

For many people, the realm of the spiritual lies at the heart of their daily living experiences. Another part of the context of daily living for millions of women is, unfortunately, the reality of domestic abuse. Canadian figures indicate that 653,000 Canadian women reported being a victim of spousal violence within a five year period, with 26% of these women being assaulted more than ten times.[6] In the United States, the Centers for Disease Control and Prevention report that nearly 5.3 million incidents of interpersonal violence occur each year among United States women ages 18 and older, resulting in nearly 2 million injuries and 1,300 deaths nationwide every year.[7]

3. Nason-Clark, "Making the Sacred Safe," 349–68.
4. Nason-Clark, "The Steeple or the Shelter," 249–62.
5. Stone et al., "A Study of Church Members," 405–421.
6. Statistics Canada, *Family Violence.*
7. NCIPC, *Intimate Partner Violence.*

On the face of it, it appears contradictory that religion and family violence would be present within the same context. But they are. In her book entitled *The language of battered women,* Carol Winkelmann[8] details her nine years of speaking with abused women in a shelter located in an economically depressed region in the upper south of the United States. She says: ". . . many shelter women express their faith plainly. They turn their burdens over to Jesus and they go on trying to survive and heal." [She goes on to say] "[c]hanges happen in brief conversations, in exchanges of gazes or embraces, in experiences of empathy and compassion. Simply listening to the sometimes seemingly unspeakable stories of shelter women can evoke shifts in outlook, priorities, principles, and faith." According to Winkelmann "[t]he sufferer must have hope and vision even in the midst of pain and suffering" (p.161). Importantly, the RAVE Project also provides resources for women of faith who are affected by abuse.

Religious leaders are those who have experienced a calling to ministry and have a sense of spiritual responsibility for the people they serve. This calling and sense of responsibility are closely tied with their identities—they are matters of faith and professional training. Yet many have experienced the challenge, and perhaps frustration, of not being able to respond to all of the various needs within their congregations. Clergy are often stretched beyond what they thought they would be doing when they made the decision to answer the call to ministry. In our research with and presentations to pastors, we know that while they are concerned about family violence, many of them feel ill prepared to address it and to respond to the needs of victims within their churches.[9]

In a recent research project with Catholic priests in several dioceses across Canada, every single one of them, when contacted to arrange an interview, said that they probably would not be of much help since they had little experience dealing with the issue of domestic violence. With persistence, and despite their belief that they had little to say, they agreed to be interviewed. It became clear in the interviews that indeed, they had a great deal of contact with people who could potentially be experiencing or have experienced situations of abuse or violence. All of them were leaders in at least one if not more churches where they had regular contact with Catholic couples and families. However, because no

8. Winkelman, *The Language of Battered Women.*
9. Nason-Clark, *The Battered Wife*; Nason-Clark et al., "The RAVE Project," online.

one had directly come to them for help in a situation of crisis, they did not see themselves as having the opportunity to deal directly with the issue. Yet it became clear that even though women had not used words like "abused," "battered," or "violent," there had probably been situations in which abusive relationships were being alluded to. It was interesting that when an interview turned in this direction, the priests began to remember other conversations or even just phrases said in passing that may have been signs of something amiss in someone's family. Once religious leaders are able to talk about various aspects of their ministry and to look at them with an awareness of the reality of domestic violence in all of its forms, they begin to see cracks or spaces where opportunities to send a message about the problem of abuse may become possible. It is during these moments that pastors begin to better understand that they do have a particular role to play in a collaborative community response to family violence.

USING RAVE RESOURCES

The Religion and Violence e-Learning Project (www.theraveproject.org) is a website designed, in part, to provide religious leaders and church members with practical resources for addressing family violence informed by the latest research and best practices for professionals. These resources can be used to expand the whole church's awareness of the prevalence and varied forms of abuse among families of faith. They can also help them to figure out ways to walk alongside religious victims and survivors on their journey to healing and wholeness. Pastors play a key role in this process because they are community leaders and set the tone for what is said and done in their churches. In this capacity, they also have the opportunity to send a message to perpetrators of abuse in their congregations that such behaviours and the attitudes that foster them are not based on either biblical or Christian theological understandings.

An initial and relatively simple step for many clergy in working to send the message that their church is concerned about family violence is a visual one. Most pastors have an office and we know that they take care in creating a particular type of space that says something about them and their approach to ministry. Religious art and symbols are often present. The RAVE website has a *Resources* tab which features a couple of downloadable posters. These tastefully designed posters, strategically placed on an office door or church bulletin board, will send a message that this clergy person is aware of family violence and that his or her office is a place where abuse can safely be disclosed. In doing this, a pastor can assume that members of the church will take note of the RAVE website address on the poster and look it up in the privacy of their home or in a community center where they have access to the internet. Having one of the many books about religion and domestic violence (such as this one!) lying on the pastor's desk or coffee table is a subtle sign that will be picked up by a victim or a victim's friend. Even setting the home page on the priest's internet browser to the RAVE Project website can be a helpful way to indicate to parish staff his willingness to talk about the subject.

Another way to gradually increase awareness about family violence in a church is through prayer. Many denominations include prayers of petition and thanksgiving in their order of worship. Including a prayer of compassion for those who have suffered from abuse, be it child sexual abuse, emotional abuse or elder abuse not only illustrates that the congregation has faith that prayer will help those who suffer but that those who suffer as a result of violence and abuse are not forgotten. People understand that we pray about things that matter. A prayer for those who act violently either requesting that they come to realize the pain and suffering that they cause others and requesting God's help in the process of learning to change, can call perpetrators of violence to account. Particular times and days of year lend themselves to remembering the lives of those who may live with the pain of family violence. Christmas can be a time of tremendous stress on families and gently reminding members of the church through prayer of those who bear the brunt of violent emotional outbursts can be valuable. Mother's Day can be difficult for women whose husband's or children treat them with contempt rather than respect. Keep the day real by praying for the mothers who are abused. The RAVE website's *Resource* tab has examples of prayers that can be incorporated into worship services on a variety of occasions.

Sermons or homilies are probably one of the most significant ways in which a minister can deliver their community a message about family violence. Preaching is crucial in the church's mission to give voice to the injustice, pain and suffering in the church and in the world.[10] Again, the RAVE website offers examples of sermons that have been preached directly on the topic of abuse in different Christian denominations. *No Place for Abuse: Biblical and Practical Resources to Counteract Domestic*

---

10. McClure and Ramsay, *Telling the Truth.*

Violence by Catherine Kroeger and Nancy Nason-Clark (2001) can help both clergy who rely on the lectionary and those who choose their own scripture passages to preach on to find connections between our contemporary society's struggle against domestic violence and the traditional stories of faith. A revised version of *No Place for Abuse* (2010) includes an entire chapter on the RAVE Project, offering several guided tours and an index of where to find specific materials. Information about the publications mentioned in this chapter and links to sites where they can be purchased on-line are available on the RAVE website.

If a church has the technological capacity, in the form of high speed internet access and large viewing screens, video clips from the RAVE website can be used to introduce the topic or illustrate points made in a sermon. The *Stained Glass Story of Abuse* can be used as a guided visual meditation during liturgy, inviting those present at worship to hold in their hearts the many situations of abuse present in the community at large and to provide a hopeful way to viewing the journey to healing and wholeness. Taking the opportunity during a homily to explain the interpretation of certain passages in scripture as they relate to marriage or family life is an important part of the clergy's role in becoming a voice against domestic violence and in favor of relationships of mutuality. Clergy can help clarify scriptural words or phrases in ways that show that the bible in no way condones abuse. Examples include the concepts of submission, obedience, sacrifice and forgiveness. Giving positive examples of healthy relationships and speaking concretely about what love is and what it is not can help listeners to think about their own intimate relationships and families.

There is rarely an opportune moment to bring up the issue of domestic violence during worship. The bible does not use that kind of language explicitly. Domestic violence was not considered to be a social problem until the 1970s when laws first appeared to address it. That does not mean that family violence did not happen prior to that. It was just not publically recognized and acknowledged as such. Violent men were often considered mentally ill and their female victims deviant in some way. It was only through the courage of countless victims speaking out about their experiences and demanding justice that we as a society came to realize that something needed to be done. Likewise, it is through the faith and courage of religious survivors of abuse that we have come to know that despite our religious language about love, compassion, kindness and care, abuse occurs in families of faith at alarming rates.

Therefore deliberately talking about the subject of family violence or explicitly raising it through symbols and video images involves taking a risk. Not everyone will hear those words or view those images the same way. For some, it will be an uncomfortable shock. For others, it will be a tremendous relief —the shame and guilt that they have been hiding as victims of abuse has been brought into the light. The message for them is that their suffering is real and it is an aspect of life that God and the church care about deeply.

Once it becomes apparent that a pastor is aware of the problem of family violence and that his or her church is a safe place for people to disclose their experiences of abuse, victims and survivors will seek them out. We all know that information in churches and communities spreads through webs of relationship and people will begin to direct their friends or family members to sympathetic ministers. In preparation for this inevitability, clergy can do a variety of things, but it must be emphasized that they do not have to become experts in counseling victims of violence or abuse. They can rely on their pastoral strength of providing a listening ear. Most people want to speak to someone who will listen to their experiences with empathy and compassion. This has been the hallmark of pastoral care and even though the issue of family violence may be new to a pastor, the tools of good ministry remain relevant. Be prepared to listen, listen and listen some more as victims work through their experiences, emotions and beliefs.

Clergy new to the issue of family violence can work through various sections of the *Online Training* tab to become more familiar with all that is involved, because there is more to dealing with victims of abuse than listening. In particular, reading through the *Mending Broken Hearts* series, based on actual stories from our research, and comparing the responses to those stories by other professionals such as police officers, advocates, counselors, social workers and criminal justice workers can help clergy to develop their own strategies for responding to a call for help when it comes. Keep in mind that the signs of abuse are more likely to present themselves indirectly rather than directly. Viewing the video clips or listening to the voices of survivors on the RAVE website will help religious leaders become more adept at recognizing potential signs of family violence. Again, it requires courage on the part of religious leaders to take the risk in asking if someone is being mistreated in her or his family. But better to ask and be wrong, than to not ask and miss an opportunity to help someone in need.

FAITH COMMUNITY CONNECTIONS

A staff member at one Northwest United States church describes the prevalence of abuse issues that come to her attention:

> And so I have been counseling at our church. I am just, I am overwhelmed at the number of people in our little congregation that have come forward . . . .

Responses of faith communities can take many forms, usually encompassing spiritual guidance, the compassionate comfort of friendship, and the practical needs of those involved. Whatever the response, acceptance and assistance from one's community of believers can indeed offer a "safe haven" for respite along the faith journey. Shupe et al.[11] report that the "most ominous use of religion occurred when men freely admitted that they had been violent but that since they had been 'saved' by Jesus Christ, all their sins and weaknesses, including explosive anger, were forgiven . . . these men simply wrote off their violence as an unimportant foible. Their faith, they said, excused them entirely." In two secular Texas batterer intervention programs, researchers[12] found that religious men appealed to the Bible to justify their violence. "The most common word they used was submit: She will not submit, she did not submit, she should submit."

An important connection for many men is that with their faith communities. Schneider[13] discusses the importance of developing social capital through relationship building amongst members of a community, often based on shared understandings and patterns of trust. He refers to this as "trusting that of God in everyone," a process that does have a recognizable impact on men of faith in recovery.

In her discussion of "what congregations do," Ammerman[14] states that "[c]ongregations are places where people take care of each other. They are a 'first response' social service agency . . . ."(p. 16) Faith communities may be sources of invaluable practical assistance and compassionate support as members deal with the myriad of consequences related to violent behavior.[15]

11. Shupe et al., *Violent Men*, 93–94.
12. *Ibid.*
13. Schneider, "Trust that of God," 269–295.
14. Ammerman, "Still Gathering," 6–22.
15. George et al., "Explaining," 190–200.

A pastor in another Northwest United States congregation describes how she tries to assist people dealing with issues of domestic violence, particularly in terms of whether they require outside counseling:

> When they come in and see me I listen to the words, you know, what is being told, what are you hearing, how are you reacting. And how I make that decision, I think it's really hard. It's very difficult, it's never a slam dunk. I often work with the person.

Meissner[16] argues that "the religious community provides a sustaining and hope-embodying matrix within which the individual can find confirmation of his own inner hope and meaning." Relatedly, Mills[17] also addresses the faith dimension of hope. In referring to hope in relation to prayer, he says "[H]ope, phrased as poetry or prayer, gives expression to pain and, in so doing, redeems the pain. The anguish becomes a fixed and limited adversary rather than an omnipresent, malevolent, lurking shadow with no boundaries."

Several men enrolled in a batterers' intervention program discuss the assistance they have received through their churches in terms of someone to walk with them, pray with them, mentor them, and offer practical support for difficult life issues.

> #08: . . . But through the death of [a close family relative] I had such an outreach of good Christian people around me that gave me that support. Trust me, don't think I didn't want to go pick up a fifth of whiskey and go out and sit on a log out in the woods and sit down there and drink it.

> #09: I always still had a strong faith that there was someone higher than me but it didn't really ever spark an interest to go back until I met the pastor of our church and it just seemed like right. When I walked in the door he knew all of my problems by looking at me and then with his sermon it was like I was up there telling him, whispering everything into his ear and then we actually had a sit down conversation and he singled me out for the whole congregation of new people. . . . I guess you could say he's my mentor, he's a great man, he's done everything he could. . . . He's played the mediator, he helped me find a place to stay with some church brothers. He's done above and beyond the call of duty. . . .

16. Meissner, "Notes," 136.
17. Mills, "An Anatomy of Hope," 49–52.

> #06: I have people that I can call within the church. We have a prayer specialist that will take you and spend time with you and talk and pray and that brought up a lot as far as the church being there for us. I think they would be 100 percent supportive. . . .

When asked what kind of additional support they might look for from others, and what kind of advice they would provide to those who wish to help someone who is impacted by violence, the men most often turn to their faith communities:

> #08: What they can do is be there for people because unless people are ready to change you are never going to change them . . . all you can do is be supportive and give prayer. I believe strongly in prayer and pray for people you know and just try to you know be there when you can.

> #16: That part of your job as a pastor is to love people and to care and shepherd them and I think that is what the word pastor means. . . . I find that a lot of pastors are, for whatever reason, really shying away from giving advice to people and holding people accountable.

George et al.[18] highlight the positive impact of church attendance for those experiencing stress. The pastors and members of the faith communities of these men offer them on-going support and encouragement, provide numerous services, make themselves available, model appropriate behaviour, and are generally just there where and when they are needed. Their arms are wide and their hearts are big and both serve as shelter for men who require that. This type of supportive network can be of enormous benefit to men who are struggling to stay on the right path.

IMPORTANT COMMUNITY RESPONSE CONNECTIONS

Clergy can become better prepared to assist victims of family violence by getting to know the resources and agencies available in the local area for victims. They can click on the RAVE website's red *Help Now* tab to obtain phone numbers for shelters in their area and anywhere throughout North America. Making referrals to the appropriate community resource and even offering to accompany a victim to her first meeting with a lawyer or an employment counselor is an appropriate role for clergy to take when asked for help.

---

18. George et al., "Explaining," 190–200.

Many community agencies for victims of family violence need the financial support and involvement that members of churches can provide. Particularly when moving into a new community it is imperative that religious leaders get to know the people that work in these agencies and talk about what they can do to be supportive. Clergy can encourage members of their congregations to support the work being done in these agencies either through asking for donations on a regular basis, promoting fundraisers organized by the organizations themselves, or suggesting that church members volunteer on a local board of directors. Religious leaders who feel competent in the practice of providing a listening ear to a religious survivor of abuse can let shelter staff know that they can be contacted when the need arises. Likewise, clergy can invited shelter staff or lawyers specializing in family court to come and speak at their churches about their work. For other suggestions on how churches can begin to build bridges with community resources in the work on family violence, check out the *Community Resources* section of the RAVE website.

Another opportunity for pastors to work to raise awareness about abuse is to address it directly with couples preparing for marriage. Many couples today who come to the church to be married have been together for a while and some are already living together. A minister can speak frankly to the couple about how they have come to handle conflict and stress in their relationship. Letting couples know that the representative of the church who is presiding at their wedding cares about the health and strength of their relationship is an important message. Both together and as individuals, a pastor can let couples know that if they need help, they can find it at the church where they were married. Often, particularly in Catholic churches, marriage preparation takes the form of a course done over a weekend or in several evening sessions. Such courses are facilitated by married couples who should not be shy about bringing up the topic of abuse. Resources available through the RAVE website, such as a brochure on marriage preparation found on the *Resources* tab, a presentation on Gender Relationships in the Introduction to Domestic Violence section of the *Online Training* tab, or the video clip "When Abuse is Worse than Divorce" which is also found through the *Resources* tab, can help couples facilitating marriage preparation courses approach the topic of domestic violence. Our research has uncovered marriage preparation courses in churches that offer a handout of local resources such as counseling services, crisis intervention lines or women's shelters along with their phone numbers to couples. Rather than seeing this as casting a negative pall over the future marriage, such practices encourage couples to seek professional help when problems arise. If a religious leader takes part in such a marriage preparation course, it is important that he or she also send a message to couples that they will be available to listen and offer guidance when difficulties are experienced in a marriage. In this way the whole church can show that it cares about marriage and family life and will be faithful, particularly when it is most needed.

Another key player in the work to shatter the silence in churches concerning the issue of family violence is the church secretary. This person represents the "front line" of the church and is often the first contact someone has when looking for help. Making sure that church secretaries have an updated list of resources in the community to assist victims of violence and abuse is crucial. Having the RAVE website book marked on their web browser will ensure easy access to shelter information and other domestic violence hotlines in their local area when they are needed. Church secretaries have been instrumental over the years in making sure that washrooms have copies of the downloadable brochures from the *Resources* tab. Victims, afraid and unsure of where to turn, can read these safely, slip them into a purse to take home, or jot down the phone number of the local shelter in private without anyone else in the church knowing. Another way of getting information on abuse and violence out to those who need it in the congregation is through the Sunday bulletin. Periodically using the bulletin to convey messages about the church's zero tolerance policy on domestic violence or to inform church members about how they can get help for anger management or drug and alcohol abuse are just a few ways that a church secretary can use the bulletin to help victims of violence or to hold perpetrators to account. Finally, the church bulletin boards are usually domains of the secretary. Consider highlighting national domestic violence awareness month once a year by printing and posting the RAVE posters found under the *Resources* tab along with a list of local agencies working with victims and perpetrators. Sample scripture verses that challenge abusive acts or prayers that offer hope could also be included.

In addition to pastors, secretaries, and laity that help with marriage preparation in their churches, there are others who can help in the church's efforts to prevent abuse and violence in intimate relationships. One of the most obvious areas of the church's ministry pertains to those who work with youth. The RAVE website's *Youth* tab features a plethora of resources that can be used in church youth group settings, the highlight of which is *The Dating Game*. Using this online video game, members of youth groups can actively engage with the lives of teen characters like Athletic Bob or Handsome Harry and Musical Mary or Sensitive Sally and others as they go on a date. Teens can choose to navigate their characters through a variety of relationship scenarios that include going for pizza, shopping at the mall, seeing a movie, or text messaging. Through play, young women and men learn to identify healthy and unhealthy relationship patterns. As developers of this game, the RAVE Project team sees it as a starting point for conversations with youth about their own relationship patterns. Abuse and violence occur in dating relationships at all ages—in fact it parallels adult violence in that it exists on a continuum from verbal and emotional abuse to sexual assault and murder. The consequences of experiencing violence in a dating relationship are long-lasting and may include damage to self-esteem, confidence and sense of safety, a negative affect on development and functioning, and, importantly, increasing risk for experiencing or perpetrating further violence in future relationships. While youth are unlikely to tell their parents or school guidance counselor about the relationship violence that they experience, they are likely to tell their friends. Church youth groups can assist in the development of young people who are able to recognize the signs of abuse and help their friends to navigate their way out of unhealthy relationships. Other activities such as a Fast Facts on Teen Dating Violence, viewing You Tube videos related to dating violence, or a structured discussion on the effects of child abuse are also available on the *Youth* tab. Keep in mind that even if a young adult does not disclose experiences of abuse at church, having seen the RAVE website means that it is likely that s/he will return to get the information needed to take the next step.

CONCLUSION

While repentance and reconciliation can be important elements in the healing journey of both women victims and male perpetrators, they are not enough to change behaviour and thinking and to keep women safe. Women victims require a blend of what Nancy Nason-Clark calls the language of contemporary culture and the language of the spirit in terms of advice and support as they deal with this crisis.

Women of faith who are victims of abuse look for hope that the violence will end but they may also look for hope that there can be reconciliation of their relationship within the context of their faith community. They live in family situations that are not peaceful and safe yet their faith tradition highlights the family unit and celebrates the divinely ordained nature of family life. In interviews with women of faith experiencing abuse, Boehm, et al.[19] noted that many of these women spoke of their spiritual anguish in the midst of family violence. To offer hope to these women it is important that the abuse they have suffered be condemned using the language of faith.[20]

Male perpetrators require intervention in order to alter their ways of thinking and behavior, and they also require informed spiritual guidance from their pastors and their faith community. Other faith-related contextual factors may play a part in changing men as well. Perhaps the support of their faith community (both in terms of their spiritual needs and their practical needs), the monitoring by their clergy member, the spiritual support found in prayer and worship, the guidance and comfort of their sacred texts, and the opportunity to talk with other men of faith in an intervention program—all of these things, and others, have the potential to make a difference in changing the thinking and behaviour of violent religious men.

Finally, Rosenbaum and Leisring[21] discuss the oft-mentioned intergenerational transmission of violence wherein violent parents beget violent children. Children internalize a culture of violence within the home and often repeat this behavior in their own peer relationships. Overcoming and recovering from the impact of witnessing or experiencing abusive behaviour during childhood is important to peaceful living throughout life.[22] The resources found under the Youth tab and the Dating Game provide assistance and opportunity for youth pastors to open dialogue and help teens with identifying unhealthy and abusive behaviors.

The RAVE Project [www.theraveproject.com] provides an excellent foundation for building knowledge and expertise related to violent relationships in communities of faith. We invite you to visit the site frequently.

19. Boehm et al., *Lifelines*.

20. Nason-Clark and Kroeger, *Refuge from Abuse*.

21. Rosenberg and Leisring, "Beyond Power," 7–22.

22. Dutton and Golant, *The Batterer*.

REFERENCES

Ammerman, N.T. "Still Gathering Data After All These Years: Congregations in U.S. Cities." In *Can Charitable Choice Work? Covering Religion's Impact on Urban Affairs and Social Services,* edited by A. Walsh, 6–22. Hartford, CT: Trinity College, 2001.

Boehm, R. et al. *Lifelines: Culture, Spirituality and Family Violence. Understanding the Cultural and Spiritual Needs of Women Who Have Experienced Abuse.* Edmonton, AB: The University of Alberta Press, 1999.

Dutton, D. G., and S. K. Golant. *The Batterer: A Psychological Profile.* New York, NY, Basic Books, 1995.

George, L.K., et al. "Explaining the Relationships between Religious Involvement And Health." *Psychological Inquiry* (2002) 190–200.

Kroeger, C. Clark, and N. Nason-Clark. *No Place for Abuse: Biblical and Practical Resources to Counteract Domestic Violence.* Downers Grove, IL: InterVarsity Press, 2001.

_____. *No Place for Abuse: Biblical and Practical Resources to Counteract Domestic Violence.* Second edition. Downers Grove, IL: InterVarsity Press, 2010.

McClure, J. S., and N.J. Ramsay. *Telling the Truth: Preaching About Sexual and Domestic Violence.* Cleveland, OH: United Church Press, 1998.

Meissner, W.W. "Notes on the Psychology of Hope: The Psychopathology of Hope." *Journal of Religion and Health* (1973) 190–139.

Mills, R. "An Anatomy of Hope." *Journal of Religion and Health* (1979) 49–52.

Nason-Clark, N. *The Battered Wife: How Christian Families Confront Family Violence.* Louisville, KY: Westminster John Knox Press, 1997.

_____. "Making the Sacred Safe: Woman Abuse and Communities of Faith." *Sociology of Religion* (2000a) 349–68.

_____. "The Steeple or The Shelter? Family Violence and Secularization in Contemporary Canada." In *Rethinking Church, State and Modernity: Canada Between Europe and the USA,* edited by D. Lyon and M. Van Die, 249–62. Toronto, ON, University of Toronto Press, 2000b.

Nason-Clark, N. and C. Clark Kroeger. *Refuge from Abuse: Hope and Healing for Abused Christian Women.* Downers Grove, IL: InterVarsity Press, 2004.

_____.(2005). "Linking Research and Social Action: Violence, Religion and the Family. A Case for Public Sociology." *Review of Religious Research* (2005) 221–234.

Nason-Clark, N., et al. "The RAVE Project: Developing Web-based Religious Resources for Social Action on Domestic Violence." *Critical Social Work,* (2009). *http://cronus. uwindsor.ca/units/socialwork/critical.nsf/main/E193B211B874DBFD852575E7002 2A92B?OpenDocument.*

NCIPC. *Intimate Partner Violence: Fact Sheet.* Centers for Disease Control and Prevention, 2005.

Rosenbaum, A., and P. A. Leisring. "Beyond Power And Control: Towards an Understanding of Partner Abusive Men." *Journal of Comparative Family Studies* (2003) 7–22.

Schneider, J.A. "Trusting That of God in Everyone: Three Examples of Quaker-Based Social Service in Disadvantaged Communities." *Nonprofit and Voluntary Sector Quarterly* (1999) 269–295.

Shupe, A., et al. *Violent Men, Violent Couples: The Dynamics of Domestic Violence.* Lexington, MA: D.C. Heath and Company, 1987.

Statistics Canada, Canadian Centre for Justice Statistics. *Family violence in Canada: A Statistical Profile 2005.* Ottawa, ON: Statistics Canada, 2005.

Stone, H.W., et al. "A Study of Church Members During Times Of Crisis." *Pastoral Psychology* (2004) 405–421.

Winkelman, C.L. *The Language of Battered Women: A Rhetorical Analysis of Personal Theologies.* Albany, NY: State University of New York Press, 2004.

16

Building Bridges between Clergy
and Community-based Professionals[1]

Nancy Nason-Clark, Steve McMullin,
Victoria Fahlberg and Dan Schaefer

INTRODUCTION

DOMESTIC VIOLENCE IMPACTS HOMES of believers and non-believers alike. As a social issue, it knows no boundaries of class, color, country or faith perspective.[2] Its prevalence around the globe, and its presence in Christian homes, cannot be denied.[3] What is often denied, however, is the role of pastors in responding to those who look to their congregation for help when violence impacts their lives. It is imperative that religious leaders are aware of the nature and severity of abuse and the unique role they have in the journey towards justice, hope and healing for both victims and offenders. Yet, many clergy are ill-equipped for the task and unable—or unwilling—to access community-based resources for those who seek their assistance.[4] Despite this, there is mounting evidence that a coordinated community response to domestic violence offers the most hope to reduce abuse and bring safety to women and children victim-

---

1. This article was previously published under the title "Clergy referrals in cases of domestic violence" in *Family and Community Ministries: Empowering through faith*, v. 23.4, (2010). It is reproduced here by permission of Jon Singletary, Editor of *Family and Community Ministries*.

2. Stirling et al., *Understanding Abuse.*

3. Kroeger and Nason-Clark, *No Place for Abuse.*

4. Nason-Clark "Shattered Silence"; "Woman Abuse."

ized by it. To be sure, collaboration between churches and community agencies presents both challenges and opportunities.

In October of 2008 the organization Peace and Safety in the Christian Home organized an international conference in Washington DC related to abuse in families of deep religious commitment. One of the panels brought together a multi-disciplinary team to discuss the issue of *Referrals between Clergy and Community-Based Resources*. The response to the panel was so enthusiastic that we have decided to share some of our remarks more widely in the hope that they might be of use to others as well.

CLERGY REFERRAL IN CASES OF DOMESTIC VIOLENCE

In order to contextualize the issue of clergy referrals to secular agencies, we need to consider some of the empirical evidence. Highlighted below are several findings to emerge from selected studies of twenty years of research on violence amongst religious families.[5]

- In a study of 343 pastors of evangelical churches, we found that many clergy were reluctant to refer abused women and other family members who seek their assistance to professionals in the community or community-based agencies; 15 percent have *never* referred an individual who sought their help to a non-clerical counselor;

- Of those pastors who have referred on at least one occasion, 39 percent report referrals in less than one in ten of the cases of individuals or couples who seek their help for marital or relationship issues, while at the other end of the spectrum, 14 percent of clergy report that they refer in at least half of these cases;

- In one of our studies involving in-depth interviews with 100 evangelical clergy, it was found that the average pastor spent 16 percent of his or her professional time providing relationship or marital counseling (two afternoons a week). Of those individuals receiving pastoral counsel, 37 percent are seen on an ongoing basis, which we defined as three or more sessions;

5. Fisher-Townsend et al., "I am Not Violent"; Nason-Clark, *The Battered Wife*; "Shattered Silence"; "Making the Sacred Safe"; When Terror Strikes"; Linking Research"; "An Overview."

- The overwhelming majority (85%) of clergy in our sample report that the demand for pastor counseling has increased and pastors regard counseling as one of the greatest stresses in their current work. Only eight percent of religious leaders feel well equipped to respond to situations involving domestic violence;

WHAT LEADS CLERGY TO REFER?

- The most frequently cited reason: a case was too difficult to deal with singlehandedly. A recurring theme that pastors discussed was the disjuncture between congregational expectations for counseling availability and expertise, and the pastor's own perception of inadequacy to provide these services;

- Pastors with more preparation, knowledge and experience about domestic violence were more likely to refer parishioners than those with little or no training;

- A few pastors (less than 10%) noted that sometimes the lack of secular resources makes a referral impossible.

ARE CLERGY SATISFIED WITH THE RESULTS OF REFERRALS?

- The overwhelming majority of pastoral counselors report that they have been satisfied with the counsel parishioners received when they followed through on clerical advice to seek the help of a secular counselor;

- Only eight percent of clergy reported dissatisfaction with the advice offered by secular sources in cases where they referred individuals or couples for non-clerical counsel.

These data identify the demand for pastoral counsel and pastoral perceptions of being ill-prepared to respond to the needs of victims and abusers in the aftermath of violence in the home. Yet, parishioner needs outweigh feelings of inadequacy amongst pastors, and so most ministers report substantial, ongoing experience counseling men, women, couples, and families impacted by domestic violence.

From our studies, we have learned that there are a number of factors that shape pastoral counseling strategies and their willingness or reluctance to make referrals to professionals in the community or community-based agencies. One that might come as a surprise is the role of personal experience, and personal crisis, in their own lives.

Personal experience: My personal experience has been very interesting because I've had both a sister and a brother that found
themselves in violent situations. . . . I realize that it can happen,
and it can happen to anybody at any time . . . training has shaped
me, [but] . . . I guess experience more than anything (Clergy interview #543).

Personal crisis: I know what it's like to be three mortgage payments behind and I know what it was like to have practically no
food in the cupboards, and if it wasn't for my wife's extreme love
for me, I would have been just another statistic, another clergy
marriage breakup. . . . I got some counseling and it was really,
really good (Clergy interview #373).

Personal pain: The major factor that influenced my counseling
was, and I have my wife's permission to say this to you, about four
years ago she began to remember incidents of abuse when she
was a child . . . the last 4 years or so the primary thing that, that
has shaped my, my counseling. . . . I've joined a spouse's support
group. . . .We've had a couple of very good counselors . . . whose
knowledge of marital counseling were always far beyond what
mine was (Clergy interview #480).

Clergy who reported extensive counseling experience (about 15% of our
interview sample of 100 conservative Protestant clergy) tended to have
views about the efficacy and nature of both pastoral and secular counseling that set them apart from colleagues who had less relationship counseling experience. In many ways, it was their attitudes about counseling
rather than their level of training that distinguished ministers from one
another.

Generally speaking, the clergy who reported extensive counseling
experience also reported fairly extensive referral patterns. As a group,
they were less pessimistic about the difficulties associated with referring a
parishioner to a secular counselor for help, and they were far more knowledgeable about what resources were actually available in their local area.
Says one pastor, a 50 year old male working within a small city context,
"When I move into an area, one of the first things I do is . . . to make
contact with other helping agencies. . . . I don't refer people to . . . secular
counselors very often unless I know the individual very well, their type
and style of counseling services" (Clergy Interview #350).

Other clergy within this more experienced pastoral counselor
group reported that there are many different agencies, including transi-

tion houses, hospitals and mental health clinics that are useful resources in the community. Some of the clergy who reported extensive counseling experience had rather formalized links with community agencies or the professionals in their community. Rev. Williams, a younger male working in an urban environment reports, "I am in connection, with the [name] Psychiatric Hospital in [small city] and I'm in connection, communication, with a number of psychiatrists who are there. I meet with the head of psychiatry in [small city] area, I would say, maybe once a month." (Clergy Interview #552)

Our data reveal that the majority of pastors have at some point referred individuals, couples, or families to a counselor or social worker, to a psychiatrist or psychologist, and/or to a mental health community agency. Yet, referrals for most pastors happen irregularly and with some degree of angst. Many pastors do not know of the community resources available and worry about what might occur after a referral has been received. Some claim only to refer to those professionals in the community who they know to be *believers*.

For the most part, clergy with the more extensive counseling experience did not differentiate in their referrals between those counselors or professionals in the community who were explicitly *Christian* and others. They made their referrals based on a knowledge of the person and their counseling or professional skills. And, for the most part, they were satisfied with the support and counsel their parishioners received when they followed through on their advice about referral. Pastors with more extensive referral networks were far more able to outline the specific role of the pastoral counselor in a coordinated community response, likely in part, because they personally had been challenged by their own networking opportunities to think through their own uniqueness. These clergy also talked far more explicitly about the spiritual emphasis of their own counseling.

Interestingly, those with limited experience in relationship counseling were the most reluctant to refer those individuals, or couples, who did seek their advice. In a sense, referrals were most unlikely to occur where they were perhaps needed most. Clergy with less experience seemed to have little knowledge of what secular resources are available and little faith in those with which they were familiar. They tended to feel that secular and sacred counselors would be likely to work at cross-purposes, yet they were unable for the most part to explain exactly what a pastoral counselor could offer to a damaged or hurting person or marital relationship. While educationally these pastors did not differ from their more experienced counterparts, their answers indicated that their ministry style set them apart. Less experienced pastoral counselors were adamant that their counseling approach was very different from the secular world, yet they were unable to articulate how this was so.

In an effort to think more fully about referral patterns, obstacles, and opportunities, we offer the points of view of three seasoned professionals: the senior pastor of a large Baptist church; the executive director of a community-based agency; and a licensed clinical psychologist.

FROM THE POINT OF VIEW OF THE PASTOR

As is true for many religious leaders, my early years as a pastor in a small rural charge were marked by both a religious idealism about devoutly religious families and a naïveté about issues of domestic violence. In my personal experience growing up in a devoutly religious family, home had always been a safe place. I presumed that violence rarely occurred in the homes of those who consistently participated in the faith community. With little training about family violence, I think that at the earliest stage of my pastoral ministry I might have considered it a personal failure to have felt the need to refer a member of my congregation to a secular resource in the community. I would also have been concerned about whether I could trust a secular agency or counselor to respect and affirm the religious faith of a member of my church. Although experience has since taught me the importance of making referrals, I would have to say that the latter concern is not always unfounded. Secular community resources are not always supportive or understanding about the religious faith of victims of domestic violence. Though I hope those instances are not common, stories about such unsympathetic responses to devoutly religious victims may serve to reinforce the reluctance of clergy about making referrals.

When I moved to a second, and much larger congregation, my illusions about the homes of church members were soon shattered. The church had an effective, thriving ministry for single parents, some of whom had been the victims of abuse, perhaps at the hands of a quite religious spouse. I recall that at an initial meeting with the two women who coordinated the ministry, they explained to me in a very matter-of-fact way that one of their initial responses when contacted by a victim of family violence was to refer them to a good, affordable lawyer. They then explained to me that they knew which lawyers in town were less expensive than others, which were more sensitive and helpful to victims of domestic violence, and which ones treated the faith of the victims with respect and understanding. Because of the very spiritual aspects of the Christian marriage vows, such understanding is a very important concern for a religious victim who contemplates separating from, or even putting an end to, a marriage to an abusive spouse. Because of my idealistic desire to preserve marriages, I was at first taken aback by the idea. As I became more familiar with the needs of victims of abuse, I came to understand how important such referrals are.

Soon afterward I was contacted by a leading mental health professional in the community who asked if he could refer a client to me. When I expressed my surprise, he explained that within his office there were a number of qualified counselors, but that not all were sensitive to issues of religious faith. In such instances, he wanted to be able to send clients to a religious leader who could provide spiritual guidance as part of the healing process. He candidly assured me that if I referred someone from my congregation to his office, he would make sure that they were directed to someone who would understand the importance of their faith and of their religious community. His willingness to include me in his network, and his assurance about how my congregants would be treated, dispelled the fears that I had had about making referrals to agencies outside of the faith community. More importantly, it enabled me to begin building helpful relationships with service providers in the secular community. Once I knew some of the people to whom I could refer people, and once they knew me, I was much less hesitant to recommend them to a member of my congregation.

As I look back now and reflect, I believe that the most significant reason why I had been so reticent about making referrals to community agencies and secular professionals was the lack of relationships with people in those agencies. I didn't know the people at the local women's shelter, I didn't know the local advocates for victims of domestic violence, and I had few contacts with secular agencies in the community. Pastors are often in this situation. I would like to say that after realizing that I needed to build those relationships, it was an easy task to carry out, but it was not. Unlike the mental health professional who contacted me, it was sometimes very difficult to build bridges to some agencies or individuals. The problem is not only that clergy may not trust secular agencies; those agencies may not trust religious leaders, and therefore they have done little to facilitate helpful relationships that could make referrals less difficult. To build bridges with some agencies and individuals, I had to be very intentional and determined. Some service providers made it clear to me that they considered the church to be a patriarchal institution that is part of the problem. By volunteering to serve on a community group organized to combat domestic violence, I was able to eventually build relationships with a wide variety of people, but it took time and patience.

One might assume that because clergy realize that they are not adequately trained to respond to domestic violence, they would be *more* likely to refer victims of domestic violence to other resources in the community, but that assumption would be wrong. Why might this be so?

- First, untrained clergy may underestimate the seriousness of the abuse. When the abuser claims to be sorry and promises not to repeat the abuse, the untrained religious leader may consider the problem solved;

- Second, untrained clergy are unlikely to understand what resources are needed by both victims and perpetrators of domestic violence. They may assume that a few words of pastoral guidance will suffice, or that a few sessions of pastoral counsel or marriage counseling will resolve the problem, instead of realizing how difficult and dangerous the situation is for the victims. Clergy may sincerely believe that the abuse has ended when it is simply being hidden from others;

- Third, untrained clergy may not know what resources are available in the community. If they are unaware of therapists, advocates, shelters, or support groups they will obviously not refer people to them. Clergy are fearful that they will put a member of their congregation in a place where their faith will be questioned or criticized. Clergy will rarely refer to someone, unless that person or agency is known to them personally or has been recommended by another trusted pastor or denominational leader;

- Fourth, some clergy simply do not know how to make referrals. It may seem like a simple thing for people who are involved in the domestic violence community, but for a pastor who is accustomed to making referrals only when it is in-house (within the congregation or the denomination) they may be quite unaware of how to make referrals, especially if those referrals are to fee-for-service professionals;

- Finally, some clergy may be skeptical about referring to agencies or professionals who are not expressly Christian. Some have had bad experiences with referrals. Some have concerns about other aspects of referrals: the costs seemed excessive, or the waiting list was long, or the person to whom the referral was made was unwilling to communicate with the religious leader or allow the pastor to be part of the healing process. Some consciously feel that referring someone seems like shuffling the victim to someone else—as if they have failed to do their job adequately—instead of understanding that a referral is intended to provide the help that the religious leader cannot provide.

As important as it is for clergy to be trained adequately about making referrals, it must not be left only to the religious leader to initiate referrals. There are important things that domestic violence advocates and therapists can do to help Churches and leaders with referral options.

- *Provide Community Resource Information.* Many religious leaders would welcome a detailed listing of trained, trusted community resources, along with clear guidelines about how to make referrals. It would be especially helpful if such resource lists could include recommendations by other local religious leaders;

- *Build partnerships.* As part of a community group seeking to address domestic violence, I was able to invite the local Ministerial Association to become involved in some significant ways. For example, the group planned to develop a pamphlet about spousal abuse to be distributed by local clergy to couples planning to be married. Instead, I encouraged the group to invite the clergy to design and write the pamphlet, which they did. In addition to making it much more likely that the pamphlet would actually be used by local clergy, by involving local religious leaders in the community response to domestic violence, a greater sense of partnership was established;

- *Network from within congregations.* There may be important community resources within local congregations that can provide a beginning to the bridge-building process. If a religious leader is hesitant about referring to someone outside his or her own congregation, is there an advocate or therapist or other resource person within the congregation or within a neighboring congregation of the same faith group to whom the pastor would be willing to refer?;

- *Meet with groups of pastors.* Pastors will be much more likely to refer to people whom they have met. Can a presentation be made to a local ministerial association or (even better) to a denominational leadership group, where resource people are personally introduced to religious leaders? Can pastors who have successfully established a network for referrals talk about how such networks have been helpful?;

- *Make referrals to religious leaders.* Community agencies must learn to make referrals to clergy. When a victim expresses spiritual concerns, rather than discounting those concerns it would be most helpful to the victim, and to the collaborative process, to be able to refer her to a pastor who understands and has experience in responding to domestic violence.

FROM THE POINT OF VIEW
OF AN AGENCY DIRECTOR

As I see it there are several challenges for religious leaders and churches with respect to the issue of domestic violence:

- Churches don't take it seriously enough because it is often kept hidden by the victims and offenders. As a result, church leaders and their congregations often are unaware of how pervasive, dangerous, and harmful domestic violence is within their congregations and the broader society;

- Clergy/congregations lack training and information on how to best address the problem so they often resort to traditional theological positions related to family relationships, such as male entitlement, female submission, and prohibitions on divorce;

- Since outrage over domestic violence came out of the secular feminist movement, and since feminism has been so demonized by some in religious circles, anything coming from the feminist movement is distrusted;

- Many clergy and members of the congregation will have personal relationships with families experiencing domestic violence. They will tend to "believe" the person (husband or wife) with whom they have the closest relationship since they do not have deeper knowledge about the family dynamic that occurs in situations like these. This will then color the response to the problem including who will be blamed and held accountable;

- Domestic violence challenges the faith of some believers. If God is in control of the Christian family, then God should be able to empower the believers to simply stop abusive behaviors, right? These questions impact their response.

There are other issues as well deriving from the agencies with which a religious leader might wish to make a referral or establish a relationship.

- Secular agencies and clergy/congregations have different ideologies and values. Secular agencies view a woman's empowerment and safety as more important than keeping families together (even when the potential danger is low). They do not believe that husbands have a right to entitlement of any kind from their wives;

- There is fear/distrust on both sides—both sides can recount "horror" stories. For example, secular agencies can talk about cases where women being beaten were told by their pastor and Christian friends that if she "just becomes a better wife" that the husband will stop abusing her, thereby laying the blame on her. On the other hand, secular agencies can be disrespectful of a woman's faith and religious beliefs that they feel are preventing her from being safe. Some shelter workers have refused to help a victim find transportation to her church. Advocates at secular organizations may see both the Bible and Christianity as irrelevant, or even harmful;

- Domestic violence organizations are generally led by women and churches are generally led by men. Working together requires a mutual respect for the leadership of each type of organization, otherwise, there will be a feeling of "superiority/inferiority" that can prevent collaboration/partnership;

- While the work of domestic violence may draw strong women to advocate on behalf of victims, it is important for those in the churches to come without preconceived notions of who the workers are and what they believe. Similarly, those who work in the domestic violence field also have stereotypes of pastors and religious people;

- Community organizations often see themselves as the domestic violence experts and want to "teach" rather than "listen;"

- Churches often want to solve everything within their own walls, no matter what the problem. Turning to an outside secular agency by some pastors is viewed as having "failed" their congregants. Referrals are thus viewed as failure on the part of the pastor.

HOW TO OVERCOME THESE CHALLENGES:

- Accept that differences will exist in theology/ideology and in leadership, gender and style. Accept it rather than fearing it;

- Create relationships with community organizations. Talk with directors of agencies about your concerns regarding their view of people of faith, how they approach helping the victim, and how they have partnered with churches in the past. There is nothing more powerful than creating personal relationships;

- Don't expect those in community-based agencies to agree with your religious views—only to respect them;

- Some people who work in agencies, like some people in the pews, are not very nice people. If you come across someone who isn't so nice, then try to build a relationship with someone else in that agency. If you have one bad experience with someone in an agency, do not assume that everyone else there is just like them;

- Move beyond stereotypes. Stereotypes go both ways—domestic violence staff often have stereotypes of pastors as well. Remember, staff working in agencies can be Christians too. Secular women, strong, opinionated women can *also* be good, kind, compassionate, friendly, and caring;

- Have confidence in the faith of your congregants. Christians have fears of being corrupted by the "world." But most Christians do not easily lose their faith in God. Whether they lose their faith in the institutional church will depend more on how they are treated by the church and its leadership than what they hear at secular agencies about Christians;

- Many staff in secular agencies have a great desire to work in partnership with churches. Some secular agencies are coming to see faith as a powerful tool in helping victims to heal.

FROM THE POINT OF VIEW
OF THE PSYCHOLOGIST

Shortly after Jimmy Carter was elected President of the United States, he appointed a task force to study mental health issues across the country. We learn from their work that a substantial number of families indicated that if they were experiencing significant emotional problems, they would consult first their pastor, priest or rabbi. While some of my colleagues were surprised to hear of these findings, it comes as no surprise to any one connected to church leadership or congregational life. But is the same true for those who experience domestic violence? I wonder. Unfortunately, many victims of abuse are unable or unwilling to approach their own pastor with stories of pain and brokenness. And those that do are often disappointed with the response.

As we have already argued in this article, many clergy do not feel well equipped to respond to those who seek their assistance in the aftermath of domestic violence. Even though accurate, helpful information is available from secular sources (e.g., books, national domestic violence advocacy groups, community-based transition houses) many religious leaders do not know where to turn to find these resources nor are they always comfortable accessing them. There are even a growing number of domestic violence resources directed towards families of faith (e.g., books, videos, and web-based training and resources, available through The Rave Project, www.theraveproject.org, PASCH, www.peaceandsafety.com, and the Faith Trust Institute www.faithtrustinstitute.org).

Acquiring knowledge about abuse is central for religious leaders who are called upon to respond to women, men, and children in crisis. It is indeed a lack of knowledge about abuse amongst religious leaders that creates such a need for local expertise, resources, and support. This is why it is so essential to have referrals between clergy and mental health professionals in the community. Yet, amongst many religious leaders, there is a reluctance to refer those who come to them for help. Sometimes, this is due to the fact that they do not know what resources are available. Sometimes, this is due to a suspicion on the part of clergy about the advice that might be given to parishioners from those who work in mental health and community-based agencies. Sometimes, though, religious leaders do not know what to do with the information they already have at their disposal—and they simply need some guidance about how to build bridges with their community.

Here are some initial steps that pastors can take:

- Start to consult with other local clergy, directly, or within local ministerial associations, about their experience with domestic violence, their response to families in need, and the community resources of which they are aware;

- Contact local community mental health centers to see if they run classes for men arrested for domestic violence. Ask some of your clergy colleagues to join you to meet with the leaders of these groups. I suspect you will be surprised at how well you will be received by the group facilitators;

- Build community relationships with agencies and their professional staff by learning from them how to be more effective and "culturally sensitive." In time, you will have opportunities to help them to be "religiously sensitive" to clients of deep faith who come to them for help. Since most DV facilitators have heard violent men in a batterer group at one time or another justify their family violence on religious grounds, your advice and support will be very helpful as they do their work. Humility first, and then wisdom.

Building bridges takes initiative, courage, and tact. Sometimes, it will be the religious leader who will initiate the process of referral or contact. Sometimes it will be an agency administrator or one of their professional staff. I offer the following example based on my own experience. The first phone call may sound something like this:

> Psychologist: Pastor Whitmer? My name is Dan Schaefer. I run groups for men in this area who have been arrested for domestic violence. We help men learn more effective ways to resolve conflict with their wives and children, so the family does not have to live with the threat of violence. And I think I need your help.
>
> Pastor: And what kind of help could I offer you, Dan?
>
> Psychologist: Increasingly we are getting referrals from the courts of church-going men who have assaulted their spouses, and I am having two kinds of problems. First, these men are very suspicious of our staff since we are not necessarily members of their church or denomination. Secondly, they are using the Bible to justify their violence. I'm wondering if I could buy you some coffee and you could give me your thoughts about how I can be more effective with these men?

Such a phone call accomplishes two tasks: you build a relationship with a community leader who has connections with, and the respect of, many men; and you will learn how to more effectively respond to people of deep faith. In the process, that pastor will learn of your services, meet you, and be confronted with the troubling incidence rates of domestic violence in your local area. This will increase the chances that he or she will effectively respond to those coming for help and increase the potential of referrals. On the other hand, you will learn first hand what the sacred texts have to say about violence in the family context. If you are smart, you will take good notes, and keep them around when you go to visit your next pastor— comparing and contrasting how various clergy and church traditions see the role of faith in responding to this social evil.

CONCLUDING COMMENTS

Bridge building takes time—time to focus on a shared vision of a community that takes domestic violence seriously; time to discover common ground that would enable progress towards this goal; time to learn the unique contributions different professionals and varying agencies in the region can offer to assist in a community-wide response. Usually one agency or one profession takes the initial lead in bringing others to the collaborative table. It could begin with a project that is sponsored by one agency, but others are asked to join in the efforts. It could begin with a single event to determine whether there is interest across the community in bridge building.

Referrals are a critical strategy in bridge-building. But learning when to refer, how to refer, and to whom to refer, is not as straight-forward as it may seem. You need to know about the resources in your community if your referrals are to be appropriate and successful. Others need to know about the skills your agency or profession brings to the table in order for referrals to be bi-directional. Training is a central component of the process of making referrals. So also is tact, courage, and humility.

SELECTED REFERENCES
(RESEARCH PROGRAM HIGHLIGHTED IN ARTICLE)

Fisher-Townsend, B., et al. "I Am Not Violent: Men's Experience in Group." In *Beyond Abuse in the Christian Home: Raising Voices for Change* edited by Catherine Kroeger et al.,78–99. Eugene, OR: Wipf and Stock, 2008.

Kroeger, C. Clark, and N. Nason-Clark. *No Place for Abuse: Biblical and Practical Resources to Counteract Domestic Violence.* Downers Grove, IL: InterVarsity Press, 2001.

Nason-Clark, N. *The Battered Wife: How Christians Confront Family Violence.* Louisville, KY: Westminster. John Knox Press, 1997.

_____. "Shattered Silence or Holy Hush: Emerging Definitions of Violence Against Women." *Journal of Family Ministry* (1999) 39–56.

_____. "Making the Sacred Safe: Woman Abuse and Communities of Faith." *Sociology of Religion* (2000) 349–368.

_____. "Woman Abuse and Faith Communities: Religion, Violence and the Provision of Social Welfare." In *Religion and Social Policy*, edited by P. Nesbitt, 128–145. Walnut Creek, CA: Rowman & Littlefield Publishers, Inc., 2001.

_____. "When Terror Strikes at Home: The Interface Between Religion and Domestic Violence." *Journal for the Scientific Study of Religion* (2004) 303–310.

_____. "Linking Research and Social Action: Violence, Religion and the Family. A Case for Public Sociology." *Review of Religious Research* (2005) 221–234.

Nason-Clark, N., et al. "An Overview of the Characteristics of the Clients at a Faith-Based Batterers' Intervention Program." *Journal of Religion and Abuse* (2003) 51–72.

Stirling, M. L., et al. (Eds.). *Understanding Abuse: Partnering for Change.* Toronto: University of Toronto Press, 2004.

17

Seminary Students and Domestic Violence —Applying Sociological Research

Steve McMullin and Nancy Nason-Clark

Ponder this . . .

- Visiting a women's shelter is the one factor that made the most difference in whether or not a seminary student feels well prepared to respond to a situation involving domestic violence;

- Male seminary students reported that they felt much less well prepared to respond to families impacted by abuse than female students;

- Seminary students understand that they will likely be called upon to respond to incidents of abuse, yet many expressed concern and fear that their inability to respond in a crisis will negatively impact their ministry and the life of the congregation.

Listen to what seminary students have to say about responding to victims and their families in the aftermath of abuse . . .

- . . . spiritually I'm not sure that we're prepared and we're definitely not prepared in terms of knowing practically what we need to do (male seminary student);

- . . . within your church probably your biggest fear is: "Is this going to destroy my congregation?" (male seminary student);

- I think it would scare us if we knew what was going on . . . (female seminary student).

When a victim of domestic violence approaches her minister for help, what happens next? For almost twenty years, that question has been keeping Nancy Nason-Clark and her collaborators and students busy. Sadly, it is too often the case that well-meaning pastors do not understand the seriousness of domestic violence, or that they provide poor or harmful advice, or that they attempt to confront the abuser or counsel the couple, or that they are unaware of how to access community resources, including women's shelters, to which they can refer victims. For some time, our team has been asking pastors about their experience, training and intervention when a woman, man, teen or child seeks their help in the aftermath of violence at home. Our results indicate that only eight percent of clergy feel well prepared to respond to a victim of domestic violence. Since seminaries are one of the foremost training grounds for pastors, it seemed like an ideal location to ask whether the next generation of religious leaders were being prepared to provide spiritual and practical assistance to those in their church and community who sought their help after abuse. This chapter examines the experience of students currently enrolled in four different seminaries across North America—where Steve McMullin met with them in focus groups and asked individual students to complete questionnaires. In the paragraphs to follow, we offer a window into their views and experiences.

HELPING TO TRAIN PASTORS

There are many unique aspects to the role of religious leaders in addressing and responding to domestic violence. Since the victim's family members, including the abuser, may also be part of the congregation, the pastor must be prepared to respond to a vide variety of personal and family needs that arise in the wake of the disclosure of domestic violence. Since congregations themselves are composed of important relationships, a disclosure of domestic violence may have complex repercussions that affect not only family members but the wider community of the congregation. In those especially troubling church situations where the abuser is a person of power and influence in the congregation, the pastor may be especially in need of resources and wisdom to know how to respond effectively in ways that will not prevent the abuser from using their position in the church to punish the victim or other church members who come to her aid.

In an effort to translate social science data from our research program into social action strategies, the RAVE website www.theraveproject.org has been designed to provide guidance and training for clergy so that they can learn some of the things that they were not taught in seminary. The online training resources on the website provide data and information about domestic violence as well as a variety of case studies that can inform a pastor who seeks to know how to respond to a victim of abuse. The website also provides contact information for shelters as well as resources from state and provincial coalitions. Our team have made presentations to thousands of religious leaders across Canada and the United States in order to make clergy aware of the free resources that are available.

These represent attempts to retrofit pastors who were not adequately prepared in seminary for the kinds of crisis situations to which most pastors are called upon to respond. A better long-term solution would be to find ways to ensure that seminary training provides the kind of preparation that will ensure that future pastors are well prepared and know how to access community resources and make appropriate referrals, that they know how to address domestic violence wisely in the congregational context, and that when victims come to their pastor for assistance they will be provided with guidance to safety and excellent pastoral care.

Seminary Data Collection

The RAVE team has carried out research at four North American seminaries—one in eastern Canada, two in New England, and one in the southern United States. Three of the seminaries describe themselves as evangelical; one is a mainline seminary. A total of 412 students participated in the study by completing a detailed questionnaire about their knowledge of violence in society, about their current understanding of how to respond to domestic violence, and about their own sense of preparedness to respond to violent situations that may arise in their future pastoral ministry. More detailed information was provided by students who participated in several focus groups at each campus.

Of primary interest for this study was to find out whether there has been any improvement in seminary education with regard to domestic violence. Based on the response of students, it is apparent that those who are preparing for ministry continue to feel very inadequately prepared to respond:

STUDENTS' SELF EVALUATION OF THEIR PREPAREDNESS
TO RESPOND TO DOMESTIC VIOLENCE (MEAN PERCENT)

N=364	Not at all prepared	Poorly Prepared	Somewhat Prepared	Well Prepared
Seminary 1	24.4	41.5	34.1	0.0
Seminary 2	20.8	47.4*	30.5	1.3
Seminary 3	26.0	37.7*	31.2	5.2
Seminary 4	10.9	37.0	39.1	13.0
All seminaries	19.8	42.0	33.2	4.9

*Two students indicated a response
between poorly and somewhat prepared.

Since students are at various stages in their seminary education, the table below focuses specifically on those students who were in the final year of their seminary education and about to graduate:

SELF-EVALUATION OF PREPAREDNESS OF GRADUATING STUDENTS
(MEAN PERCENT)

N = 66	Not at all prepared	Poorly Prepared	Somewhat Prepared	Well Prepared
Seminary 1	10.0	23.3	53.3	13.3
Seminary 2	15.1	34.0	43.4	7.5
Seminary 3	7.4	29.6	44.4	18.5
Seminary 4	9.1	22.7	50.0	18.2
All seminaries	13.6	34.8	43.9	7.6

As the above table shows, there is a slight improvement in the students' self-assessment of their preparedness to respond to domestic violence as they approach graduation, but with only 7.6 percent of students in their final year of seminary believing that they are well prepared to respond, it is urgent that seminaries be equipped to address the need to more adequately prepare their students. Nearly half of the graduating students still believe that they are either poorly prepared or not prepared at all.

The students' responses indicate that students are expecting seminary to prepare them to respond to domestic violence and feel that the seminaries have failed them in this regard. Most first- and second-year students indicate that they are not at all prepared or poorly prepared to respond, but that they expect to be somewhat prepared when they graduate. However, the expectation of third-year students dropped, with most believing they will be poorly prepared at graduation. In other words, the questionnaire results show and the focus groups confirm that first- and second-year seminary students anticipate that before graduation they will receive adequate training, but when students in their final semester of seminary were surveyed they indicated that their preparedness had improved very little.

This was confirmed several times in the focus groups: "I don't feel as prepared because it's just my second semester but hopefully in two years I will be ready" (female student). "Next term we are taking a course called 'Family Care, Counselling, and Therapy.' So maybe something's going to come out of that course and I would like to think, by that title, that something will" (male student).

SEMINARY STUDENTS' AWARENESS OF DOMESTIC VIOLENCE

With remarkable consistency in spite of the considerable geographic and doctrinal differences among the seminaries, the students in all four seminaries estimated the extent of domestic violence in families within congregations to be significantly lower than it is in families in the wider society:

STUDENTS' MEAN ESTIMATE OF PERCENTAGE OF COUPLES EXPERIENCING VIOLENCE

	Among All Couples in the Community	Among Couples In the Church
Seminary 1	33.1472	23.6941
Seminary 2	32.6410	25.0426
Seminary 3	33.1544	24.5009
Seminary 4	38.7679	26.0959
All seminaries	34.1201	24.9635

At the same time, most students do realize that domestic violence is a problem that affects many families both in the wider society and within local congregations. When this information is combined with their own sense of lack or preparedness to respond, it is not surprising that one of the important themes that emerged from the student focus groups was a sense of their fear about addressing and responding to domestic violence.

WHAT MAKES THE MOST DIFFERENCE?

As researchers, we are interested in identifying factors that contribute to a seminary student's sense of preparedness to respond to a victim of domestic violence. We asked specific questions about their knowledge of women's shelters, we asked about whether they knew people (either in their church or in the community) to whom they could refer victims, and we asked about their knowledge of the Religion and Violence e-Learning (RAVE) website resources that have been developed by our team. Information about the RAVE website had not been provided to students before they completed the questionnaire.

Knowledge of Community Resources

Many students lack knowledge about women's shelters. Only 33.58 percent know where the nearest women's shelter is located, and only 55.47 percent even know how to contact a shelter. Just 33.1 percent of the students had actually visited a woman's shelter. Only 58.6 percent knew of any resource person in their community to whom they could refer a victim, while 49.6 percent knew someone in their church to whom they could refer a victim. The percentage of students who had visited a shelter varied from 19.1 percent at the Canadian seminary to 46.8 percent at the mainline seminary. It should be noted that the mainline seminary had a much higher percentage of female students than any of the evangelical seminaries. A faculty member at the Canadian seminary told me that when he included a visit to a women's shelter as an assignment for his students, some shelters did not allow or made it difficult for male seminary students to visit.

An analysis of the data indicates that among all of the factors we surveyed having made a visit to a women's shelter makes the most significant difference in increasing the likelihood that a student feels well prepared to respond to domestic violence:

SELF-ASSESSED PREPAREDNESS TO RESPOND TO DOMESTIC VIOLENCE

	Students who have visited a shelter	Students who have not visited a shelter
Not at all prepared	9.3	24.8
Poorly Prepared	36.4	44.7*
Somewhat Prepared	42.4	28.9
Well prepared	11.9	1.6

*Two students indicated a response
between poorly and somewhat prepared.

Gender and marital status were also important factors. The ways that married and single males and females responded are listed in the table below by percentage in each category:

PERCENTAGE WHO FEEL PREPARED BY GENDER AND MARITAL STATUS

	Single Male Students	Married Male Students	Single Female Students	Married Female Students	Divorced or Separated students
Not at all prepared	31.0	15.2	21.1	12.7	5.3
Poorly Prepared	44.8	40.4	50.0*	36.4	26.3
Somewhat Prepared	23.0	42.4	25.6	41.8	42.1
Well prepared	1.1	2.0	3.3	9.1	26.3

*Two students indicated a response
between poorly and somewhat prepared.

Overall, female students feel better prepared than male students, and married students feel better prepared than single students. Thirty-one percent of single males believe they are not at all prepared and only 1.1 percent of single male students feel well prepared to respond. Only

12.7 percent of married female students feel not at all prepared, while half of married women believe they are somewhat or well prepared to respond. Although only 19 students (16 female, 3 male) indicated they are separated or divorced, it is noteworthy that those students rated themselves as much better prepared than other students with 68 percent feeling either well prepared or somewhat prepared.

Since a visit to a women's shelter makes such a major difference in preparing seminary students to address and respond to domestic violence, it would be helpful for shelters to provide opportunities for seminary students to visit and understand the work of the shelters and meet with shelter staff. Since previous study has shown that for many religious victims of domestic violence, their pastor is the most likely person they will seek out first for help, it is important that the pastor be able to express confidence in the shelter and its staff when referring a victim from the faith community. We have discovered that pastors are most likely to refer to those whom they know and trust.

Knowledge of the RAVE Website

Among the 45 students who had knowledge of the RAVE website, 65.31 percent knew how to contact the nearest women's shelter compared to 54.02 percent of the students with no knowledge of RAVE. Among the 25 students who had accessed the RAVE website resources, 75.86 percent knew how to contact the nearest shelter compared to 53.83 percent of those who had not accessed the website. The RAVE website lists contact information for every North American woman's shelter, so pastors can easily access the nearest shelter.

STUDENTS' FEARS

Neither in the survey questions nor in the focus group questions was there any allusion to fear, yet fear was a striking and consistent element in the focus group discussions, with comments such as: "It scares me, just to think of what goes on out there" (male student). "My first thought [about addressing domestic violence in a sermon] was 'no' just because of the whole fear thing" (female student). "Fear of the unknown" (male student). "It would scare me to stop and think about what is going on" (female student). A range of fears were expressed as students considered their level of preparedness to respond to incidents of domestic violence.

Personal fears

Some students expressed fears that were directly related to their own personal history. At the end of one focus group, a male student said that he had been afraid that I would ask questions about family violence in his background. He talked about growing up with a violent father and mother, and expressed that his childhood experience made him so fearful that he had delayed seminary to make sure that he had dealt with any issues of anger that might affect his future relationships. Two additional students disclosed in focus groups that there had been violence in their families, and three students, as they submitted their completed questionnaires, said that they had been victims. Such unsolicited disclosures lead to the question about what seminaries are doing to help students work through issues of abuse in their own past.

Ministry-Related Fears

Students expressed fears related to their future roles as pastors. Two students (one male, one female) expressed concern about personal safety when responding to an incident of domestic violence. A male student expressed fear about male pastors being stereotyped—that society thinks they will respond by defending male headship and authority. A female student expressed fear that addressing the issue in a sermon would result in victims coming to her for help: "It could be a sense of fear that if it's brought up then people in the church will come forward, you're not ready for it, and then you're kinda screwed" (female student).

A female student expressed fear that her ill-informed response might actually make a situation worse by putting the victim in greater danger:

> If I hadn't thought this through until right now and I would've been in that situation I might have told the husband that the wife had talked to me and not have realized until after something happened that, oh yeah, I just put her in greater danger. Cause it didn't actually occur to me until I was saying it out loud . . . and so here I would have been the pastor making the situation worse (female student).

Quite animated responses resulted from discussions about the implications when a church leader is the abuser. First, students were fearful of the extent of the problem in churches. According to one female student,

> I think it would scare us if we knew what was going on and . . . we're talking in very general terms, we're talking family violence, or battering, but there are so many degrees and levels. And so where do you stop? Like is it okay if a spouse is verbally abusive? . . . Do we let them serve on the committee? Where do we draw the line? Because this is a really nuanced topic when you're talking about it, when do you cross that line?

A male student expressed fear that the implications of exposing abusive behaviour in the life of church leaders could have serious repercussions for the church:

> Especially if . . . the husband is well respected I think I would face a fear of, oh my goodness the next thing I say is going to be, is going to have huge implications. And I'd like, I know, that I will need to overcome my fear and . . . say whatever is necessary to make sure the woman, the wife is safe, but that being said, emotionally, spiritually I'm not sure that we're prepared and we're definitely not prepared in terms of knowing practically what we need to do (male student).

Another male student expressed fear that the ministry of the church could be destroyed:

> I think probably one of the biggest things with the fear is like, "How big is this fire going to escalate?" And within the church, especially if you're a pastor of the church . . . within your church probably your biggest fear is, is this going to destroy my congregation? Is the destructiveness of this sin going to destroy my congregation? (male student)

RELIGIOUS IDEALS

The focus groups revealed some interesting differences among the students at the four seminaries. Especially striking at one evangelical seminary was the frequency with which students appealed to the Biblical discussion of marriage in Ephesians 5. In both focus groups at that seminary, reference was made to the comparison of marriage to the relationship between Christ and the Church. In one group, the passage was referenced by a female student:

> Ephesians, instructing the man about how Christ loved the church and served the church and the church is his bride as Christ loves his bride. This is what a man needs to do and a clear, a clarifying of what the scripture means about women submit unto your husband, this doesn't mean being a doormat and this doesn't mean that the man has authoritarian headship over the wife and the family, but that he is to serve the wife and to put the wife's needs and desires first and he does this and serves as Christ did. She's going to respond in like manner in respecting him and loving him and the two of them be able to come together in a better union (female student).

In the other group, Ephesians 5 was a central part of the group's conversation. After two allusions to the passage, a male student explicitly commented on the relevance of the words of Ephesians:

> I still love Ephesians 5 just in terms of the picture of how husbands should treat their wives. So if the wife is at all having a fractured view of how she should be treated, Ephesians 5 is a great picture of, you know, she's to be treated with the same love and care as the body of Christ by Christ. So there's no higher image of the value of her being loved and treated well. So even just to, you know, affirm what we've been saying about how to mend that fractured view of herself, I think Ephesians 5 is huge, just in terms of the love that she is worthy of and should be receiving from her husband and so that would help in that sense (male student).

In response, a female student in the group added:

> I guess I agree with the Ephesians passage. To help her to see how Christ shows love, because the Bible talks about Christ, about the Church being the bride, or Christ being the groom and the Church being the bride, and show how, in a marriage relationship, how the husband is supposed to love as Christ does the Church. To try to understand that (female student).

After discussion about the implications of the passage, a male group member summed up the comments: "well I guess there's a consensus expressed with the idea that Christ and the Church is the model." Seeing marriage as a covenant meant that on the one hand they saw domestic abuse as a heinous crime because it violated the covenant that was God-ordained, while on the other hand they considered the marriage covenant as being of such Biblical importance that reconciliation in the family, and the preservation of the marriage, was a high priority as they considered how they would respond. A male student summed it up this way:

> In this case there has been both that special sacred marriage violation that something is horribly wrong and then there's also two members, both as one body, in discord, but then also there's two people of the church, two members of the body also in discord, and that we are also called to certain steps there to mediate that (male student).

Because of their understanding of marriage as a divine covenant, the students did not address abuse as an incidence of violence so much as they addressed it as a marriage issue. The breaking of the covenant of marriage was the sin to be addressed, not the violence—for those students, the act of breaking the divine covenant is more serious than an act of violence.

REALITY

Students at all four seminaries mentioned that their schools provide little course time for the issue, except in specific courses usually taken by students in counselling or social work tracks. The students at the three evangelical seminaries expressed that conservative congregations expect a very high level of expertise from pastors—especially extensive Biblical and theological knowledge—and that seminaries have difficulty fulfilling that expectation in a three-year Master of Divinity program. At those three seminaries, faculty members who are supportive of our initiative have nevertheless emphasized the constraints that make it difficult to carve additional time from the classroom schedule.

OVERALL ASSESSMENT

Fear is a central construct in understanding a victim's experience of domestic violence. It is the number one reason why women do not leave abusive partners and violent homes. An abused woman fears for her future, fears further violence and fears for the emotional and physical safety of her children. In reality, fear permeates almost every aspect of a battered woman's life, her waking hours as well as her sleep. Moreover fear sometimes hampers women's ability to see the choices they have to enhance personal safety or to choose to live free from the abuse of the past. Fear, in large measure, keeps women from escaping danger and motivates them to spend what energy they have keeping secret the abuse.

What this present seminary study has revealed is that fear is intertwined with how seminary students understand domestic violence as well. They are fearful about addressing it in a congregational context and fearful about their response to those who seek their help in its aftermath. Sometimes that fear is based on their own narrative, sometimes on a gap between the training they believe they need and the response of the seminary to provide it, and sometimes it is linked to their own worry that they may thwart the healing journey by doing, or saying, the wrong thing. With limited experience or knowledge related to the topic of abuse, many seminary students have reason to be fearful. Yet, these data reveal that the knowledge of resources and a familiarity with referral sources reduces the fear seminarians report. Here a little information goes a long way to dispelling myths and providing empowerment for men and women training for ministry. There is no doubt that those who find themselves in a congregational context in the future will be called upon to respond to violence in families of faith. The question is simply: will they be prepared to respond?

To help students, faculty and administrators at seminaries think about how they can respond to the challenges raised in this chapter, we offer a few suggestions.

WHAT CAN ONE STUDENT DO?

- Choose to research the topic of domestic violence as part of preparing to write a paper for a course;

- Ask a faculty member if they can suggest some sources relevant to their course(s) that cover the issue of domestic violence;

- Contact a women's shelter in your local area and ask if you can meet with the Executive Director or the staff about their resources and obtain any printed information they have available;

- Google "domestic violence and religion" and begin to read some of the articles that appear in newspapers across the country. Search your seminary library for relevant books;

244 RESPONDING TO ABUSE IN CHRISTIAN HOMES

- Check out our RAVE website www.theraveproject.org. Identify webinars or seminars that discuss domestic violence and decide that you will take advantage of one training opportunity this academic year;

- Suggest a chapel speaker that can preach a message related to domestic violence;

- If you are a peer mentor, or a youth worker, or a resident fellow in university-owned facilities, suggest training in *relationship abuse* as part of your orientation;

- Place a poster (or shoe cards or pamphlets) on domestic violence in public washrooms around campus (after receiving permission to do so);

- Volunteer to organize a student-initiated panel discussion on domestic violence at your seminary;

- Ask the don of residence life or campus pastor at your seminary if there are support groups for students struggling with issues of domestic violence (from their past or in the present).

What can one faculty member do?

- Choose to include the topic of domestic violence as part of at least one lecture in every course that you teach;

- Raise the issue of domestic violence at a departmental or faculty meeting and ask how your seminary might take seriously the results discussed in this chapter;

- Volunteer to organize a panel discussion on domestic violence at your seminary;

- Consider how your department or faculty could partner with the don of residence life or the campus pastor to offer resources to students personally impacted by domestic violence;

- When you are called upon to pray at chapel, remember those whose are struggling with issues of abuse—from their past or in their present;

- Identify what resources are available at your seminary to raise awareness on the subject of domestic violence. Order some new resources for the library if you can locate only a few;

- Ask your dean or provost how your seminary might take the challenge of preparing students for this form of ministry—to the broken-hearted;

- Identify some pastors in the local area that have been trained in the area of domestic violence and let students know of their expertise;

- Suggest the topic of abuse awareness when planning for a faculty retreat or continuing education for graduates;

- Decide that this academic year you will read one book that highlights the problem of abuse in families of faith;

- Organize a class field trip to a battered women's shelter so that ministry students and shelter staff can meet one another and better understand how to partner with each other to combat domestic violence and assist victims.

WHAT CAN ONE SEMINARY DO?

- Partner with an organization that understands domestic violence and issues of faith and plan one or more events on campus to raise awareness;

- Encourage faculty members to include the topic of abuse as part of the curriculum in Biblical studies, Old Testament and New Testament scholarship, counselling, social justice, urban ministries, family studies, psychology, race and ethnic studies, gender and sexuality, and church history, to name but a selection;

- Ensure that all residences and public washrooms around campus have posters (and pamphlets) about domestic violence and information on where to seek help;

- Make the campus a safe place to disclose that you have been a victim of domestic violence and ensure that there are resources to offer to those who have disclosed abuse in their past or present;

- Ensure that abuse awareness is part of the training for peer mentors, campus security, counselling services, and those who work in the residence system;

- Identify abuse as the subject matter for at least one chapel service per academic year;

- Ask all academic units to discuss how they are going to meet the challenge of preparing seminary students to help individuals and families whose lives have been impacted by domestic violence;

- Require a compulsory course on domestic violence of all ministry students;

- Offer to send several faculty members each year to a seminar, workshop or conference that discusses issues of abuse in the family context;

- Consider expertise or experience in the subject of domestic violence as a priority for at least one faculty hire.

18

Conclusion

—Carrying the Torch Forward

Nancy Nason-Clark, Catherine Clark Kroeger and Barbara Fisher-Townsend

IN JANUARY 2004, A newly founded evangelical organization, called PASCH, was formed. While the word denotes the Passover or time of new beginnings, PASCH also stands for peace and safety in the Christian home. During February of 2005, PASCH held its first international conference in Newport Beach, California. Attended by 250 men and women, the conference sought to sound out a call to bring those interested in creating peace and safety in Christian homes across North America to one place at one time. A second conference was held in the Spring of 2006, at Gordon Conwell Theological Seminary, just outside of Boston, Massachusetts. Based on several plenary sessions and workshops held at these two conferences, an edited collection entitled *Beyond Abuse in the Christian Home: Raising Voices for Change* was published in 2008, under the House of Prisca and Aquila series of Wipf and Stock.

Like our first PASCH edited collection, this current collection of essays has been organized around some of the plenary sessions and workshops at our 2008 conference in Washington, D.C. and a smaller workshop held in the Boston area in August of 2009. In the pages of *Responding to Abuse in the Christian Home* we have attempted to celebrate successes within the Christian community in identifying and responding to abuse in its many and varied forms. Throughout the chapters, we have also identified hurdles to be overcome as congregations, their leaders and the women and men who support them consider the prevalence and severity of the problem of abuse. Interwoven throughout the pages you have just read is the role of the Christian Scriptures in calling Christians to social action to address this evil amongst us.

We are sympathetic to churches and their leaders who find themselves caught between a high value placed on family unity and the reality of so many families in crisis. We have attempted to incorporate both theoretical insights and practical suggestions as we discuss the many challenges faced by people of faith and the congregations where they worship.

Ultimately, we hope that this collection of essays offers a prophetic call to the evangelical church to slumber no longer. This is the day to shatter the silence and end the holy hush as it relates to violence in the family context. This is the day to call abusers to accountability. Today is the day to open our arms to those who have been victimized. With God's help change is possible: tomorrow can be a new day. We need that new day.

In the future, there will be more PASCH conferences, more edited volumes, more workshops and more voices around the world, informed by Christian principles and supported by the Scriptures, that stand firm to their resolve that there is no place for abuse. Join us on the journey.